Aztlán and Viet Nam

AMERICAN CROSSROADS

Edited by Earl Lewis, George Lipsitz, Peggy Pascoe,
George Sánchez, and Dana Takagi

Aztlán and Viet Nam

Chicano and Chicana Experiences of the War

Edited and with an Introduction by
GEORGE MARISCAL

University of California Press

BERKELEY / LOS ANGELES / LONDON

University of California Press
Berkeley and Los Angeles, California

University of California Press, Ltd.
London, England

© 1999 by
The Regents of the University of California

Illustration credits: p. 13—Augustine Acuña, *The Grind*
(courtesy U.S. Army Center of Military History); p. 47—
Malaquías Montoya, *Murió una muerte natural* (courtesy of the
artist); p. 185—*Raza sí, guerra no* (artist unknown, from *Triton
Times* [University of California, San Diego], April 11, 1972);
p. 213—Malaquías Montoya, *Fuera de Indochina* (courtesy of
the artist).

Library of Congress Cataloging-in-Publication Data

Aztlán and Viet Nam : Chicano and Chicana experiences of
    the war / edited and with an introduction by George
    Mariscal.
        p.   cm. — (American crossroads; 4)
    Includes bibliographical references.
    ISBN 0-520-21404-8 (alk. paper)
    ISBN 0-520-21405-6 (alk. paper)
        1. Vietnamese Conflict, 1961–1975—Participation,
    Mexican American.   2. Mexican American soldiers—
    Vietnam.   I. Mariscal, George.   II. Series.
    DS559.8.M39A95   1999
    959.704'3'0896872073—dc21   98-39737

Printed in the United States of America
9 8 7 6 5 4 3 2 1

To the scores of Chicanos who died in Southeast Asia—que en paz descansen—and to the thousands of Chicanas and Chicanos who protested to stop the war.

O Lord, if you can hear my prayer now,
Please help my brothers over in Vietnam.
The poor boys fightin' and killin' high and low
May be killin' their own brother they do not know.

—J. B. Lenoir, "Vietnam Blues" (1966)

That farm boys, Mexicans, and Negro boys are in Vietnam
is but one thing I think about.

—José Angel Gutiérrez, "22 miles" (1971)

Chicano slum kids don't come from middle-America's
clay, or spirit. I mean, what fuckin' Iowa pig farmer, Mississippi sharecropper, Westchester County Jew, California
grape grower, Harlem spade, or Spokane shop owner is
gonna admit bein' of the same clay and spirit as some
dumb wetback who got his ass ripped in Nam?

—Charles Durden, *No Bugles, No Drums* (1976)

¡Puro pedo! We don't live in Mexico. We live in the States.
You ever worked in the fields, *pinche,* Martínez? You ever
lived on the border? If you ain't, *ese,* you ain't seen shit."
Somebody else called out, "Our *jefitos* worked to build the
States. My old man fought in WWII. My uncle Tino died
in some shitty field in Korea. We got rights just like anybody else. . . ."   —Daniel Cano, *Shifting Loyalties* (1995)

CONTENTS

Part 2 / ¡Raza sí, guerra no!

ACKNOWLEDGMENTS

"From the Halls of Montezuma to the shores of Tripoli"—
whenever the "Marine Corps Hymn" boomed from the television at the end
of a John Garfield or John Wayne picture, my father would rise from his
armchair and stand at attention. We all laughed because we knew he was
joking. But years later it occurred to me that maybe he wasn't. His time in
the Corps during the final years of World War II and the Occupation of
Japan had been important to him. In our garage, an old M-1 rifle, a Japanese flag, and a samurai sword hung on the wall as reminders. A first-
generation Mexican American from East Los Angeles, my father, like so
many others, might not have seen the world beyond Southern California if
not for that conflict. The irony in his case was that, having grown up in an
ethnically diverse community of which Japanese Americans were an important part, he would be sent to the Pacific to fight the Japanese. Little did we
know that, twenty-four years after my father's experience overseas, I too
would become a participant in another U.S. war against Asian peoples.

Growing up, we heard many stories. The ship my Uncle Andy was on
in the Pacific theater—sunk by a kamikaze attack. My father's cousin Al-
fonso—shot in the face in Korea: "The bullet went in his mouth, bounced
off a tooth, and rolled around inside. He spit it out and survived." The stories took on a life of their own, but the essential message was the same—
military service was a family tradition. The photograph of my father in uniform, standing with his beaming parents in front of their *imprenta* (print
shop) on Fourth Street near Roosevelt High, speaks volumes about the
complex process of immigration and acculturation. The long road traveled
by one family, from Hermosillo, Sonora, to Calexico to East Los Angeles to
Camp Pendleton to Sasebo, Japan, and back, would continue through me
in such exotic and unfamiliar places as Compton, California; Fort Gordon,
Georgia; Long Binh, South Viet Nam.

In a newspaper column attacking affirmative action programs, Repub-
lican presidential candidate Pat Buchanan wrote: "Hispanics were never

enslaved in America for 300 years. Nor were they victims of 100 years of racial discrimination. There were few Hispanics even in the United States 40 years ago. How, then can the feds justify favoring sons of Hispanics over sons of white America who fought in World War II or Vietnam?" (*Washington Times,* January 23, 1995). Despite this incredibly ignorant statement, Buchanan is not an ignorant man. As a candidate for office, he knew that an attack on the "Hispanic" community would not be met with public repudiations by those with power in government and the media. He knew that he could inflame voters against affirmative action programs by using the entire Latino community as his scapegoat. In fact, other than short-lived protestations from Chicano organizations like the GI Forum, Buchanan did not receive the public drubbing he deserved. His statement went unchallenged, and the decades of sacrifice made by Latinos in U.S. wars once again were erased. I am grateful to Buchanan for making me angry enough to finish this project in a timely fashion.

My thanks to the University of California Institute for Mexico and the United States (UC MEXUS) for providing a grant to support the production of this book. I also want to thank the following individuals for their inspiration and support throughout the years: Rick Berg, who in 1979 led a small group of UC Irvine graduate and undergraduate students out of the Viet Nam vet closet; Alda Blanco, *mi carnala,* who made me see that there was no contradiction in loving Trio Los Panchos, Santana, the Beach Boys, and Taj Mahal; *aquel vato loco,* Charley Trujillo, for keeping our stories alive; George Lipsitz, who in an age of postmodern attacks on humanism and "master narratives" provides a model for ethical scholarship; *mi carnal* Patrick Velásquez, a Chicano from Nebraska who inspired me to be an academic who is also an activist; Iris Blanco, Don Wayne, Susan Davis, Michael Meranze, Rick Maxwell, and Dionne Espinoza, *por su amistad* and keen intelligence; Renny Christopher, for sharing with me her vast knowledge of Viet Nam War literature and veterans; Rosalío Muñoz and Ramses Noriega, who helped create a Movement and twenty-five years later recounted their experiences to my class on Chicano culture in the Viet Nam era; the people at Project YANO of San Diego, especially Rick and Carol Jahnkow, who for almost thirty years have lived the difficult life of anti-militarism organizers inside the belly of the beast; my undergraduate students at UC San Diego, especially Victor Nieblas, Augie Orozco, Monica Copado, Poncho Guevara, Juan Astorga, Monica Villafaña, Leticia Juárez, Gabriela Juárez, Kathia Romo, Abigail Delgado, and Mike Rodríguez, who reminded me that the

Movimiento never ends; and *los bibliotecarios*—Brigida Campos of the East Los Angeles Public Library, Christine Marín of Arizona State University, Richard Chabran of UCLA, Lily Castillo-Speed of UC Berkeley, and Cecilia Puerto of San Diego State University. Thanks also to Amy Einsohn and Rose Vekony for their careful editing. A special *gracias* to Malaquías Montoya for granting me permission to use his powerful art. To all those who allowed me to include their work in the anthology or who agreed to be interviewed—I have felt the intensity of your experiences and I thank you for sharing it.

My love and gratitude to Elizabeth for putting up with me while I revisited my past. As always, my appreciation for the unconditional support of my parents. Finally, to my children Emma and Samuel—for three consecutive generations our family has been touched by war: the Mexican Revolution, World War II, and the American war in Viet Nam. My wish for you both is that your lives are filled with peace.

GEORGE MARISCAL
San Elijo, Califas
[*Cardiff by the Sea, California*]

AZTLÁN AND VIET NAM

The earliest indigenous Mexican chronicles refer to a region to the north of present-day Mexico City known as Aztlán. Although the region's exact location was never specified, in writings of the sixteenth century Aztlán was associated with what today is the Southwest region of the United States. Alternately referred to as *el lugar blanco* ("the white place"), *el lugar de las cañas* ("the land of canes"), and *el lugar de las garzas* ("the land of herons"), Aztlán was the place of origin of the first ancestors.

Throughout the nineteenth and twentieth centuries, Aztlán became a powerful myth with diverse political and cultural usages. At the height of the Chicano Movement in the 1960s, Aztlán garnered tremendous symbolic weight as the stolen homeland and future nation of the Chicano people. If Aztlán was the U.S. Southwest, then it was precisely that part of Mexico lost to foreign invasion and conquest after 1848. While many groups took the recuperation of the territory of Aztlán as a realistic political objective, others used the concept as a rallying cry around which a reinvigorated Chicano identity might take shape. As the poet Alurista recalled in a 1981 interview: "The myth of Aztlán, as I saw it in the 1960s, was just a way to identify a people, a land, and a consciousness that said, 'Struggle. Do not be afraid.'" [1]

Aztlán thus signifies the community of people of Mexican descent living in the United States and subject to its government's domestic and foreign policies. It refers to a region and communities that have historically been erased from foundational narratives of "American culture" and that continue to be misunderstood and misrepresented by the government, historians and scholars, the media, and the nation at large. Today, Aztlán continues to be a relevant "space," not in the fight to regain a lost land but in the ongoing struggle for economic and social justice.

As a Viet Nam veteran whose grandparents were Mexican immigrants, I have been struck by the invisibility of Chicanos and Chicanas in the histories, oral histories, and literary anthologies of the Viet Nam War era. Only a handful of these works on the war contain contributions by or about Chicano GIs, though a disproportionately large number of U.S. soldiers were of Mexican descent. And though some of the largest anti-war rallies of the late 1960s and early '70s were organized by Chicanos and Chicanas, the story of these protests is little known outside the Southwest.[2] With few exceptions, the study of the Viet Nam war era has become, like the rest of American studies, largely the domain of middle-class European-Americans. That this should occur in the study of a war fought in great part by working-class people of color is an intellectual and political problem of some magnitude.

In this volume, I have brought together writings from Chicano veterans who fought the war in Viet Nam and from Chicano and Chicana activists who fought the war at home. This combination will not sit well with some readers; old animosities are not easily overcome. But if we want to understand what Viet Nam meant—and means—to Americans of Mexican descent, we must look at the figures of both the GI and the protester and at the issues of color, class, gender, region, and generation that divided *la Raza,* as they divided the nation, during the war years. The present anthology brings together pieces of this story, as told by the novelists, poets, journalists, short story writers, and memoirists of Aztlán.

In addition to offering a body of creative work representing diverse voices within Chicano communities, this anthology provides a starting point for the discussion of several historical and social issues that are central to our understanding of the sixties and its legacy. For example, in part 1, the autobiographical and fictional accounts by the veterans offer us the sights, sounds, and emotions of technological warfare as well as representations of the structures of interethnic relations in Viet Nam, both within the U.S. military and between the U.S. soldiers and the Vietnamese people. The debates within Chicano communities about the conduct of the war, the racist practices that informed the military and the draft, the meaning of patriotism, and the meaning of manhood are exemplified by selections in both part 1 and part 2. Finally, the readings speak to broader political issues: the complex relations between ethnic identity and class identity; the solidarity, or lack of solidarity, between various peoples of color; the question of how to move beyond identity politics; and the struggle to live with the personal tragedies brought on by the war.

In selecting texts for this volume, I decided to omit readily accessible works, such as the anti-war *actos* of the Teatro Campesino, and to focus primarily on works that I found in libraries, personal collections, and archives in California. Of course, as the selections illustrate, many Spanish-speaking communities sent men and women to Southeast Asia. For example, the poet Pedro Pietri, a Nuyorican veteran, explores many of the same themes as the authors represented here.[3] At the other end of the political spectrum, Felix Rodríguez, an anti-Castro Cuban mercenary, tells of his participation in a variety of right-wing operations ranging from the Bay of Pigs to Iran-Contra, including covert activities in Viet Nam.[4]

Johnson and Rodríguez

> *The warrior's knowledge as expressed in memoirs, novels, poems and plays by the soldiers, together with reports by oral historians and essay journalists, posits a literature about the war that contradicts the war-managers at virtually every level. . . . Race and ethnicity also constitute important social divisions in the warrior's knowledge.*
>
> James William Gibson, *The Perfect War: Technowar in Vietnam*

Two of the surnames that appear most often on the wall of the Viet Nam Memorial in Washington, D.C., are Johnson and Rodriguez. These two names tell us something about the composition of the U.S. military during the war, especially the combat units. What they teach us, however, cannot be learned from reading the historical accounts of the war. "Johnson" combines the Caucasian and African American sacrifices. It locks into a single name the black/white opposition that structures virtually all discussions of race relations in the United States. "Rodriguez" stands for the Latino experience during the war—Chicanos from the Southwest, Puerto Ricans and Neoyoricans, Cuban Americans, and even Mexican nationals. "Rodriguez" functions as a third term or supplement that disrupts and complicates the black/white dichotomy. Histories of the war and cultural representations of the war have yet to hear the voice of "Rodriguez." This book is intended to give voice to one segment of that suppressed Latino chorus.

In the death and casualty lists of U.S. servicemen in Southeast Asia, all Mexican Americans are listed as "Caucasian." (The armed forces had abandoned the use of the category "Mexican" in 1949 in response to objections to the term by Mexican American advocacy groups.) Thus it is virtually impossible to know how many Chicanos served in Viet Nam.[5] Briefly told, a heavy load was carried by U.S. soldiers of Mexican descent in a war in which the burden was disproportionately borne by working-class people of color.

To date, no history of Chicano participation in the Viet Nam War has been published.[6] The only oral history of the war focused on the Chicano experience in Viet Nam is the one written and self-published by Charley Trujillo, a veteran whose manuscript was rejected by major publishing houses because they felt his subject matter was too narrow.[7]

In the years immediately following the war, some regional publications chronicled the deeds of local Chicano heroes, but none of these reached a wide readership. It is unlikely that these tributes could have been written by anyone other than intimate friends of the deceased, yet their motives seem to extend beyond the personal. In fact, they are shaped by a structure of experience that functions only in the most insular of communities: the need to construct monuments to lost heroes in order to reaffirm the community's patriotism and loyalty.[8]

One poignant example is Sol Marroquin's *Part of the Team: Story of an American Hero,* which honors Alfredo "Freddy" Gonzalez, a recipient of the Congressional Medal of Honor who died in Hue City in 1968.[9] The book is dedicated to "those who gave their lives to preserve our freedom" and is replete with traditional images of patriotism, loyalty, military glory, and masculinity (Gonzalez had been a high school football hero). Mexican Americans are referred to as "Latin Americans," thereby obscuring their status as U.S. citizens; in an exaggerated rhetoric of assimilation, the term "Chicano" is avoided. Gonzalez's own views of the war, however, were more complicated: Before returning to Viet Nam for his second tour of duty, he reportedly told a friend that he dreaded the thought of killing Vietnamese people because "they worked the fields and lived simple lives, like most Hispanics from the [Rio Grande] Valley."[10]

The Chicano Press

With few exceptions, the journals, newspapers, and literary magazines published by the Chicano Movement in the late 1960s and early '70s made only infrequent references to the war. (The exceptions were mostly in cities with a tradition of political activism; *El Informador,* in Berkeley, California, editorialized against the war as early as December 1967.) Newspapers published in relatively conservative Mexican American communities reproduced the patriotic rhetoric of World War I and World War II. In Houston, for example, the *Compass* newspaper ran columns on Mexican American winners of the Congressional Medal of Honor. *El Chicano,* published by Marta Macías McQueen in San Bernardino, California, did not include any articles or editorials critical of U.S. foreign policy until three people were killed in the aftermath of an anti-war demonstration in East L.A. on August 29, 1970—this despite the paper's staunch support for the United Farm Workers and *chicanismo* in general. In more radical publications, the occasional poem or public opinion survey was embedded among commentary on what were considered to be the more pressing issues of ethnic origins (e.g., Mexican and pre-Columbian culture), police brutality, educational reform, and cultural nationalism. As if somehow these important issues could be separated from what was happening in Southeast Asia, the Chicano press was largely silent on the topic of the war and Chicano participation in it.

One striking exception was *El Grito del Norte,* a Movement publication produced in the rural city of Española, New Mexico, and edited by Elizabeth "Betita" Martinez. A Chicana with extensive experience in the Civil Rights movement, Martinez created a journal that combined local issues, such as Reies Tijerina's land-redistribution campaign, with a strong internationalist focus. Chicano struggles were linked to political conflicts in Latin America, Cuba, and around the world. In late 1969 *El Grito del Norte* ran the first installment of a series on Vietnamese society and culture. The author, who used the pen name "Valentina," introduced the series by addressing the following questions to Chicano soldiers:

> Why, why are you going to fight in this war? Is it because that's the only way you can find to make a living? Or is it because you're tired of your little hometown and parents and you want to "see the world"? Or maybe because you want to impress the girls with your uniform? Or because you're afraid to have your buddies and girlfriends call you chicken?"[11]

The magazine's special issue for August 29, 1970, had a striking cover that drew upon the growing sense in the Chicano community that Vietnamese peasants and Mexican farmworkers had much in common. Six photographs are displayed in two columns headed "Their People ..." and "Our People ...": A group of Vietnamese children are juxtaposed to a group of Chicano children from northern New Mexico; "campesinos of North Vietnam" are side by side with "campesinos of Northern New Mexico"; and a North Vietnamese woman faces the image of "La Chicana."

In the same issue, Elizabeth Martinez reported directly from North Viet Nam. In a two-part series, "Lo que vi en Vietnam" ("What I saw in Vietnam"), she drew a connection between the Vietnamese peasant who had lost his land to large landowners and the situation faced by poor Mexicans throughout their history: "La historia de la guerra en Vietnam empezó por la tierra. Muchos años pasados, los campesinos perdieron sus tierras a los grandes terratenientes, hombres poderosos estos últimos (como les pasó a nuestros antepasados)." (The history of the war in Vietnam began because of the land. Many years ago, the peasants lost their lands to the large landowners, the latter very powerful men [just like what happened to our ancestors].) [12] Martinez then described the physical beauty of Viet Nam, its people, and its culture. Upon her return, Martinez unsuccessfully attempted to arrange for another visit to North Viet Nam by a large group of Chicano and Chicana activists. The majority of anti-war organizers she contacted felt that they would lose whatever credibility they had in their communities were they to participate in such a visit. [13]

Another effort to discuss the war in Movement publications was initiated by Octavio I. Romano V., a professor at the University of California at Berkeley and editor of the important Movement journal *El Grito*. In the Spring 1968 issue, law student Philip Jiménez wrote an essay on the illegality of the war according to international conventions. The same issue included a group of drawings by Esteban Villa entitled "¡Viet Nam!" The next year, Romano published a roll call of all the Latino casualties in Viet Nam, listed by place of origin: Texas, Puerto Rico, California, New Mexico. [14]

In 1973, as the war was winding down, Dorinda Moreno Gladden, a San Francisco Bay Area activist, published a collection of writings primarily by Chicanas, *La mujer—en pie de la lucha ¡y la hora es ya!* (Mexico City: Espina del Norte). Bringing together artistic and political agendas, Moreno's anthology included a chapter on the war in Viet Nam.

It is worth noting that the Chicano intellectual community—unlike the African American intellectual community—did not produce a group of highly visible anti-war activists. Writers who composed the first cadre of canonical Chicano authors, such as Rolando Hinojosa, did write about Viet Nam, but the core authors of the first Chicano canon (Anaya, Rivera, Hinojosa) were of an older generation, and their ties to the anti-war movement were not as strong as those of their counterparts in the African American community. Thus there were few nationally known Chicano public intellectuals to stand beside Martin Luther King, Jr., Julian Bond, James Baldwin, Amiri Baraka, or Huey Newton.[15]

Fiction

During the 1970s and '80s, the aftershocks of Viet Nam repeatedly surfaced in Chicano literary works that were not specifically about the war. For example, in the late '70s, the plight of the Vietnamese boat people was captured in a short poem by Juan Manuel Bernal, "A Thanh Le" ("To Thanh Le"):

> Carnal, carnalito, vietnamés:
> Sufres el mismo mal que todos
> los POBRES.
> Andas por los mares, como peregrino,
> queriendo beber, saciar tu hambre,
> con un palmo de agua en las manos.

> (Brother, my little Vietnamese brother: / You suffer the malady of all poor people / Roaming the seas like a pilgrim / wanting to quench your thirst / to feed your hunger / with a little water in your hands.)[16]

We also hear the echoes of Viet Nam in short stories such as Jack López's "Easy Time" and Dagoberto Gilb's "Nancy Flores," which refer to sons and brothers lost in the jungles of Southeast Asia yet still present in the memory of their families. Rosaura Sánchez's "The Ditch" reminds us that surveillance technologies developed during the war are now used by the INS and the Border Patrol in their campaigns against other poor people of color along the increasingly militarized U.S.-Mexico border.[17] In Eve Bunting's children's book *The Wall* (New York: Clarion, 1990), the central figures are a Latino father who takes his son to visit the Viet Nam Memorial in search of his own father's name—George Muñoz.

In literary works by non-Latino writers, Latino characters are relatively rare, and the few Chicano characters who do appear tend to be either gross stereotypes or unrecognizably assimilated.[18] I want to comment on three examples that are noteworthy in that they depart in different ways from conventional representations.

My first example is John M. Del Vecchio's novel *The Thirteenth Valley* (1982). Del Vecchio offers us a large group of characters, a cross-section of American society, including several Chicano GIs of different social classes. Early on, First Sergeant Eduardo Laguana, for example, is juxtaposed to radioman and college graduate Rafael "El Paso" Pavura, who questions Laguana's authority: "That stupid asshole. He doesn't have any right to tell me to trim my mustache. Son-of-a-bitch. Gives us Chicanos a bad name. Can't even speak English."[19] The child of first-generation Mexican immigrants, El Paso becomes a figure of intellectual, rather than military, authority in the novel. El Paso had been educated and mentored by a local priest, and he is extremely well-read in Vietnamese history and culture, the history of U.S. imperialism, and Chicano/Mexicano history. As the mediator between rival factions in the company, he bridges the black/white opposition and becomes a kind of soldier-philosopher with moral influence over his peers. The narrator explains:

> There was a simple law in the southwest and along the border where the Anglo oligarchy controlled the lands: No man is guilty of anything unless he is a Mexican. It was the same law against which El Paso revolted many years later when it was applied by Americans to Vietnamese—the It's Only-A-Gook Law. In the southwest the society was so structured as to continue the vicious circle of poverty, to trap the menial labor force in their mosquito-infested *barrio bajo,* a reinforced plague of illiteracy and unemployment. From this grew violence and revolutionary politics and to this Rafael was attracted.
>
> (p. 240)

This analogy between domestic racism and its imperialist counterpart appears in many writings by Chicano soldiers and anti-war activists. Despite the peculiar "Spanish" surnames Del Vecchio gives his Chicano characters, his representation of Chicano GIs is among the most complex offered by a non-Chicano author.

My second example is Isabel Allende's *El plan infinito* (1991). In an interesting departure from her earlier works, the popular Chilean novelist sets her text in the United States and includes several Chicano/a characters in principal roles. But it is a non-Chicano, Gregory Reeves, who figures as the Chicano Viet Nam combatant and veteran. Although not of Mexican descent, Reeves was raised in a Mexican American neighborhood, speaks Chicano

Spanish fluently, and in essence identifies himself as a Chicano. After enduring the trauma of the war, he returns home a cynical and self-centered hero. While in Viet Nam, he reflects on race relations in the military: "But racial tension burns beneath the superficial camaraderie: whites hang out with whites, blacks with blacks, Latinos with Latinos, Asians with Asians, all with their own language, music, rites, superstitions. In the camps the barrios have inviolable boundaries." [20] What is left out of Allende's account are those moments when ethnic and racial boundaries break down and a sense of solidarity emerges between members of diverse groups. This precarious solidarity is one of the major concerns of the present volume.

While the Viet Nam War and Chicano experiences of it are not the central theme of Allende's novel, her representation of Chicanos and race relations in the barracks and on the battlefield may be among the most influential because her novels enjoy a large readership in Spanish-speaking countries and are widely translated into English and other languages. This situation, in which (once again) Chicanos do not speak for themselves but are spoken for, raises a number of contradictions having to do with the production of a "Hispanic" literature and history that erase the specificities of each Latino community and its struggles. It is not a question of whether Allende "gets it right," but whether her readers will search out or have access to a variety of texts that discuss Chicanos and the war.

My last example is Joe Klein's *Payback* (1984), an account of five GIs' experiences after their return to the States. In this novel, a Chicana surfaces as the "foreign" female to whom a white veteran is attracted: "Eve [Holguín] was a junior, an accounting major from Los Angeles. She was a Mexican-American, and Steiner was intrigued by the contrast between her looks, which were exotic—long dark hair, dark eyes and olive skin—and her personality, which was unpretentious, friendly, funny and kind." [21] Why the juxtaposition of Latina features and a "friendly, funny, and kind" personality constitutes a "contrast" is not immediately clear. The one plausible reading, unfortunately, is that the veteran shares the kind of racializing attitudes that to a great extent drove U.S. policy in Southeast Asia, only here it is an American woman of Mexican descent who is the object of his colonialist desire.

Reading Chicano/a Writings on the American War in Viet Nam

The quest for a critical alternative would have to begin by asking what kind of service historians, or people with an education in history, can perform to support the subjectivity of individuals in their historical perception of themselves.

Lutz Niethammer (in collaboration with Dirk Van Laak),
Posthistoire: Has History Come to an End?

Above the text of her beautifully written remembrance of her brother who died in Southeast Asia (Reading 24), Chicana author Norma Elia Cantú places a photograph like those found in thousands of Mexican American homes since World War II. It is the standard photo issued upon graduation from armed forces basic training; its subject—a handsome and vibrant Chicano young man—is decked out in a brand new U.S. Army uniform, the tired smile on his face perhaps having less to do with masculine pride than with the sheer relief of having survived the ordeal of military indoctrination.

It is the relationship of the American war in Viet Nam to that photograph and writings about the war that haunts this anthology. For a community that has given many of its young men and women to the building of the United States, unacknowledged sacrifices begin to lose their meaning. For many in a community whose working-class and recently immigrated members continue to be caricatured and exploited for economic and political motives, the image of one more Chicano in uniform begins to lose its patriotic power. This is not to suggest that the U.S. military has ceased to be an important path to assimilation. Take the case of Luis Gómez, for example. One of four brothers currently in the Marine Corps, Gómez was born in Sonora, Mexico, and moved to California as a young boy. As he puts it: "Coming from another country, the Marines allowed me to pay back the United States for allowing me to go to school and grow up here." [22] Thirty years after the fact, the legacy of Viet Nam simply drops out of Gómez's narrative; for others it produces the bitter ironies that lay in wait for the reader of this anthology. What sets the two positions apart—unexamined patriotism versus critical consciousness—are the differing historical identities of Spanish-speaking communities in the contemporary United States.

Angie Chabram has argued that the first wave of Chicano-authored literary criticism took something called the "Chicano experience" as its master code, and "authenticity" and collective identities as its trademarks.[23] For those coming of age in the late 1960s, the war in Viet Nam and the efforts to stop it were a fundamental component of that experience. By the mid-1980s, however, something called postmodernism had unceremoniously shoved the idea of historical experience itself off the intellectual stage. Because postmodernism (and its academic precursor, poststructuralism) chose to "bracket" history and reject "master narratives" about collective action and social change, discussions about cultural representations of the war focused on the ways in which those representations reproduced the main characteristics of an already given "postmodern condition." Clichés abounded about Viet Nam as the first postmodern war: youth subcultures, technology, and the very nature of a guerrilla war, we were told, constituted a new, postmodern rendering of war literature. In effect, a canonical way of reading representations of the war was inaugurated and continues to hold sway to this day.

It is ironic, then, that the leading U.S. scholar of postmodernity—Fredric Jameson—was one of the first thinkers to point out the unique status of literature about the American war in Viet Nam. In his analysis of Michael Herr's *Dispatches* presented at a conference on the war held at UC Irvine in 1980, Jameson argued that what would later come to be called Viet Nam representation "forces us to confront the issue of the relationship between culture and reality—a political issue—more directly than we have the habit of doing with artistic and cultural representations generally. . . . It raises the question of the political effects of works like these in a situation . . . in which the rewriting of the past and of Vietnam plays a crucial role."[24] Jameson's insight—that writing about the war might necessarily require some form of the earlier cognitive mode called realism—sets up an uneasy tension between our sense of the Viet Nam debacle as "the first postmodern war" and our intuition that such assertions trivialize the profound human experiences of that moment and the cultural representations that seek to capture them. While it is true that the self-referential language of now canonical texts such as *Dispatches* partakes of a postmodernist aesthetic even as it echoes in realistic fashion the self-enclosed speech acts of American GIs, many of the texts in this anthology employ a different kind of realism, one that rather than mirror the incommunicable horror of the war attempts to delineate the historical causes that produced it.

Literature written by Chicanos and Chicanas both during and after the war unsettles our preconceptions about the postmodernity of Viet Nam representation. Because they are for the most part grounded in working-class understandings of community, nationality, and lived experience, these writings refuse to abandon their grounding in history and the real. Because they are inextricably bound up with issues of nation, class, and race, many of them force a reevaluation of those inherited forms of patriotism, white supremacy, and the "classless" nature of U.S. society that produced the war itself and has determined the treatment of Chicanos and Mexicanos at least since 1848 and the U.S. conquest of the Southwest. Like the photograph above Norma Cantú's text, the subjects in each of the readings draw us into the reality of a deeply felt experience, now some thirty years past. Despite the passage of time, both the living and the dead continue to insist: "Aquí estamos y no nos vamos" ("We're here and we're not leaving").

Part 1 / Standing at the Wall

Introduction

But from Oliver Stone, you would think that all our boys looked like Tom Cruise.

Bárbara Renaud González, "The Summer of Vietnam" [1]

In a speech on the floor of the U.S. Senate in 1972, future presidential nominee George McGovern spoke of Mexican Americans as "the most invisible of all our minority groups": "Whites count. Blacks count. Indians count. But due to the inexplicable ways of the bureaucracy, Mexican-Americans don't count." His speech included a timely, but unheeded, plea for Chicano veterans:

> I have been increasingly concerned lately with the difficulties facing veterans of our ill-conceived involvement in Vietnam. The unemployment rate among returning Vietnam veterans between 20 and 24 years of ages is 12.4%. These difficulties are even worse for veterans from minority groups, including Mexican-Americans who have contributed more than their fair share to this war. Fifteen percent of California's casualties, and ten percent of all casualties in the Southwest, have been Mexican-Americans. What Mexican-Americans want to know is why are they first in war but last in peace? Why are they good enough to lead men in combat in Vietnam, to carry the heavy responsibility of life and death, but not good enough to handle a desk in Washington? [2]

Although Chicano GIs found many common issues around which to organize, their experience of Viet Nam was not homogeneous. U.S. citizens of Mexican descent, or *la Raza* as they were grouped together by the Chicano Movement, have always constituted a heterogenous community whose members have had different historical experiences, the result of class, gender, region, generation, and other factors. In a poem written in 1977, Olivia Chumacero, one of the original players in El Teatro Campesino (the cultural arm of Cesar Chavez's United Farm Workers union), compared some of the features of Chicano culture in Texas with those in California:

What's the difference
between Califas y
Texas.
In Califas you know
ah, that's the way it is
you know
y en Texas
luego cambia la onda
tú sabes.
Aunque quieras o no
estamos más agabachados
en Califas
que en Texas.
Everybody digs on
Stevie Wonder and
Santana
y Linda Ronstadt
but not necessarily
in that order
luego siempre andamos con el
give me five!
Meantime back in
el Rancho Grande
están
   Los Royal Jesters
      Snowball y Compañía
         Los Alegres de Terán
           y para no
              hacer lo menos
                 Little Joe y la familia
                    qué locotl no.
Los pochos get down
con salsa y disco
Los tejanos
con cumbias y polkas
y rancheras
el famoso Tex-Mex sound.
Pero no hay fijación
porque
todo es puro movimiento
you dig.

(What's the difference between California and Texas. In California you know, ah, that's the way it is, you know, and in Texas,
then the scene changes, you know. Whether you like it or not
we're more assimilated in California than in Texas. Everybody
digs on Stevie Wonder and Santana and Linda Ronstadt but not
necessarily in that order and we always go around with the high
five! Meantime back on the Rancho Grande are The Royal Jesters,
Snowball and Company, Los Alegres de Terán, and last but not
least Little Joe and the family, how cool. The Americanized ones
get down with salsa and disco, the Texans with cumbias and
polkas and rancheras—the famous Tex-Mex sound. But there's
no problem because it's all nothing but movement, you dig.)[3]

In this poem, Chumacero puts to humorous effect the fact that in many of its
aspects Chicano culture in Texas remains more closely tied to the Spanish language and Mexican music than does Chicano culture in California. But the
final lines pull the diverse elements together in the universalizing *movimiento*
of the music, which also refers to the political movement that reached its apex
during the Viet Nam era.

In Rolando Hinojosa's *The Useless Servants* (1993), a fictional journal written by Rafe Buenrostro, the narrator comments upon the regional differences
among Mexican American soldiers during the Korean War:

Saw one guy I thought was a Texas Mexican. Turned out to be a Coloradan;
called himself Donald Trujillo. Says his people came from Spain, and then
Charlie and Joey asked him if those were the Spaniards that landed in Virginia and then trekked across the South until delivered safely and soundly
to the Promised Land. This is the third Coloradan we've run across, and
they all claim to be Spanish. Well, that's the first Mexican of any kind I've
ever met named Donald. We spoke Spanish to him, but he answered in
English.[4]

These same differences are used for comedic effect by Daniel Cano (see Readings 8 and 9): "*Pinche,* Woodland Hills, *Californio,* you *vatos* spend all your lives
with Mickey Mouse *y la* Marilyn Monroe *y* John Wayne. That ain't life, *ese.*
C'mon down to the Rio Grande Valley and learn what's it all about."[5]

While regional and linguistic difference can be used to create humor
in scenes such as these, more serious differences based on class, gender, and
levels of assimilation produced in Chicana/o writings about the American
war in Viet Nam a wide range of figures whose complex identities take shape

at the intersection of contradictory and often mutually exclusive categories, for example, the imperative of combat versus Catholicism's condemnation of taking a human life. The texts included in this anthology illustrate a range of reactions to the political and cultural changes, strong feelings of community and solidarity, and the violence and exhilaration that characterized the period. Thus there are writings by Chicano veterans that express a nascent solidarity with the Vietnamese people, an experience not shared by Chicano soldiers who were prisoners of war or career military personnel (see Readings 11 and 12). Yet it is precisely where these texts diverge most from conventional accounts that we may begin to understand the particularities of the "Chicano/a experience" of this country's longest war.

Toxic Liberalism

Much has been made of the fact that the Viet Nam War has not been, and perhaps cannot be, absorbed by official U.S. history. Despite attempts to "get beyond Viet Nam" by conducting "more successful" wars against developing nations, the specter of Viet Nam continues to inhabit the national psyche. Books such as Myra MacPherson's *Long Time Passing: Vietnam and the Haunted Generation* (1984; rpt. 1993) play upon the notion of lingering trauma and tragedy, but I would argue that the war cannot be "figured out" nor "factored in" at least in part because it marked the end of uncontested "white" hegemony and radically destabilized the meaning of what it is to be an American. The racial, ethnic, and class composition of U.S. combat units and the final Vietnamese victory together revealed the hypocrisy and inefficacy of the white male ruling class and its particular brand of liberalism. That a disproportionate number of combat troops were poor, brown, and black should have forced (but did not) a rethinking of American identity and the rights and responsibilities of citizenship. The ramifications of this break in the liberal tradition continue to be felt in the late 1990s through neo-conservative charges of "reverse discrimination," the "oppression of the white male," and other self-serving fantasies that motivate the roll back of the minimal gains of the Civil Rights era.

In early 1967, in a brilliant moral and political analysis of the war's disastrous effects, Martin Luther King, Jr., spoke in Manhattan's Riverside Church:

As I ponder the madness of Vietnam and search within myself for ways to understand and respond in compassion my mind goes constantly to the people of that peninsula. I speak now not of the soldiers of each side, not of the junta in Saigon, but simply of the people who have been living under the curse of war for almost three continuous decades now. I think of them too because it is clear to me that there will be no meaningful solution there until some attempt is made to know them and hear their broken cries. . . . In order to atone for our sins and errors in Vietnam, we should take the initiative in bringing a halt to this tragic war. . . . We must continue to raise our voices if our nation persists in its perverse ways in Vietnam. We must be prepared to match actions with words by seeking out every creative means of protest possible.[6]

Dr. King's plea for an end to American ethnocentrism, his repudiation of Johnson's war policy, and his call for renewed efforts by the anti-war movement would be silenced by the assassinations of 1968 and the election of Richard Nixon. But his claim, in the same speech, that the war in Viet Nam had been the primary cause for the derailment of the domestic war on poverty would be picked up by Johnson himself and become a generally accepted axiom.

The bankruptcy of traditional liberalism exposed in Dr. King's speech deserves our attention. For if poor whites and poor people of color were being victimized at home because of misguided national priorities, poor whites and poor people of color were also the ones thrust into fighting the war. It is the point at which Johnson's War on Poverty entered into an unholy alliance with the Pentagon that the government created a direct conduit from the barrios and ghettos to the killing fields of Viet Nam. The primary architects of the policy were Secretary of Defense Robert McNamara and Daniel Patrick Moynihan, then best known for his analysis of what he called the "disorganized and matrifocal" structure of "the Negro family." Military service, Moynihan argued, was the perfect cure for poverty: "Very possibly our best hope is seriously to use the armed forces as a socializing experience for the poor—particularly the Southern poor—until somehow their environment begins turning out equal citizens."[7] How the "environment" of the "southern poor" (i.e., poor African Americans) would "somehow" eventually create better citizens was never specified.

The plan to socialize poor people through military service had its origins in the Task Force on Manpower Conservation report submitted to President

Johnson in January 1964. Established by President Kennedy two months before his death, the task force was commissioned to investigate the fact that half the men tested by the Selective Service System were deemed unqualified for the armed forces. In Kennedy's opinion: "A young man who does not have what it takes to perform military service is not likely to have what it takes to make a living. Today's military rejects are tomorrow's hard-core unemployed."[8] As a member of the original task force, McNamara was well positioned to make the deadly connection between "curing poverty" and supplying additional men for the military. Men who had been rejected for either mental or medical reasons were to be retested for their suitability to enter what Selective Service director General Lewis Hershey called "a program for the guidance, testing, counseling, training and rehabilitation of youths found disqualified for military service."[9]

During Johnson's first years in office, this plan gained new urgency as military leaders realized that the draft pool would have to be expanded, either upwards (to include middle-class college students) or downwards. In August 1966, at a time of escalating manpower needs, Secretary of Defense McNamara announced the creation of Project 100,000, thus named because its goal was to enable the induction of 100,000 previously unqualified men each year. By presenting Project 100,000 as another jobs and training program linked to the Great Society, McNamara followed Kennedy in claiming that disadvantaged youth would be well served by the military, that they would learn valuable skills: "The poor of America have not had the opportunity to earn their fair share of this Nation's abundance, but they can be given an opportunity to serve in their country's defense and they can be given an opportunity to return to civilian life with skills and aptitudes which, for them and their families, will reverse the downward spiral of human decay."[10]

The goal of 100,000 inductees was to be met by drastically lowering standards and accepting men with low scores on the Armed Forces Qualification Test. Standards for advanced training programs, however, were not adjusted. As a result, tens of thousands of poor and poorly educated minority soldiers were recruited, assigned to infantry units, and dispatched to Southeast Asia. Over 50 percent of the "new standards men" fought in Viet Nam; over 50 percent of these men were African American.[11]

Because the military did not keep separate statistics for Mexican American or Latino servicemen, no one can calculate the effect of Project 100,000 on Chicano communities. In 1967 a presidential commission, reporting that a disproportionate number of "Negro" soldiers had died in combat (22.4% of all those killed in action during the first eleven months of 1966), concluded: "There is reason to believe that many of the statistics relating to the Negro would be comparable for some other minority groups, although specific information to establish this is not available." [12] Data on men previously rejected by the services on "mental" as opposed to physical grounds (over 90 percent of all Project 100,000 inductees) show the largest percentage coming from Puerto Rico and a disproportionate percentage coming from south Texas and other southern states. Many men whose first language was Spanish did not score well on the military qualification test, which placed them in the ranks of the new standards men.

The extent to which the Selective Service interpreted cultural and linguistic difference as "mental inferiority" is impossible to reconstruct. In a report prepared in late 1964 and published by the Department of the Army in 1965 (some eight months before the announcement of Project 100,000), "marginal men" were separated into physical, mental, and moral categories. Following up on studies conducted by the Army in 1953 ("Fort Leonard Wood study") and by the Air Force in 1952 ("Project 1000"), the report summarized research on whether men who would otherwise be rejected from military service might be given special training in order to increase their "usefulness." An entire chapter was devoted to "Army-wide Utilization of Puerto Rican Enlisted Men." [13]

The case of Puerto Rico is suggestive. Since the 1950s, the Department of the Army had operated special English-language programs in Puerto Rico. Once they attained minimal language proficiency, the participants were transferred to the mainland for regular basic training. By the Army's own admission, these programs were less than successful: through 1964, the drop-out rate was 56 percent. As manpower needs escalated and Project 100,000 was enacted, the government discontinued the language proficiency program; the new lower standards eliminated the need for pre-induction remedial programs. Although Puerto Rico ranked approximately twenty-sixth in population among the fifty states during the Viet Nam era, Puerto Rico ranked fourteenth in casualties and fourth in combat deaths. It was not until 1970 that a federal judge ruled against the Army in the case of *portorriqueño* Carlos J. Rivera-Toledo, finding that the Army had not complied with its own regulations regarding the testing of non-English-speaking inductees and that the Army had failed to provide adequate training. Rivera-Toledo was subsequently released from military service.

One of the few novels to refer to Project 100,000 is Charles Durden's

No Bugles, No Drums (1976). A traditional combat narrative set during one soldier's tour of duty, Durden's novel is at the same time a curious blend of anti-war sentiments and stereotypical caricatures of minority GIs. Narrator Jamie Hawkins arrives in Viet Nam and joins other new guys in a platoon that includes four new standards men—three African Americans and a Chicano:

> Garcia 'n' the Drill Team, like Jinx, were dubious benefactors of McNamara's brainchild. McNamara's 100,000. It has a ring, like Fortune 500, or 10 Downing Street (which, when I saw it on TV, really wasn't very impressive from the outside). McNamara's 100,000—pulled from the compost heap of America's hopeless. That sounds bitter, but I don't know if I really care much, one way or the other. Maybe I blame McNamara for what happened. I might as well blame God. I don't expect to ever get a chance to talk to either one of 'em. But it was McNamara, not God, who put his name to the program—retrainin' the retards. Takin' people who couldn't read or write well enough to pass the Army's basic entrance exam (geared to a sixth-grade level) and puttin' 'em through a cram course. Teachin' 'em to read 'n' write just enough to pass the test for cannon fodder. Teachin' 'em to write their name so they could sign their own death warrant.[14]

Durden's anger at another social engineering program and its disastrous effects on poor minorities does not preclude his using Garcia primarily as comic relief. A poor Chicano from San Diego, Garcia speaks fractured English and harbors a dream of becoming a bullfighter. He dies in a gruesome yet ridiculous scene in which he challenges a water buffalo by waving his jacket and shouting "Toro, toro." Even his corpse is an object of mockery: an enterprising GI disposes of Garcia's body in order to ship home a large quantity of marijuana in the coffin. Toward the end of the novel, the narrator points his M-16 at a herd of local pigs, takes aim at the one that the GIs had named McNamara, and blows it apart.

Project 100,000 stands as one of the landmarks in the failure and fundamental dishonesty of the liberal project. Although none of its principal architects would have considered himself racist, the consequences of their actions were unquestionably racist. Liberal discourse was structured upon racialized categories, and racial language permeated policymaker circles to such an extent that even a relatively "progressive" dove like George Ball could write the following, in a memo to President Johnson:

The South Vietnamese are losing the war to the Viet Cong. No one can assure you that we can beat the Viet Cong or even force them to the conference table on our terms, no matter how many hundred thousand white, foreign (U.S.), troops we deploy.

No one has demonstrated that a white ground force of whatever size can win a guerrilla war—which is at the same time a civil war between Asians—in jungle terrain in the midst of a population that refuses cooperation to the white forces (and the South Vietnamese) and thus provides a great intelligence advantage to the other side.[15]

"White" forces versus people of color—the lines of battle could not be drawn more starkly.

Today conservative politicians and intellectuals are riding the wave of resentment felt by "white males" who claim to be a new persecuted minority. Attacks on affirmative action programs and multicultural education are mounted on the back of the claim that people of color are somehow practicing "reverse discrimination." Although the balance of social and economic power continues to favor white males overwhelmingly, white male supremacy no longer holds the unquestioned privilege it once did—and this, it seems to me, is a direct consequence of the kind of thinking about race, class, and power that began during the Viet Nam War. To cite one important example: On December 26, 1971, fifteen Viet Nam veterans barricaded themselves in the Statue of Liberty, calling for an end to the war. Their statement to the press echoed an analysis that Latino and African American activists had developed early on: "The reason we chose the Statue of Liberty is that since we were children, the statue has been analogous in our minds with freedom and an America we love. Then we went to fight a war in the name of freedom. We saw that freedom is a selective expression allowed only to those who are white and who maintain the status quo."[16]

Structures of Experience

In her groundbreaking study of U.S. and Vietnamese literature about the war, Renny Christopher summarizes the complex epistemological disjuncture between experience and narrative: "Overriding faith in the validity of individual experience causes us to read Viet Nam narratives as historical documents rather than as literature. The relationship to reality is assumed to be unmediated."[17] Readers, in other words, mistakenly assume that writings by veterans are close to the truth of what happened. But because most published texts on the war have been written by European American males, the "reality" of the war as received by readers is hopelessly narrow and too often ethnocentric. This approach to veteran-authored texts also establishes an unassailable authority ("if you weren't here, you can't understand") and excludes alternative "experiences."

The highly mediated nature of narrative, its distance from some irrecoverable "real," has a special bearing on war stories, including accounts of the anti-war movement. That literary texts constitute a second-level reality composed of inherited forms and languages is a fundamental tenet of criticism, one that in its most recent manifestations produced the fashion for "interrogating representations." The pitfall is that by narrowing the critical focus to the constituent parts of a given representation, one loses sight of the fact that "something" actually did happen before the production of the text. In other words, while it is true that the "real" or historical itself is not recuperable, it is also true that the aftershocks of the real are the precondition for any textualization. This rather commonsense notion, however, is necessarily an issue for debate for the discipline of cultural criticism, especially in the case of war literature, which, as Fredric Jameson argues, "forces us to confront the issue of the relationship between culture and reality—a political issue—more directly than we have the habit of doing with artistic and cultural representations generally. In particular, it raises the question of whether a work of art can be judged in terms of its accuracy to life, whether it can convey the experience of the war and of the veteran, and even more basically, whether it can communicate that experience to people who have never had it."[18]

The "you had to be there" position typical of many veteran-authored texts founders because not even the participant who retells his or her story can tell an unmediated truth. Yet no one can doubt that the physical and psychological contexts of a veteran's experience diverge radically from those of the nonveteran. The point, however, is not to privilege one experience over another, even as we concede that the "something that happened" to the veteran will influence his later actions (and in the case of writers, his texts). In a like manner, the experience of the anti-war demonstrator, or that of someone whose relative was killed in the war, still affects his or her present condition in ways that those who did not share that experience will not immediately comprehend.

It is not that literary representations are history, but that literary representations are always historical insofar as they are deeply embedded in the
raw material of historical praxis.[19] "Within" the texts by Patricio Paiz (Reading 14) and Norma Elia Cantú (Reading 24), for example, lie the very real
deaths of two young Chicanos—Arturo Tijerina, twenty-one years old, and
Florentino Cantú, Jr., nineteen—both killed by small-arms fire in early 1968
in the Republic of South Viet Nam.

Rather than claiming that each "individual" experience is unique, however, I want to argue that even the most intimate experience cannot be re-
duced to individual action but rather is the result of complex social conjunc-
tures. In this way, we can begin to speak of Chicano/a experiences of the Viet
Nam War. I take the term "structure of experience" from Raymond Williams
in order to insist that "something" always precedes the text ("experience") and
also to emphasize that "experience" is a product of social and cultural structures. Williams's use of the term remained underdeveloped precisely because
of its close connection to the more ephemeral concept of "structure of feeling"
as he defined it in *Marxism and Literature*. There, Williams sought to describe
those moments when "experience, immediate feeling, and then subjectivity
and personality are newly generalized and assembled."[20] Arguing at one
point that such moments were often, though not necessarily, linked to specific
generations or to the emergence of social classes, Williams obscured the
term's meaning by in essence collapsing it back into the concepts of ideology
or worldview. Nevertheless, his initial insight remains useful because it allows
us to consider the kinds of unsettling experiences leading to the radical rethinking of inherited "common sense" that the war produced in the Chicano
community. Williams argues that the tension between everyday experience
and received forms is not always clearly understood:

> The tension is as often an unease, a stress, a displacement, a latency: the mo-
> ment of conscious comparison not yet come, often not even coming. And
> comparison is by no means the only process, though it is powerful and im-
> portant. There are the experiences to which the fixed forms do not speak at
> all, which indeed they do not recognize. There are important mixed expe-
> riences, where the available meaning would convert part to all, or all to
> part. And even where form and response can be found to agree, without ap-
> parent difficulty, there can be qualifications, reservations, indications else-
> where: what the agreement seemed to settle but still sounding elsewhere.
>
> (*Marxism and Literature*, p. 130)

It is precisely this "sounding elsewhere" produced by the dissonance between traditional forms of patriotism, masculinity, and assimilation and the actual experience of the war that resonates throughout the readings in this anthology. By isolating specific structures of experience within these texts, I hope to begin the preliminary analysis that will lead to a rethinking of the so-called Viet Nam War canon in U.S. literary studies and a reevaluation of a particular moment in the development of Chicano literature. What we find in many of these writings is a profound questioning of ethnocentrism, white supremacy, Cold War mythology, and traditional forms of masculinity. Because most Chicana/o writers are situated outside the dominant intellectual and artistic circles, and because their communities are invisible to government and economic elites, many of them have been able to view American society with a critical eye and a righteously indignant pen.

"Our kids don't have blue eyes"

In a photograph of a 1968 rally during the Los Angeles high school "blow-outs" (demonstrations for educational reform), one sign strikes with special force: "Our kids don't have blue eyes, but they go overseas to die." Some would say that the sign-maker's mistake was to use the conjunction "but," for it is precisely *because* they did not have blue eyes that young Chicano men were sent overseas. But the sign-maker's point was a different one: "Give us credit for dying for our country. We too are Americans."

Since the turn of the century, Mexican Americans have served in the U.S. armed forces in disproportionate numbers.[21] One factor that complicates the service of this community is the thorny issue of assimilation, its connection to patriotism and to the promise of full citizenship in the nation. For members of groups already marked as not fully "American," the desire to fit in—to not call attention to one's self by refusing to practice conventional behavior—is especially strong. Even the first anti-war plays staged in the late 1960s by El Teatro Campesino embody the tension produced by the desire to assimilate. In the 1971 *acto* (one-act play) *Soldado Razo* (*Buck Private*), the narrator describes the departure of a young Chicano soldier: "So Johnny left for Vietnam, never to return. He didn't want to go and yet he did. It never crossed his mind to refuse. How can he refuse the gobierno de los Estados Unidos? How could he refuse his family?"[22] The suggestion that his family's wishes coincide with those of the U.S. government, that the refusal to serve would disappoint both equally, reminds us that Latinos, like other "unmeltable" ethnic groups, are under immense pressure to fit in and submit to the demands of state authority.

The drive to assimilate through military service is exacerbated by one of the most pernicious legacies of Mexican culture: warrior patriotism. The idea that masculine behavior must include a readiness to die for "la patria" is powerful in Mexican nationalist ideology. When transferred to the Chicano context it is especially dangerous since the Mexican male's rhetorical claim that he is willing to die anytime anywhere becomes a fatal reality once it is linked to U.S. imperialist projects. As the son declares in the "Corrido del padre de un soldado," by famed *tejano* composer José Morante, "Soy purito mexicano / y no le temo al morir" ("I'm one hundred percent Mexican / and I'm not afraid to die") (Reading 1). To cite a more recent example: In the wake of the Persian Gulf War, the *tejano* musical group Little Joe y la familia combined national icons from both the United States and Mexico, and invoked clichés like "Voy a la guerra contento" ("I go happily off to war") and "Mi raza sabe morir dondequiera" ("My people know how to die anywhere").[23]

In the short story "Feliz Cumpleaños, E.U.A." ("Happy Birthday, U.S.A."), published in 1979, Rolando Hinojosa wrote against the patriotic grain and asks his reader to imagine the unimaginable: "Sí, y como dije, después vino Korea y de repente, como si tal cosa, vino el Vietná . . . y allí va la raza de nuevo . . . ah, y esta vez muchos de los bolillos rehusaron ir—sí, raza—que no iban y no iban y no fueron . . . ¿qué tal si la raza no hubiera ido, eh? Se pueden imaginar." ("Yeah, like I said, then came Korea and then, just like that, came Vietnam . . . and there went Chicanos again . . . and this time a lot of white boys refused to go—yes, my fellow Chicanos—they weren't going to go and they didn't go . . . What would have happened if Chicanos hadn't gone? You can imagine.")[24] The implied listener here is a traditional Mexican American community aghast at the thought that someone, anyone, had refused military service. If Chicanos were to resist, how would the state respond? More important, how would the community react? In Luis Valdez's play *The Dark Root of a Scream,* the death in Viet Nam of the character Indio is attributed in part to the pressure to serve he felt from the community:

GATO: He rapped against the war, but his time came and he had to go
a huevo [of necessity] just like everybody else.
PRIEST: He was concerned what the barrio would think if he refused
induction.

GATO: If he'd gone to the pinta [prison] instead of the army, all the barrio would have said he was chicken.

PRIEST: He was considering fleeing the country, but he knew he'd never be able to return as a community leader.[25]

In massive numbers, Chicanos faced with the prospect of going to Viet Nam reacted with the same sense of duty or fatalism that had inspired their fathers, cousins, and uncles in World War II and Korea.[26] The case of the small town of Silvis, Illinois, exemplifies the sacrifices made by Chicanos in the armed forces. The town, which sits along the Mississippi River, near the Iowa border, became home to Mexican railroad workers who had journeyed north to labor on the Rock Island line. During World War II, Korea, and Viet Nam, a single block in that community (renamed Hero Street in the 1960s) sent eighty-seven young men to war. Among those who died were men like Tony Pompa, a Mexican citizen who enlisted under an assumed name. As of 1994, over one hundred residents of Hero Street had served in the U.S. military.

In discussing Mexican American participation in U.S. wars, we must focus critical attention on the social networks that allowed some groups to resist the war while others were unable to do so. The conflation of duty to family and duty to country is strikingly present in one Chicano veteran's explanation of why he served: "I didn't have much of a choice. If I had refused to get drafted, what was I going to do? It would have been just as hard to refuse the draft as it was to go into the army. Where was I going to go? I had nowhere to go. That would have been real hard on my *jefitos* [parents]."[27] The chant "You don't have to go!" offered to minority draftees by the relatively privileged student leaders of the campus anti-war movement wholly ignored the intense pressures and contradictions felt by members of working-class communities of color.

The material conditions of poverty, job discrimination, and educational tracking together with what was felt to be the overwhelming obligation to serve and prove one's loyalty according to traditional notions of nation and masculinity were responsible for the relatively low number of Chicano draft resisters during the Viet Nam era. Nevertheless, Chicano men slowly joined the ranks of those who refused to participate in the killing. Ernesto Vigil, of Denver, was the first to refuse induction, stating that he would not fight against his "brown brothers in Vietnam."[28] This sentiment and language was echoed by other resisters like Rosalío Muñoz, David Corona (son of long-time Chicano activist Bert Corona), Fred Aviles, and Manuel Gómez. In a letter to his draft board in 1969, Gómez wrote: "The Vietnamese people are not my enemy, but brothers involved in the same struggle for justice against a common enemy. We are all under the same sky. East and West are one."[29] A combination of the language of Chicano nationalism and mythic images of a prelapsarian nature, Gómez's letter previews the major tropes of Chicano anti-war literature in the early 1970s.

By the late 1960s, it became evident to many in Mexican American communities, as it had to many all across the country, that U.S. involvement in Viet Nam was not a battle to defend democracy, as World War II had been. The shift from an earlier generation's unqualified patriotism to the Chicano generation's ambivalent attitudes toward the war is illustrated by a letter written by a World War II veteran and LULAC (League of Latin American Citizens) activist father to his son, Douglas MacArthur Herrera, who was in the military but had refused to obey orders to ship out to Viet Nam:

> Dear Son: Your Mom and I were very shocked to read your letter and you know we have never had a Herrera yet who has refused to serve his country. Your family will never live it down and your life will be ruined. You should not question your country's motives and its foreign policy, and in the overall picture someone must suffer.... Your objections will be widely publicized here in Texas and your family will probably have to move out of Texas to get over the embarrassment and humiliation of what you are doing. Knowing your feelings your entire family will be more proud of you now if you go back and finish the few short months that you have to go. Think of your AGGIE BUDDIES! Your school has a glorious tradition almost as long as the Herrera family of serving our country always without question. There has not been a single Aggie Buddy that has refused to serve, there has not been a single Herrera, don't be the first one son, don't make us ashamed of you. Go back and serve your country. Don't break our hearts. Please call us and tell us that you are going to do the right thing to your country and to your family.[30]

From the father's point of view, the son has brought such profound shame upon his family that they will feel compelled to leave their home, even to move to another state. In effect, by disrupting the long line of Mexican American service in U.S. wars, the younger Herrera threatens to destroy one of the most important roads to assimilation.

Ralph Molina's short pieces (Reading 20), written in dialogue with the memoirs of Octavio I. Romano V., a Chicano Movement *veterano* and

World War II veteran, reflect the differences between the worthy cause of World War II and the uselessness of the sacrifices in Southeast Asia. For both Molina and Romano, however, a constant is the racism directed toward people of Mexican descent and the ironic situation of the Chicano GI who "fights for America" even as America's dominant institutions oppress his community. Molina's soldier in Viet Nam reads accounts of the police actions against demonstrators in East L.A.; Romano's soldier overseas reads accounts of the Zoot Suit riots of 1942, when roving gangs of sailors and marines attacked Mexican American youth throughout Southern California.[31]

Nowhere are the contradictions inherent in the Chicano soldier's position more explicit than in the story of Everett Alvarez, Jr., who was held as a prisoner of war for eight and a half years in North Viet Nam. Alvarez's participation in the U.S. war in Southeast Asia spans the early 1960s, when he became a Navy aviator, through the Gulf of Tonkin incident, and on to the release of the POWs in 1973 and the dedication of the Viet Nam Memorial in 1982. Alvarez's account of this twenty-year period, the autobiographical *Chained Eagle* (Reading 12), is at once a conventional tale of heroism, an apology for the war, and a compendium of mutually exclusive positions regarding its meaning.[32]

Alvarez's prologue is a stunning example of patriotic discourse as it was reformulated in the 1980s by Reaganite ideologues and a large sector of Viet Nam veterans. In their view, the problem with the war was that the men who fought it were not allowed to win. The fact that such an interpretation, as well as the following analysis, was offered by a member of a relatively disempowered minority group, the grandson of Mexican immigrants, makes it both predictable and paradoxical.

If wars bring the ultimate destruction, they also present the noblest challenges. Prolonged captivity under brutal conditions in a hostile land pits a man against overwhelming odds. My survival depended on much more than trying to satisfy a craving for food, and overcoming the emptiness of isolation and the pain of torture. My strength came from holding fast to my faith in God and belief in the values enshrined in our Constitution: duty, loyalty, unity, integrity, honor, allegiance, courage and hope. Without my absolute belief in these core virtues of our heritage I don't believe I would have pulled through alive and sane.

(*Chained Eagle*, p. 2)

The juxtaposition of military values and the U.S. Constitution marks Alvarez's text as the product of a career Navy officer. But it also suggests the easy connections made by many Americans between the modern responsibilities of citizens and ancient patriarchal and religious codes of conduct. As he stepped off the plane upon his return, Alvarez told the assembled crowd: "God bless the president and God bless you Mr. and Mrs. America" (p. 312).

The chapter from *Chained Eagle* reproduced here represents the divisions that split U.S. society in general and the Alvarez family in particular. Although Alvarez was being held by the North Vietnamese, both his mother (Soledad) and sister (Delia) came to publicly oppose the war. The family was torn (and torn apart) by loyalty to its eldest son, belief in the promises of U.S. culture, and serious questions about the morality of the war. As Delia Alvarez put it: "Everett will return when Vietnamese children will be able to look at the sky and clouds and not fear that a bomb will drop that will burn and tear their bodies."[33]

The second passage reproduced here from *Chained Eagle* is an imaginary novel described by Alvarez during his captivity. Alvarez never explicitly mentions his Mexican American ethnicity in this narrative, elaborated over a six-year period and recounted to his fellow prisoners as part of an exercise to cope with boredom and fatigue. The story of a young "Hispanic boy"[34] contains elements found in countless Chicano novels of education: The boy is orphaned at an early age and travels to the East Coast, where he has contact with and "adopts" the dominant U.S. culture; after violent encounters with racism in the Southwest, he "returns" to Mexico and searches for his origins, the utopian dream realized in California. Although the author claims that there is nothing autobiographical in this imagined setpiece, it is as if Alvarez's unconscious had finally been allowed to speak.

Roy Benavidez's *The Three Wars of Roy Benavidez* (1986) is the account of another Chicano Viet Nam War hero who, despite childhood memories of discrimination and a grueling rehabilitation after being seriously wounded, concludes that he "would do it all again." Benavidez's text is perhaps less introspective than Alvarez's, but he speaks more openly about racism aimed at Mexicans in the Southwest during the late 1940s and early '50s. In one flashback, in which he describes segregated moviehouses in South Texas, Benavidez provides a glimpse of the ethnic- and class-based reasons that have motivated some Mexican Americans to attempt to "prove themselves" through military service:

Once in the balcony, the division was down the middle—blacks on one side, Mexicans on the other. Below, gringos milled about, sitting where they wanted.

Often, I edged past the usher and took my seat in the middle of the whites. I was a small kid, a thin barefoot boy who couldn't hide the color of his skin, even in a darkened theater. Soon, I would feel the tap on my shoulder. "Okay, muchacho, get up. You don't belong down here. Go on upstairs where you belong."

I got into scores of fights just because I resented—and envied—the white kids who had new shoes or who could afford to buy an ice cream cone any time they wanted. There was no joy in being poor and no pride in my heritage. I was a spic, a tamale-eater, a greaser; nothing more— except angry. The rage and frustration were all there for the makings of a bully, and I went a long way toward getting there.

It was important to me to prove that I wasn't afraid of anything, much less anybody. I guess it was the machismo nature of the Hispanic male mingling with the Indian blood of my Yaqui mother. My mother was a member of an Indian tribe which settled in Mexico and then refused to bow to the Spaniards in the seventeenth century or the Mexicans in the nineteenth century. Defying army after army, only starvation had defeated them at the turn of the twentieth century.[35]

Benavidez's analysis falls apart as he attempts to reduce complex issues of class, ethnicity, and masculinity in an oppressed Chicano community to the category of blood, that is, his Yaqui lineage. But elsewhere in his text he subtly describes the bigotry and exclusion suffered by African Americans and Mexicanos in the years immediately preceding the Civil Rights era. Such background material makes the conclusion of Benavidez's text all the more stunning. When asked by a congressman whether or not he would serve again in Viet Nam given everything that had happened to him, Benavidez replies: "Sir, to answer your question properly and honestly, I would say yes . . . yes sir, I would do it all over" (*The Three Wars of Roy Benavidez,* p. 288).

"Color is not the game"

The two structures of experience I have mentioned thus far would seem to be mutually exclusive: the young Chicano's refusal to fight an unjust war (Herrera) or his identification with non-Americans of color (Gómez) stand in an uneasy relationship to the patriotism and desire for assimilation present in many Chicano communities (Alvarez and Benavidez). Let us try to move beyond this apparent contradiction by naming a third structure. This structure produces a new trope that is implicitly linked to the building of coalitions among people of color in the United States. The political impulse in this case is no longer tacit acceptance of nationalist mythologies nor the transitory clash of conflicting values; rather, it is a critical analysis of class and race relations rethought in the light of the Chicano's participation in an imperialist war.

It is somewhat of a commonplace in literature about war that the intensity of combat temporarily erases differences of race and class. What sociologists label "primary-group relationships" have been commented upon by philosophers and represented by creative writers in a variety of genres. Dr. King referred to the situation of men from varied class and racial backgrounds thrown together in Viet Nam as a "brutal solidarity." [36] J. Glenn Gray described this provisional unity in *The Warriors:* "This confraternity of danger and exposure is unequaled in forging links among people of unlike desire and temperament, links that are utilitarian and narrow but no less passionate because of their accidental and general character." [37] Without inventing a false racial harmony among American GIs, I want to suggest that what in other contexts has been dismissed as male bonding and homosocial relations is in fact a preliminary model for group solidarity with important potential for progressive political agendas.

During the war, especially in the rear areas, race relations among U.S. troops were often tense if not openly hostile. As veteran Lou Lacariere recalled:

It depends on where you were. I spent time in the field and time in the rear. In the field there wasn't much of a problem between blacks, Hispanics, and Caucasians. We all knew that we were fighting a common enemy and that we had to depend on each other. In the field color seemed to disappear. We became real close no matter what color of skin we had. They seemed to take us in even though we were white. It didn't seem to matter, and that was different from their experience stateside. The movies that make a big deal about racial problems in the field I don't think are accurate. After I was in country for 10 months I was wounded and got a job in the rear in the Long Binh area. There I saw a lot of segregation in terms of blacks hanging out with blacks and whites hanging out with whites, and the same thing with Hispanics. There was a lot of division and some animosity. [38]

Despite these differences between the "field" and the "rear," the combat zone was not a utopian space of undifferentiated community. There are too many stories of U.S. soldiers putting bounties on the heads of reckless or incompetent officers, of fraggings and "accidental" deaths, for us to romanticize social and race relations in combat. The hierarchies and the injustices back "in the world" obviously informed how different groups of GIs viewed one another. The most basic tension was encapsulated by the formula black versus white, but some men were attentive to class differences and understood the inadequacy of a simple analysis based on "race." As one black veteran said, "But you know how it is—the whites got to have their way or else. Or else—someone's got to suffer, whether it be the American black man or the poor white man or Mexican American."[39]

What we find in some Chicano/Latino and African American writings about Viet Nam confirms Lacariere's sense of a solidarity born of mutual dependence. One black veteran, interviewed by Malcolm Boyd, put a provocative spin on the same intuition: "I think Vietnam is the best thing that ever happened to a white man. He's been able to associate closer to the black man here. He's in a position where he can see the black man *for a man*."[40] A Chicano veteran viewed the war as an experience that freed him from narrow ethnocentrism: "I mean, they [Anglos] were my enemy back home. Everybody who was white was my enemy and with my experience in Vietnam and meeting and knowing and getting very close to a lot of Anglos, close enough to say that I trust them with my life, I learned a lot more than I would have if I never got out of my neighborhood."[41]

This sentiment is poignantly expressed in the recollections of Robert Sanders, an African American veteran. But Sanders's concept of an inclusive community stumbles over the issue of sexuality, and his concept of "family" is homophobic:

It takes a tragedy to bring people together. In our particular case, that tragedy brought us so close that I felt closer to everybody in that unit at the time than I do my own blood sisters and brothers. Because it was us. We'd seen hard times. We'd seen fear. It was THE family. I mean, it was us, man. It wasn't like a regular family that may not have enough food or jobs. In our particular family, we knew that in a few minutes everybody could be dead. We was close, without being "funny." I mean like gays. We was so close it was unreal. That was the first time in my life I saw that type of unity, and I haven't seen it since. And that was ten years ago. It was beautiful. It sort of chills you, brings goose bumps just to see it, just to feel it, cause the family is guys from all the states, from New York and California, Chicago, Mississippi, 'Bama, everywhere. At first, you got all these funky types of personalities hooking up into one military unit. Everybody had their own little hatreds, their own little prejudices, biases. But after four, five, six months that disappeared. You just saw total unity and total harmony. It was really great, man. It was beautiful. That was the only thing that really turned me on in Vietnam. That was the only thing in Vietnam that had any meaning.[42]

For those who fear that finding any meaning at all in the American destruction of Viet Nam will lead to a reinstantiation of the ideologies that produced the war, Sanders's remembrance of racial solidarity in combat will ring false. Clearly, the point is not to claim that what the U.S. war machine did either to the Vietnamese people or to American society is somehow mitigated by the fact that American GIs in combat sometimes "got along." Nonetheless, any provisional transcendence of prejudice and racial hatred ought not to be dismissed as necessarily in collusion with myths of American exceptionalism and therefore regressive. If such tentative moves "out" of racism lead to a wider critique of imperialism and corporate greed, so much the better.

It is this third and crucial structure of experience that distinguishes *The Oddsplayer* (1989), a novel by Chicano veteran Joe Rodríguez. The novel describes a squad of infantrymen—poor whites, blacks, Chicanos, and Puerto Ricans—who confront not only the dangers of combat but also the abuse of an unusually brutal sergeant. The soldiers' coming together under duress is motivated by mutual protection and the need to survive, and from it emerges a shared understanding of just who the real enemies are. When Pérez, a Chicano soldier, is welcomed into his new unit by a small group of Latinos and blacks, the Puerto Rican short-timer Fernández speaks first:

"Oye, hermano, you'll die quick if you lose your head." Fernandez offered Perez his canteen. Perez' hands were scraped and bleeding from the [sand]bags.

The small circle of men murmured their assent. In the light from the battlelamp, their faces gleamed eerily.

"The suckers in charge have slick ways to beat you down," Johnson said and put his hand on Perez' shoulder. "At least the incoming is straight up. The Man will grease you on the hottest point of the perimeter. He'll work your ass the whole day, then nail you to the night roster. He wants you to make a mistake and check in your piece. His conscience is White and you're bagged meat."

"Remember what that fucking Slater tried to do to us?" Fernandez asked the group. "He told Cooper that I was bad-mouthing Blacks. Then he turned around and told me that the Blacks were reaming Mestizos. Cooper and I talked and found out his downside ride."

"That redneck took a ride," Johnson burst out. "Why should we Rainbows fight among ourselves and do the Man's work for him? Color is not the game. Power and money bleed everyone."[43]

In this dense passage, the analysis moves from one based strictly on racial and ethnic separatism (the Man's conscience is White) to one that incorporates questions of economic exploitation and the power of capital to strategically divide disempowered groups. The idea that Rainbows, or working-class people of every color, might band together against the technocrats, white supremacists, and corporate managers points tentatively toward a solidarity of purpose of which there are few examples in U.S. history.

"Oye, vieja, esas gentes son iguales que nosotros"

In her important history of the war, Marilyn Young suggests that it was difficult for U.S. soldiers to identify with the Vietnamese peasants they encountered:

A Japanese reporter, Katsuichi Honda, understood the distance between American soldiers and the ordinary scenes of Vietnamese rural life they witnessed daily without ever comprehending. It was hard to see a house of mud and thatch as more than a temporary dwelling; hardly a home in the American sense. Rice cultivation—labor intensive, back-breaking, closer to gardening than any farming even soldiers from farm country had ever seen—simply did not register with the troops, for whom neither the labor, nor the crop, nor the people who planted and depended on it were real.[44]

In fact, many American GIs in Viet Nam were able to bridge the cultural distance between themselves and the Vietnamese. For many GIs of color, the reality of daily life in Southeast Asia was hauntingly close to what their own lives had been in the United States. For example, the Chicano veterans in

Charley Trujillo's collection of oral histories, *Soldados* (*Soldiers*), were all from Corcoran, a rural community in central California. One feature that links the experiences of these veterans to the experiences of other veterans of color is what I call the structure of recognition.

Most of the veterans interviewed by Trujillo came from families of first- and second-generation Mexican agricultural workers. For these particular soldiers, the Vietnamese peasant evoked a certain empathy or a fleeting recognition that in most cases dissipated as the men were desensitized to their violent surroundings. Eddie Rodriguez, for example, remembers his tour in 1965:

> They used to send us to the garbage dump to get rid of all the trash and the whole dump was full of people. . . . Those people were like human buzzards. . . . Some of the guys would put C-rations cans in the middle of the barbed wire around our perimeter. The kids would crawl between the wire to get the cans, and they would scratch the hell out of themselves. I wouldn't do that, but some sadistic gabachos [Anglos] would do it. . . . At first, I felt bad about those poor people but afterwards I didn't give a shit anymore. I just got used to it."
>
> (*Soldados,* pp. 5–6)

Whereas this Chicano soldier initially distinguished himself from his Anglo counterparts on moral grounds, his fragile empathy with the hungry children dissipated over time. Moreover, although Rodriguez did not participate in the cruelty, he was never in a position to protest his comrades' behavior.

Another Chicano veteran, Frank Delgado, tells of his initiation into the violence of the war. Confronted by a North Vietnamese soldier with a live grenade, Delgado is unable to react, but his fellow squad members open fire on the enemy and hit him with over two hundred rounds. Delgado remembers:

> His brains just went all over my boots. Everybody just busted out laughing. They thought it was the funniest thing in the world. . . . When I was laughing, I was thinking to myself, why in the hell am I laughing, this isn't funny. That's when I started realizing that I wasn't the same person that I was a year ago back in Corcoran. I realized something had changed in me. I don't think it was for the better, it was for the worse! I hadn't been raised up that way, to be out killing. To find humor in death is when I started realizing I was living like an animal. And pretty soon, you started acting like one.
>
> (*Soldados,* pp. 24–25)

As Delgado's account makes clear, it would be a mistake to argue for a heightened moral consciousness among all Chicano soldiers in Viet Nam. Chicano GIs were as susceptible as others to the brutality and random violence of a guerrilla war waged in large part against civilians and also as capable as others of great compassion and an abhorrence of violence. The infamous My Lai massacre, the most notorious atrocity of the war, was perpetrated by Lt. William Calley's platoon under the command of Captain Ernest "Mad Dog" Medina, a Chicano from New Mexico and the son of a farmworker. Medina was court-martialed for the murder of 102 Vietnamese civilians. He was acquitted but later admitted to suppressing evidence and lying under oath. One of the worst offenders at My Lai, guilty of multiple murders and rapes, was nineteen-year-old *tejano* Esequiel Torres. Among the soldiers who reportedly refused to participate in the killing and who aided Vietnamese civilians were two African Americans (Harry Stanley and Herbert Carter), two Chicanos (George Garza and Leonard Gonzalez), and an Irish-American (Michael Bernhardt).[45] Certainly, atrocities could be committed by members of all ethnic groups; nevertheless, many Chicano (and virtually all Asian American) narratives about the war express a moral ambiguity that is the product of an uneasy recognition of shared experiences with the Vietnamese.

The stories in Trujillo's important collection contain the raw emotional material that took aesthetic form in *Vietnam Campesino* (*Vietnam Peasant,* 1970), a one-act play staged by the Teatro Campesino at the height of the war. The young Chicano soldier (called *el hijo,* the son) is ordered into battle:

GENERAL: I want you to burn the house of these farmworkers, boy.
HIJO: Yes, sir!

The soldier moves toward the campesinos, who hold up a paper cut-out of a small labor camp shack. They wave at him.

CAMPESINOS: Hello, hijo.
HIJO: (*Turns back to general*) Hey, I can't burn my parents' home.
GENERAL: Not *those* farmworkers, stupid. (*Points at Vietnamese*) These farmworkers.[46]

The Cuban-born poet Elías Hruska y Cortez makes a similar association when he imagines himself on a bombing mission over Viet Nam and observes "his brother playing far below" (Reading 31).[47] Or as Johnny the buck private in *Soldado Razo* writes to his mother: "'Amá, I had a dream la otra noche [the other night]. I dreamed I was breaking into one of the hooches. . . . I went in firing my M-16 porque sabía que el village estaba controlado por los gooks [because I knew the village was controlled by gooks]. I killed three of them right away, but when I looked down it was mi 'apa [my father], el carnalillo [my little brother] and you, jefita [mom]. I don't know how much more I can stand. Please tell Sapo and all the vatos [guys] how it's like over here. Don't let them . . ."[48] Johnny's nightmare that the dead Vietnamese were in fact his father, mother, and brother concretizes the recognition of "the enemy," and is transformed into an anti-war message aimed at his friends back home. In *A Barrio Tragedy,* a play written by Joe Olvera, Leo Rojas, and Raul Estrada, the character Johnny Jimenez voices a similar sentiment to his fellow GIs in Viet Nam: "Guacha, a mí nomás me falta una semana pero cuántos carnales van a venir atrás de mí? Cuántos van a hacer la misma chingadera que hice yo?" ("Check it out, I only have a week left but how many brothers are coming over after me? How many are going to fuck up the way I did?")[49]

Unlike Delgado's and Rodriguez's recollections, which contain only the vaguest intimations of a political analysis, the Teatro Campesino's *Soldado Razo* dramatizes several underlying issues: the exploitation and murder of poor people in both Vietnam and the United States, the fleeting potential for solidarity between colonized and exploited groups, and the ideological manipulation of those groups by corporate and military managers. When Hijo is killed by a Vietnamese peasant, the general urges Hijo's farmworker parents to attack the peasant for being a communist. The *acto* unmasks an identification with the oppressor, premised on Cold War mythologies, that undermines the potential for solidarity among exploited communities and that even today is a crucial driving force behind participation by minorities in the military.

This complex system of experiences is what cultural historians have yet to sort out. The structure of recognition is that characteristic of Chicano representations of the war in which the Chicano community sees in the Vietnamese enemy a "reflection" of its own class or ethnic positions. The words spoken by the father of Hijo to his wife about the Vietnamese peasants—"Oye, vieja, esas gentes son iguales que nosotros" ("Look, wife, those people are just like us")—for example, are echoed by the character of the returned veteran, Ernesto, in a play by Nephtalí de León: "Isn't it enough that I was nearly bumped off in Viet Nam? Here I go halfway across the world to die in someone else's field. As if I couldn't die in these goddamn cotton fields."[50] At the same time, we are confronted by the ease with which that same community was manipulated by the desire to assimilate and by red-baiting tactics. A few moments later in *Vietnam Campesino,* Hijo's father cries out: "Desgraciados comunistas! Mataron a mijo!" (Damned communists! You killed my son!")[51]

Despite the power of Cold War ideologies, the exposure of anti-communist rhetoric as a smoke screen for the prosecution of the war in Southeast Asia did take place in many Chicano communities. In a personal testimonial from 1970, María Carriaga described this slow and painful process:

> Our people are taught to hate Vietnamese for all our boys killed over there. I have to admit I used to feel that way too. My brother was one of the unlucky ones, he died in combat there. I also have two sons in the service, one is stationed in Vietnam. But I have come to realize that the blame is not really with the Vietnamese, so now I put the blame where it really belongs, on the U.S. government.
>
> (*El Grito del Norte* 3 [May 19, 1970]: 6)

I will return to this emergent structure of experience in my introduction to part 2.

In 1984 Erwin R. Parson, a psychiatrist, studied the effects of recognition or identification between GIS of color and the Vietnamese. Despite Parson's choice of the obscene term "gook-identification," defined as "the conscious and unconscious emotional identification with the devalued, maligned, abused, and helpless aspects of the Vietnamese people," his findings corroborate the sentiments expressed in oral histories and literature by veterans of color.[52] In interviews reported by Parson and a coauthor, African American, Latino, Native American, and Asian American veterans discuss their sense that minority soldiers were in effect "fighting themselves" in Viet Nam. A Native American vet says: "We made the connection that in Vietnam, we were involved in the same kind of colonization process that was carried out by whites in this country."[53]

The experience of the Asian American GI was particularly troubled by such overwhelming contradictions.[54] The Department of Defense estimates that some 35,000 Asian/Pacific Islanders served in Viet Nam, with the highest numbers coming from the Filipino and Japanese American communities. Japanese Americans often found themselves caught in a circuitous route that led to the U.S. military and the war. One of the most disturbing examples is that of Shojiro Yamashita, who was born in the Heart Mountain Relocation

Center in 1945 but who returned with his family to Japan immediately after the World War II. In 1968, after graduating from Fukuoka University, Yamashita returned to the United States to join his brother. The following year, he was drafted. Six months later, he died during the invasion of Cambodia.[55] Asian Americans were at times placed in segregated units such as the so-called Team Hawaii, formed in 1969 and also including Native Americans, in order to conduct operations deep in enemy territory. Very few texts about the war by Asian American authors have been published, but many of the ones we have contain the same structures of recognition that we find in Chicano narratives.

Filipino-American author Melvin Escueta, for example, writes: "Everything about the country was very Filipino. I knew these rice paddies, my uncles had rice paddies just like them; I knew the water buffalo, my family had them; I knew those huts, I had lived in them. Everything about Vietnam struck my soul, but I locked it away."[56] The protagonist of Escueta's play *Honey Bucket* (1976) develops the idea of shared experiences and dramatizes the racism directed at Asian Americans from within their own ranks. Chinese American veteran David Chung remembers: "The first day I arrived [in Viet Nam], an American soldier called me a 'gook'. . . . It was very strange to land in Vietnam, look around and realize that you looked like the enemy. I was going to be shooting people who looked like my parents, my relatives, and me."[57] Upon his return to the states, Chung was told that his membership in the local VFW (Veterans of Foreign Wars) had been denied because his presence would upset World War II and Korean War veterans.

Telling the story of having been the butt of repeated racist attacks by a Caucasian sergeant, Sam Choy recalls:

> I couldn't take it anymore. One day I got so mad I threw a knife on the floor after he called me a chink. He ordered me to pick it up. I refused. He started yelling at me. I still refused. He kept yelling all kinds of remarks like— slant-eyed Chinaman, gook, chink, and he went on and on. I just got madder. So he went to get the staff sergeant. I went to get my rifle. I waited for them to come back and when they did they started to sweet talk me to give my rifle up. I said if you come closer, I'll shoot. I fired a warning shot and they froze. Then I left the tent and the corporal came after me. He tried to grab my rifle. I fired once and he froze, he was scared as hell. Then the M.P.'s came and I shot at them too. I had bad eyes, so I missed. By this time I was near the perimeter of the base and, was thinking of joining the Viet Cong; at least they would trust me.[58]

In its most dramatic form, then, the tenuous solidarity between the U.S. soldier of color and the Vietnamese could produce a "crossing over" in which GIs considered abandoning or did abandon U.S. military installations in order to live with the enemy. While many such stories may be apocryphal, the mere suggestion of individual soldiers carrying the preliminary act of recognition to its ultimate conclusion would be enough to undermine traditional practices of nationalism, patriotism, and anti-communism. In the short story "Somewhere Outside Duc Pho" (Reading 8), Daniel Cano tells of Chicano GI Jesse Peña who has disappeared in-country and who had been sighted leading Viet Cong patrols. But according to local legend, Peña's radical critique of the U.S. war effort was not unique: "The story of an American leading a Vietcong squad was not uncommon. Everyone had heard it one time or another during his tour. Usually, the American was blond, tall, and thin. No one who told the story had ever seen the guy. The story was always distanced by two or three narrators, and it was more of a fable or myth, our own type of antiwar protest, I guess." In a concluding scene, a group of Chicano soldiers remark upon the irony of "fighting for democracy" in Southeast Asia when their own families in the United States continued to endure discrimination and economic injustice.

The empirical evidence of GIs crossing over to fight alongside the enemy is slight, though such reports are common in U.S. military history and include infamous cases like the defection of Irish Catholic soldiers (los San Patricios) to the opposite side in the Mexican War or the switching of allegiance by minority soldiers in the Spanish-American War.[59] The pressures of combat and the constraints of ideological conditioning surely preclude any easy identification with the enemy. But the figure of the phantom GI fighting for the other side reappears in literature and testimonials about the war. Richard Holguín recalls: "Salt and Pepper were these two American Marines, one black and the other white, who had turned traitor and went to the Viet Cong side. I had seen both of them with my own eyes."[60] In Cano's *Shifting Loyalties* (Reading 9), the story of Jesse Peña is retold from various points of view:

"You believe that shit, man. The Tiger Force," Langley had said, smirking, "was on a listening post, keepin' an eye on a squad of dinks movin' along the trail, and there, right in the middle of the VC column, they see Jesse— or a chubby Mexican-looking-type guy in fatigues, black headband, rucksack, and M-16. Dig this, Almas. The dude ain't a prisoner. He's like a . . .

a commie, man, walking right along with them gooks. A fuckin' stroll in the park, man."[61]

Some twenty years earlier, Charles Durden's *No Bugles, No Drums* included the story of an African American soldier, Jinx, who is known to be living with the Viet Cong. Jinx is a new standards man with a difference, for he has carried recognition and identification to a lethal conclusion. Immediately before he deserts, he explains to Hawkins, the narrator:

> "So much for McNamara's Hundred Thousand, huh?"
> "Get a nigger behind the trigger . . . then give 'im a ticket to Nam. Dig it? But some of us gonna survive. Sooner or later some of us niggers goin' home."
> "They got some poor-ass white people with that program, too."
> "Yeah, but it was us they wanted. Get the young blacks off America's city streets and into Nam's backwoods. They finally figured a way to kill spades 'n' slopes at the same time." He emptied the last of his beer down his throat. "If we was smart we'd get together. Niggers of the world, unite!" He banged the bottle down on the bar top. And laughed.[62]

When Hawkins later realizes that Jinx is fighting with the Viet Cong and calling in artillery on his former platoon, he searches him out and kills him. In the world of growing anti-war sentiment within the U.S. military, Jinx made a tenuous connection to other poor people of color and acted upon it. In the literary universe of crossovers, Jinx follows the trail of the "Phantom Blooker," a Caucasian fighting with the Viet Cong in Robert Roth's *Sand in the Wind* (1973), and clears a path for the deserter Cacciato, who occasionally surfaces with units of the National Liberation Front (NLF) in Tim O'Brien's *Going After Cacciato* (1978), as well as for Cano's Jesse Peña and other characters who cross the ultimate boundary by going over to the enemy.

It is certainly possible that almost all the accounts of desertions to the NLF are little more than wartime legends, yet when the U.S. military abandoned Saigon in 1975 approximately one hundred previously unaccounted-for GIs mysteriously resurfaced. One facet of the CIA's Phoenix Program was to track down and "terminate" American soldiers living with the Vietnamese.[63] Deserters, referred to as "renegades," were hunted down and given the option of committing suicide or being assassinated. They were then reported as either killed or missing in action.

The cultural representations of GIs who "crossed over" serve to interrogate traditional U.S. ethnocentrism and discourses of white supremacy. When the African American protagonist of Walter Dean Myers's novel *Fallen Angels* (1988) remarks that a Vietnamese girl "looked like a little doll with dark black eyes that dominated a round, brown face. She could have been black, maybe Puerto Rican" or that a wounded Viet Cong had "thin arms not much different in color than mine," the traditional war narrative and its attendant tropes of nationalism and violent masculinity are momentarily subverted.[64] The transference of such fleeting textual subversions into everyday life could be subtle but meaningful. As one Chicano veteran said on his return to the United States: "I think because we experience racism ourselves and even though we're saying those goddamn dinks, those slopes, it's making something inside here, there's this kind of understanding that we're taco benders, greasers and wetbacks."[65] It is in moments such as this that patriotism's capacity to bracket differences of class and ethnicity falls apart. Exactly what "we" as an idealized American family are all willing to die for suddenly becomes a question whose answer may have grave consequences for the nation.

It would seem unlikely that this kind of recognition between people of color was reciprocal inside the combat zone. From the perspective of the Vietnamese who did not support the Saigon government, all U.S. soldiers were more than likely viewed as equal participants in the invasion and destruction of Viet Nam, regardless of their ethnicity or race. Nevertheless, incidents such as the Saigon taxi boycott of 1964 suggest that, at least early in the war, some Vietnamese did distinguish among various groups of GIs. In their weeklong selective strike, taxi drivers refused to pick up all foreign passengers except American blacks. Anecdotes from the field also suggest a desire on the part of some Vietnamese combatants to recognize differences among U.S. soldiers. A recurrent topic in many war stories is that the Viet Cong would shoot "white" GIs but allow blacks to live, though stories such as these are probably apocryphal.[66] More often than not, such distinctions were used by enemy prisoners as a survival tactic: "The VC did most of the talking, trying to make common cause of their color—you and me, GI, brown and black against white. 'We no want to fight soul brother,' he said. 'You go home. This white man's war. You soul brother, you go home.'"[67]

In what is perhaps the most famous of all Viet Nam War narratives, Michael Herr's *Dispatches,* the Latino soldier is granted only a ghostly presence, despite Herr's appropriation of the Chicano term "la vida loca" to describe the insanity of the war. We are told simply: "Mendoza was here. 12 Sept

68. Texas."[68] Like the Mexican American soldier who appears in Norman Mailer's World War II novel *The Naked and the Dead* or even the GIs Padilla and Chavez in Pierre Schoendorffer's award-winning documentary *The Anderson Platoon* (1966), the presence of the Chicano "Mendoza," invoked through his graffiti at Tan Son Nhut airport in the final section of *Dispatches,* is fleeting at best. The reader can only imagine what Mendoza's story might have been, for Herr does not recount it.

For those of us interested in tracking the elusive figure of the minority soldier, one other scene in *Dispatches* strikes us with special force. Attempting to determine the identity of a two-month old corpse in a U.S. uniform, two GIs argue: "'Shit, this is a gook! What'd they bring him here for?' 'Look, Jesus, he's got on our uniform.' 'I don't give a fuck, that ain't no fucking American, that's a fucking gook!' 'Wait a minute,' the other one said. 'Maybe it's a spade . . .'" (p. 161). Whatever the ethnicity of the dead man, skin pigmentation is the primary sign to be deciphered. Or as a character in Joe Rodríguez's *Oddsplayer* remarks: "The color of the skin fixed the enemy" (p. 63). The dead "gook" may well have been a U.S. Latino or Asian American and was most assuredly an American soldier of color. It is almost too horrible to consider in depth the racist connotations of this scene and its consequences for the historical record. Whoever the dead man was in reality, his life and death are forever lost in the four-letter racist epithet "gook."

This startling scene from *Dispatches* is reproduced in Chicano veteran Roy Benavidez's autobiography, only now as historical fact. Gravely wounded and lying among both American and North Vietnamese dead, Benavidez is unable to speak as he is loaded on to a helicopter for evacuation:

> I retreated to the darkness behind my eyelids. Soon, I felt arms lifting me and sensed the sunlight fall across my face as they handed me through the doorway.
>
> "Just put him over here with the other three on the ground," said the voice belonging to the arms holding my legs.
>
> The other three? "Oh, Christ, No!" my mind cried as realization dawned. Half of the blood I had just dumped over Southeast Asia belonged to the Yaqui Indian nation. More than once my native American features had been mistaken for Oriental. Now, by God, they were going to get me dumped with the enemy dead.
>
> (*Medal of Honor*, p. 4)[69]

Benavidez is eventually recognized by a fellow sergeant and escapes being left to die with enemy soldiers. At such moments, when life-and-death decisions were made on the basis of skin color and other physical features, the tenuous connection between GIs of color and the people of Viet Nam took on a macabre and chilling dimension.

Corrido del padre de un soldado

Soy un padre como hay muchos,
que no hallamos qué pensar
pues tenemos nuestros hijos
allá peleando en Viet Nam,
Virgencita milagrosa
devuélvelos como se van.

Diosito santo te pido
que tengas más compasión
de nuestros hijos queridos
que andan en otra nación.
Bien sabes que se llevaron
parte de mi corazón.

Virgen divina,
Virgencita de San Juán,
protege a todo el soldado
que nos defiende en Viet Nam.

Adiós mis padres queridos,
nos dijo casi al partir,
dijo no se queden tristes
que pronto he de venir.
soy purito mexicano
y no le temo al morir.

Se despidió de su novia,
de sus hermanos también,

le dió un abrazo a su madre,
y a mí me dió otro también.
Se encomendó ante nosotros,
y ante Diosito también.

Diosito santo, tu sabes
lo que una madre sufrió
para darle vida a su hijo
hasta la vida arriesgó
a cambio de la de mi hijo
mi vida te ofrezco yo.

(Ballad of a Soldier's Father: I am like many fathers who
don't know what to think because we have our sons over
there, fighting in Viet Nam. Miraculous Virgin, return them
as they left. Dear God, I ask you to have more compassion
for our dear sons who are in another country. You know
that they took with them part of my heart. Divine Virgin of
San Juan, protect all the soldiers who defend us in Viet
Nam. Goodbye, my dear parents he told us, just as he left;
he said don't be sad for I'll be back soon. I'm one hundred
percent Mexican and I'm not afraid to die. He said goodbye
to his girlfriend and to his brothers too. He gave a hug to
his mother and one to me. He asked for our blessing and
God's too. Dear God, you know what a mother suffered to
give a son his life. She even risked her own. In exchange for
that of my son, I offer you my life.)

Translation by George Mariscal

2 / MAGDALENO AVILA (Juan Valdez)

My Uncle Sam

Yesterday my Uncle Sam wrote.
It wasn't pretty
It wasn't long.
He doesn't write much
But each time his letters
Send my heart a jumping.
He says he wants me
I think he's wanted me
for 4 × 52 weeks now;
Like Satan wanted Adam
Long before he ate the apple.
My Uncle Sam is a funny man
I never asked for him
I never loved his ways
But yesterday my Uncle Sam wrote.
He says he wants me.
He didn't say much else
He never does.

Sea of Freedom

Look at my blood as it
spills into the streets of
Saigon or San Antonio,
It does not really matter
where the war was started
But it's here and we're fighting,

look at my blood as it
leaves this dying moreno,
Damn you Democracy
you sit on your pompous ass
waiting to finish us off.
If you can't use Asia then
southern Texas will do
or how about Colorado
or Utah and if you have
time visit Michigan
with your stupid equality,
Now with our blood in the sea
we say Chicanos want to be free.

---

moreno– dark-skinned man

3 / PEDRO ORTIZ VÁSQUEZ

Las cartas de Martín Flores

septiembre 13, 1966

Dear son,

We got your letter dated September 9 which makes us happy to hear that you are fine. Everyone of us are ok. Be alert son and do the things the best way you can. Your sargent knows best so do what he tells you to do. It will make us happy to hear that you are doing allright with your training. Remember that if other fellow doing good you can do it to. We bet you look very good with your uniforms. Be patient and have faith in our Lord. Try to select your friends and don't forget to go to church and pray. Everyone says to tell you hello. The neighbors are very proud of you son. By the way you know that they going to make the post office biger. Right now is located in the corner of Spruce and Washington. It is two block from the orange packing house. Amelia came to the house yesterday. She misses you. She is a nice girl. I think this will be all. Be strong and alert. Everybody remember you around here. The first when you left was kind of hard for us because we miss you. As I said before have faith in God and yourself and everything will be allright.

Be careful and be good
Dad and Mom

P.S. Don't forget to go to church. We always pray for you.

---

cartas— letters

My name is Martín Flores, or Chuki, as my friends back home call me. I was born twenty-three years ago in El Paso, Tejas. I only started to keep this diary two days ago. The first two pages, May 2 and May 3 are blank. Today we lost four men and killed or wounded thirteen of the enemy. Perhaps this page should also remain blank but I have too many feelings and no other voice to express them. And what is worse, I have no one here to relate them to. In the week that I have been here I have come to see death and to smell it in the air. Today I felt it touch me. As easy as snapping my fingers is pulling the trigger. Quicker yet is seeing a lifetime reflected in the twisted features of a man suddenly ripped apart by the unceasing fire of a glowing steel weapon. A weapon whose only reaction is the thin shadow of smoke that rises from its barrel. Sargeant ———— says that I will make a good marine and that I will get used to the killing and accept it. I don't know. All I can do is run from the others and vomit behind a tree until I am rid of the knot in my throat. It is not as easy to rid myself of the gnawing guilt that grows like cancer when all is quiet and I am alone.

Tomorrow we will head towards the village of ————. Only God knows what is waiting for us there. Of the thirty men that arrived on the plane with me from the States, only eighteen remain, and I have come to recognize the many faces of each one. On these fields of war we have been sent to assume different identities and I wonder if the enemy also must play this role. Or is he as Sargeant ———— says, a suicidal maniac without any heart. Jompi González, who is also from Tejas and the only one here who calls me Chuki, says he thinks the enemy also has a song to sing.

"*Tienen un canto, Chuki,* like you and me, only we never stop to listen." I think Jompi is listening. Today, although he fired his weapon, he hit no one and we all know he is the best shot in the unit. Perhaps I will someday learn to listen and like Jompi, I will hear other *cantos.*

Tienen un canto—They have a song

diciembre 11 1966

Hijo

Espero en Dios que al resibo de esta estes bien. Aqui todos bien grasias a Dios, nadamas con mucho aire pero muy fuerte. Ayer te puse una cajita aber si te gusta lo que te mande. Y ayer resibimos tu carta y los siento biente dollares. Tu dady puso sincuenta en el banco y se compro un nuebo rifle para ir acasar. Hijo cuidate mucho en este tiempo feo que viene para que no te enfermes. Aqui ya enpiesan los catarros y la tos. Ya sabes que el domingo estube todo el dia esperando tu llamada y para en la noche perdi la esperansa. Aqui me tienes muy preocupada pensando miles de cosas, que te pasaria algo que estaras enfermo o que te tengan castigado por algo malo que ayas echo. Dime cual es el motibo es mejor saber que estarme pensando lo peor. Escoje tus amistades y no te olbides de ir a misa. Bueno espero saber pronto de ti. Reside mi bendisiones y que Dios te cuide en todo.

te quiere tu
mamá

Son, I pray to God that when you receive this letter you are well. Thank God we're all fine here; it's just been very cold. I sent you a package yesterday. I hope you like it. We received your letter yesterday with the $120. Your dad put $50 in the bank and bought a new hunting rifle. Son, take good care of yourself with the bad weather coming. Don't get sick. The cold and cough season has started here already. You know, I waited all day Sunday for your call but I gave up by evening. I'm so worried, thinking a thousand things, what will happen, if you get sick or if you get punished for doing something wrong. Tell me what's going on. It's better to know the truth than to think the worst. Choose your friends carefully and don't forget to go to mass. Well, I hope to hear from you soon. Receive my blessings and may God keep you. Your mother who loves you.

We did not move today as scheduled. It will be best to wait until the rains have stopped. I notice that even in the ugliness and horrors of war there is beauty intermingled. Sometimes the rain falls heavy, beating against the jungle greenery like a drummer in a marching band, other times it settles softly as a blanket placed over a sleeping child. During the pauses when it does not rain, I can almost feel the jungle stirring like one who is about to awaken. A low rustling sound grows, and just when it appears ready to shout "I am alive," it begins to rain again and the jungle sleeps.

On days like yesterday when it did not rain, the sun scorches the earth dry until I can hear its skin, crisp and brittle, crack under the pressure of each footstep. The heavy dryness of the air, like its brother the humidity of a hot rain, wraps itself around me and squeezes, perhaps in self-defense. In the clear patches of land just outside of the jungle, the sun lends a golden hue to the dust in the air and the slightest wind sends it scattering like broken pieces of colored glass. At night when the moon appears, it casts its light off of the leaves and when it is not present, it is darker than any darkness that I have ever seen. It is in this darkness that I feel naked and at the mercy of the jungle. Sargeant ———— says that not even the fear of the enemy can compare with being afraid of the jungle, and yet it does not harm unless it is harmed. I think it is our own created fear that strangles us, and tonight in this black moonless pit, the jungle watches and waits.

marzo 6 1967

Dear son

    We received your letter today everybody is ok around here. Hoping that you are fine. Thank you for the money it is in the bank right now. Also I sending you the insurance to sign it. Be very careful and don't let anyone know you have money. They will want to borrow some. Listen to your sargent. This is all for now. Be careful.

Dad and Mom

P.S. Don't forget sign the insurance. Is very important.

The village is dead. There are no survivors, even among the living. We are 13 men and 4 are seriously wounded. They will not make it and we know it, yet we lie to them. As I sit as far from the smell of burnt flesh as I can, I hear Jompi singing. He always sings when he is sad. He also cries when he is like this. I know because I have cried with him. Last night in the rain we surprised the enemy hiding in the village. I remember crawling through the mud until we were close enough to the huts to hear voices. When Sargeant ———— gave the order we charged into the center of the village firing into the straw huts and throwing grenades into them. Not even the rain could squelch the fires that devoured the small buildings and the people inside. Still the enemy was able to return our fire and we lost some men. How easy it is to say that. *We lost some men.* What have they lost? Three old men, five women, seven children and one soldier. All Sargeant ———— could say was "Son of a bitches got away but we'll get them tomorrow." Jompi and I cried into our vomit. Is this animal response our only reaction to seeing a pregnant woman split open and burning while a young child runs naked unable to scream because his face has been blown into a mangled mess of red and bone? "You write, Chuki, and I'll sing," said Jompi, and we both continued to vomit.

abril 10 1967

Querido hijo

Manana lunes si Dios me permite to boy a poner una cajita, yo porque a
tu dady le toca trabajar. Solo que amanesca llobiendo no podremos salir. Ya
sabes que feo es el tiempo. El biernes es la boda de Amelia Y Jose. Dise Amelia
que ban a ser dosientos inbitados, muchos berdad? Tambien ban a tener tres
barriles de serbesa. Fijate que tiene uno que dar presente. Aber si puedes man-
darnos unos dollares para darles algo en tu nombre. Cuidate mucho y aber si
puedes benir pronto, bueno hijo que Dios te cuide y te bendiga.

mamá

Aqui tu amigo Rafael te manda una carta.

Dear Son, God willing, I'm sending you a package Monday morning. I'm doing it because Dad
had to work. We won't be able to go out though if it's raining in the morning. You know how
bad the weather is. Friday is Amelia's and Jose's wedding. Amelia says there will be two hundred guests. That's a lot, isn't it? They're also going to have three kegs of beer. You know, we
have to give them a present. Can you send a few dollars so we can give something in your
name? Take care and I hope you can come home soon. Well, son, may God keep you and bless
you. Mama. I'm including a letter from your friend Rafael.

Chuki,

How's it going, mi general? Don't have your address so I'm sending this with your mamas. Sorry about Amelia que se fue con otro barco but at least you're free capitan. Saw your ruedas and your jefe's keeping it like showcase, all polish and ujule. Say sergeant, my primo from Osten is over there. A real crazy vato, man, Jompi Gonzalez is his cue. Maybe you'll run into him. You'll like him, he's kind of like you, a real coco loco. Bueno freno private Flores, take care mano. Y como lo sabes, Chuki, aqui o mas alla, ay nos vidrios.

tu carnal
Rafas
ooo

---

que se fue con otro barco— ran off with another guy
ruedas— car
jefe— father
ujule— cool
primo— cousin
vato— dude
coco loco— crazy guy
Bueno freno— That's it
mano— bro'
Y como lo sabes— And you know
aqui o mas alla, ay nos vidrios— here or over there, we'll see each other
tu carnal— Your brother

They came from nowhere, screaming and waving their hands and shooting their guns. Sargeant ——— cursed and hollered. We all grabbed for our
weapons and tried to defend ourselves. There was no place to run or hide. I
saw men fall everywhere. I heard screams that came from a place darker than
any jungle and I saw live blood bubbling warm from broken bodies. Now
that the fighting is over I see men lying on the ground, their eyes open, staring into the mud. What can they see in their dead reflection? An enemy soldier stumbled over a body and jumped back startled. He mumbled to himself
and bent over the form. It was one of his own. I saw him lower his head and
his body shake. He was crying. Suddenly a shot rang out and the man fell
over his companion. His legs jerked, and then he was still. Sargeant ———
staggered up. I heard another shot and he too fell into the mud.

*The enemy has left. I am lying under a bush. I feel nothing. A light flickers in the
darkness, the last ashes of fire. I can hear a soft voice singing. It is a gentle, joyful song.
"Jompi, is that you, Jompi?" All is quiet . . . . the sun seems to pierce the
jungle . . . . thickness . . . . . . bright colors flash . . . . . everywhere . . . . It is
funny . . . . how people fear . . . . . . the coming . . . . . . of . . . death . . . . . I . . am
ready . . . . I . . . . have . . . . . been . . . waiting . . . . for . . . a . . . long time . . . .
I . . . feel . . . . so tired . . . . I'm*

I'm . . listenin . . . to . . . Jompi . . . . I . . . . . am . . . .listen . . . . to Jompi

Hijo

Te pongo estas cuantas letras esperando en Dios que estes bien desde ayer quise escribir pero se me paso el tiempo. Parese que nunca ay tiempo para nada. Ace mucho calor que ayer el biejo besino se desmayo y lo llebaron al ospital. No creo que dure la semana ya que es tan biejo. Tengo tanto miedo que algo te pase hijo. Resale a Dios que te permita benir pronto. Oy mismo el padre Felipe ba ofreser una misa en tu nombre. Tu dady y yo bamos asta comulgar. No te escribo mas porque quiero que esta salga oy. Cuidate mucho y que Dios te guarde.

te quiere tu
mamá y dady

Sabes que tu amigo Rafael murio ayer en un acsidente que lastima. Te lo escribo todo mas tarde.

Son, I'm writing these few words hoping that God willing you are well. I meant to write yesterday but didn't have time. Seems there's never enough time for anything. It's been so hot; yesterday the old man next door fainted and they took him to the hospital. He's so old I don't think he'll last a week. I'm so afraid something might happen to you. Pray to God that he brings you home soon. Father Felipe is offering a mass in your name today. Your Dad and I are taking communion. I'll stop now because I want this to go out today. Take care and God keep you. Your mother and father who love you. Your friend Rafael died in an accident yesterday. What a shame. I'll write you all about it later.

4 / ROBERT PEREA

Dragon Mountain

Dragon Mountain did look like a reclining monster from a distance. We were coming up to the LEPER COLONY sign as we approached the mountain. None of us had ever been up that dirt road turn-off.

"Bet ol' Charlie never bothers them," said the Lieutenant as we hit a bump in the road.

"What, Sir?" answered the First Sergeant who was driving.

"Those lepers, that leper colony, bet no Victor Charlies have ever attacked that place," repeated the Lieutenant.

"They'd be crazy to, Sir," said the First Sergeant as we hit another bump in the road. Actually the road wasn't that bad, we just happened to be hitting all the bumps.

The big mountain loomed over us. I got a strange feeling looking up at it. I was wondering if there were any local legends about the mountain, it seemed so awesome.

But the mountain was important from a military standpoint. Our engineer battalion was extending the road south from Pleiku and the road-building camp was out of radio contact with our base camp. The mountain was the highest point for miles around and perfect for a radio-relay station. Although the base camp could not make radio-contact with the road-building camp directly, both could make contact with Dragon Mountain which was located almost dead center from each site. That would be my job, relaying messages from each site.

As we approached the winding dirt road that led up the mountain's side, a group of Vietnamese, mostly old men and women, rushed our jeep trying to sell us things. Their main customers were convoys that passed by.

"You like? Very nice souvenir," said one old mama-san holding up a handful of cheap peace medallions.

"You got M.P.C.? You got food? We trade," said another.

"Here G.I., I give you good buy," said a third old lady as she shoved a pair of Ho Chi Minh sandals into the First Sergeant's face.

"Say, these ain't bad. Made from old tires, how much you want?" said the First Sergeant.

"Five hundred piastre or five dollar M.P.C.," answered the old lady smiling, her teeth blackened from chewing beetle nut, "You buy? Very nice."

"Let's get outta here," said the Lieutenant half-yelling. The small, noisy crowd was starting to irritate him, "We haven't got time for this kind of stuff!"

"Sorry mama-san, but we gotta dee-dee mow," said the First Sergeant.

"You cheap, you no good, you numba ten," the old lady answered looking rather dejected.

"You numba fuckin' ten," added an old papa-san who had been watching everything.

"Step on it!" yelled the Lieutenant, and we left the crowd in a small cloud of dust as we headed up the side of the mountain.

It took us about three or four minutes to drive up the winding road. Near the top was a small hut where a Vietnamese sentry stood. He waved us by. On one side of the mountain top lived three squads of Vietnamese infantry whose job it was to keep control of the mountain and protect our radio-relay station. Every night about twenty of them would stand guard and patrol the base of the mountain.

We drove past some wooden barracks and then headed to the other side of the mountain pulling up in front of the radio-relay hootch. I'd been up here before to help bring the same type of supplies we now had in the jeep; c-rations, water and gas for the generator.

"Hey Busby! Get your ass out here and give us a hand," yelled the First Sergeant. Out of the hootch stepped a tall, well-built boyish looking private.

"Good to see ya, we're getting low on gas," was Busby's reply as he came over to help us.

It took us about ten minutes to unload everything. Afterwards we stood near the doorway drinking water and catching our breath. I noticed how really simple the whole set-up was inside. There were two bunks and on a table, two radios. The hootch was rather small, twenty by twenty feet, I imagined. One of the radios was set on the frequency of the base camp and the other set on the frequency of the road-building camp. There was a switch-device that connected the two frequencies, but because it often didn't work most of the actual relaying was done by voice. With a microphone in each hand, the job consisted of receiving a message in one radio and repeating it into the other.

So while the base camp and the road-building camp could exchange messages, the only voice they ever heard was that of the relay-operator on Dragon Mountain.

I walked out back. There was an even smaller hootch there which had a small store of hand grenades, smoke grenades, flares and M-16 rounds. The generator that supplied power for lights and for the radios was also out back.

The view was fantastic. These Central Highlands could match scenery with any place I'd ever seen. It was a soft, beautiful green as far as the eye could see. Off to the North I could make out the outlines of Pleiku, a distance of five clicks or so. A few clicks to the West was a Mountainyard village. Everything was a very pleasant green that held me spell-bound. The view made me think that my two months up here might not be so bad. Besides, there would be even less stateside-type bullshit up here. At base camp we rarely saluted, rarely shined our boots and never had inspections. Up here it would be even better. As long as there was somebody at the radios twenty-four hours a day, we would be pretty much on our own. It would be Busby and I, with three squads of ARVN soldiers protecting us.

Three weeks passed and we had a routine going. One of us would watch the radios and generator in the daytime while the other would do whatever he wanted. I liked to hitch-hike from the bottom of the mountain into our base camp which was about five clicks north of Pleiku. It was my chance to shower and get a cold beer. I'd get rides with whatever came by; trucks, jeeps, armored personnel carriers, anything that moved and had room. The only thing I had to worry about was being back before dark. The Central Highlands was ours by day, but ol' Charlie owned it at night.

I heard an explosion outside, but wasn't too startled.

"God damn it Busby, quit wasting grenades!" I yelled sticking my head out the doorway of the hootch.

"We got plenty," Busby yelled back.

"Well, just make sure nobody's comin' up the mountain when you throw them."

Busby had been in the Army almost three years, counting the year he'd spent in Leavenworth for punching out a major, and was still trying to make it past Private. However, he was the acknowledged company expert on fixing generators. He also had a knack for getting extra supplies from base camp, especially cans of pork and beans which was about the only tasty thing in the c-ration boxes. So I tried to ignore his war games.

His height, about six foot two, was also an asset because it kept away the ARVN soldiers. He was twice as tall as most of them, or so it seemed, and the ARVN soldiers were somewhat in awe of him. They used to pester us for c-rations, cigarettes, coffee and whatever they saw that we had. Busby put an end to that.

The only Vietnamese we allowed into the hootch without first knocking was Sergeant Le Trung Minh. Sergeant Lee, as we called him, was sort of our liaison with the other ARVN soldiers because he spoke English. He was our friend and had helped us when we needed it. Once when lightning struck our hootch and burned out the wiring, Sergeant Lee showed us how to rewire everything.

Just then Sergeant Lee walked in with Busby.

"Hey Sergeant Lee, how you doing? Have a seat."

"Got cigarettes? I all out," he said.

"Sure, we got bou coup. Busby just brought up a couple boxes of c-rations, help yourself."

"Winston taste good, like cigarette should," he said talking a big puff and smiling.

"Hell, where'd the fuck you learn that?" asked Busby.

"Oh, I read in American magazine when I in Cam Ranh Bay hospital," he answered. Sergeant Lee had told us about his month stay at the American Army hospital in Cam Ranh Bay. He used to be a paratrooper, and during one jump he landed in a patch of pungie sticks. One pungie stick ripped a big hole in his foot and he had to be medevaced to Cam Ranh Bay. He had a few other battle scars, but the huge ugly scar on his right foot was his real pride.

"Won' see big scar again?" asked Sergeant Lee pointing to his foot.

"That's alright," said Busby, "we've seen it enough times already."

"Sergeant Lee, it sure seems like it's been quiet at night lately. Have the patrols been goin' out?" I said changing the subject.

"Yes, but no see nothing. O.K. by me," Sergeant Lee answered.

"Me, too."

"It's kinda boring if you ask me," added Busby.

"Well, nobody's asking you. You want to be a hero like those ARVN soldiers we see in Pleiku? Arms and legs missing."

"I ain't afraid a' no fuckin' gooks," was Busby's reply.

"What him say? I no bick," said Sergeant Lee.

"You shouldn't use that word around Sergeant Lee."

"You heard him. He just said he don't know what it means," answered Busby.

There wasn't much traffic on the radios, just commo checks, so we sat around talking. Sergeant Lee was always asking about the states. We couldn't convince him that there were poor people in America. He said they couldn't be as poor as those in Vietnam. We agreed.

"It late, I go now," said Sergeant Lee getting up.

"Take some more cigarettes from the c-ration box. I never smoke those things."

"Many thank. You numba one," said the Sergeant as he headed for the door, "night."

"Night, sarge," we replied.

As we got ready to sack out, I walked over to the radios and turned the volume knob up. If somebody called during the night, we'd wake up.

"You know Rodriguez, it's kinda strange," Busby said to me as he pulled a blanket over himself, "but I tried to get Wendy to bring up some gals from Pleiku tonight, and she said all the Madam K's she knows were busy."

Wendy was a Vietnamese girl, probably no more than seventeen. She lived in Pleiku, but spent most of her time with the vendors at the bottom of the mountain. We never knew her real name and probably couldn't have pronounced it anyway. She was friendly and talkative and rather cute. Wendy never went to bed with G.I.'s, but had on occasion brought up some Madam K's to spend the night.

"Did you tell her we've got bou coup c-rations?"

"Yup," Busby answered.

"Maybe they were busy?"

"It still seems a little god-damn weird, if you ask me," continued Busby.

"Well, nobody's asking you."

"Aw, go fuck yourself," was his reply.

I leaned over and turned off the light. I'd just closed my eyes when I heard footsteps outside the hootch. Sergeant Lee quickly entered. He was shaking slightly and out of breath. He had his pistol in his hand.

"What the fuck's going on?" asked Busby as we both started putting on our boots and pants.

"Someone out there, someone out there! I hear someone, I hear someone!" were the words the Sergeant sputtered.

"O.K., O.K., sit down and take it easy," and I grabbed his arm and made him sit down. He sat on the edge of the bunk and took a deep breath. Busby put a lighted cigarette in his hand. He took a few puffs and looked somewhat calmer.

"O.K., now who is out there and where?"

Sergeant Lee told us he'd been walking to his hootch on the other side of the mountain when he'd stop to piss. While pissing he'd heard a noise coming from a nearby abandoned shed. He said he was sure someone was in the shed, possibly a sapper. He hurried back as fast as he could without making a noise.

"I'll be right back," I said as I went out the back. I grabbed a few M-16 ammunition clips from the storage hootch and returned.

"Sergeant Lee, where'd Busby go?"

"Him go out front door fast," replied the Sergeant.

"That stupid. . . ."

I grabbed my M-16 and flipped off the safety. We went out the door and crouched down by the side of the hootch. Sergeant Lee had his pistol ready. We got behind a pile of sandbags. The shed was a couple hundred yards in front of us, but it was too dark to see anything. Just then we heard rounds go off from the direction of the shed. Someone was running toward us.

"Is that you Busby?" I yelled.

"Yeah, don't shoot! It's me!" he answered.

He jumped over the sandbags and crouched next to us.

"You stupid . . . "

"I got him! I got the sapper! I got me a gook!" Busby said excitedly, "I yelled for him to come out and then I opened fire."

"Hold it, what's that?"

"Somebody shoot," said Sergeant Lee pointing in the direction of the shed. We heard more rounds from that direction. Then, we heard a couple of thuds hit the sandbags.

"They're, they're shootin' at us," said Busby almost standing up.

"Get down!" yelled Sergeant Lee to Busby, "You dinky-dow or something?" as he hit Busby on the side of the head.

"I . . . I . . . I . . . I'm sure I got him," stuttered Busby. But before we could say anything to him, Busby got up and started running down the back side of the mountain leaving his M-16 behind. We heard a crashing sound in the tall grass and knew he'd made it to the woods. They'd never find us there I thought, as I felt the panicky urge to run, too. But, Sergeant Lee grabbed my arm.

"That no good, Busby not smart," he said.

"You're right," I answered as the urge to run left me. More rounds started coming. We ducked down. Sergeant Lee asked me where our grenades were and I told him out back.

More rounds started whizzing overheard. More thuds could be heard in the sandbags. The feeling of panic started coming back.

"I'll go get some grenades," I told Sergeant Lee. But I couldn't move. My right leg was shaking. I couldn't control it. I didn't know what to do, the leg just kept shaking. Sergeant Lee looked at my helpless position.

"You shoot, I go get grenades," he said. I saw him low crawl back to the small hootch. He came back a few minutes later with some grenades. I'd managed to get off a few rounds even though my leg was still shaking.

Then we heard some voices. Somebody was yelling in Vietnamese from the shed. I asked Sergeant Lee what they were saying.

"Them our ARVN soldiers," he said, "they say G.I. shoot two ARVN soldiers in shed."

"Ask them how they know it was a G.I.," I said, my leg finally stopping. Sergeant Lee yelled back and got a reply.

"Them say one ARVN soldier dead, other wounded, but still live. Him hear American words before bullets come," Sergeant Lee answered.

"God-damn that stupid Busby!" I said, thinking out loud.

"What we do now?" asked the Sergeant.

"Sergeant Lee, they're not after you . . ."

"No sweat. I stay and help you," he replied. If I make it out of this I thought, nobody will believe me when I tell them an ARVN soldier didn't run.

"Ask them to hold their fire. Ask them to give us a few minutes." Sergeant Lee yelled again and the ARVN's answered.

"Them say O.K., but in tee-tee time them come and get us," the Sergeant explained.

I went inside the hootch and then grabbed the hand-mike to one of the radios. I could barely hold on to it, my hands were so sweaty. I noticed sweat was dripping from my forehead and my jungle fatigues felt clammy. I was completely soaked in sweat.

"Whiskey-Mike Two this Relay-One, do you read me? Over."

"Read you loud and clear, over," was the answer from the base camp.

"Where's four-four? Over."

"He's right here, over."

"Put him on right now, it's urgent, over."

"Roger, over."

"Go ahead Relay-One, this is four-four, over," said a voice I recognized to be the Lieutenant's.

"My partner shot some friendly's. One's dead and the rest are after us. What do I do? Over."

There was a silence. Outside I could hear Sergeant Lee yelling something to the ARVN's. I repeated my message to the Lieutenant.

"Hold it a sec', I'm thinking, over," was the Lieutenant's answer. A few seconds passed.

"Did you tell them they can't do this. We're on their side. We're here to help them, over," the Lieutenant continued.

"Roger, out."

I threw down the hand-mike in disgust, grabbed my M-16 and went back outside to where Sergeant Lee was crouched. He'd stopped yelling.

"You got twenty-five dollah M.P.C.?" asked the Sergeant.

"What?" I answered in surprise.

"You got twenty-five dollah M.P.C.?" he repeated.

"Yeah. Why?"

"ARVN's say for twenty-five dollah M.P.C. and two cases c-rations everything be O.K." the Sergeant said.

"You're kidding?"

"Twenty-five dollah and two cases c-rations," he said for the third time.

"Tell 'em yes. Tell 'em hell yes! Tell 'em fuck yes! Tell 'em they can have the radios if they want 'em. Tell 'em they can have the whole god-damn hootch if they want it!"

Sergeant Lee yelled back.

"Them say call for medevac chopper," the Sergeant said to me.

"Fine, fine, we'll do it. They can bring the wounded ARVN to the hootch if they want. We've got some first aid stuff inside that might be of some help."

I ran inside to radio for a medevac while Sergeant Lee answered again.

I came back out. In a few minutes we heard footsteps. My M-16 was ready, just in case. Two unarmed ARVN's appeared out of the darkness carrying a wounded man. We helped carry him into the hootch and put him on a bunk. His leg looked badly shattered and was covered with blood. Sergeant Lee started cleaning it, while I handed one of the ARVN's twenty-five dollars in military script.

The radio started blaring. The medevac was radioing in to say that they were approaching the mountain. I went outside and let off a couple of flares.

The blinding light made out of night. The whole sky seemed lit up. A couple of minutes later the whooshing sound of the chopper could be heard overhead. It landed and two medics came running from the chopper.

"You guys alright?" asked one.

"I am, but there's two who aren't. One's inside."

They put the wounded ARVN on a stretcher and carried him to the chopper. I had to keep a hand on my bush hat, it seemed like we were in the middle of a small wind funnel. I sent up another flare as the medics returned.

"What about the other one?" they asked.

"I think he's over by that shed."

"Be right back," said one as he took off in a slow jog toward the shed. In less than a minute he was back.

"Top of his head's missing," he said nonchalantly, "you wanna check it out?" he added, smiling.

"No thanks," I said, my stomach starting to feel uneasy.

Sergeant Lee and I watched the medics get back into the chopper. The wind funnel subsided. We walked back into the hootch and got two cases of c-rations and all the cigarettes we could find and handed them over to the ARVN's. They left and I made a quick call to the base camp to tell them everything was O.K. and to send someone up in the morning to take Busby off the mountain.

"Sergeant Lee, you can use Busby's bunk if you're too tired to head back." He did look awfully tired. I felt completely exhausted myself.

"We no go look for Busby?" he asked.

"He'll come back in the morning if he's not in Saigon by now."

I reached out my hand and offered a handshake to Sergeant Lee. "Thanks. Thanks a lot."

"No sweat, G.I.," he said smiling, "you numba one anyway."

"Yeah, but you're number fuckin' one."

♪ / Joe Rodríguez

From *The Oddsplayer*

Unreal city where death reigned above and men went underground killing by remote control. Command Headquarters, the dispensary, any location where troops gathered was dug into the earth and piled thick with sandbags, dirt, even concrete. At this northern outpost, the incoming was unpredictable and unrelenting, Cooper told Perez hurrying him along—darting from foxhole to entrenched position. Cooper doubled back through the compound and showed Perez two key locations once more: the first-aid station and the armory. "Bullets and bandaids, Blood. Those two keep us alive. We can eat fear and shower in the dust."

Finally, Cooper took him to the living quarters. The entrance snaked into the earth and Perez knew the curve was to stop the fragments and blast from a direct hit at the mouth of the fortified hut. Smoky and ill-lit, he saw shapes.

"You know better than to bring a cracker in here, Cooper," someone said.

"This is Perez, troops, Latino and a disciplinary transfer. He almost took off a sergeant's head for naming him bad."

"*Pérez,*" another voice echoed. "Coño," the shape said moving forward, "Are you 'Rican?"

"No," Perez replied. "Chicano."

"Hey, Pana, we got us a connection. Mexican-American to my New York Puerto Rican. I'm *Fernández*," he said, grasped his hand and they shook out the salute. "Vaya! Hermano, there's one bet—nothing worse can happen to us. I'll take him from here, Cooper."

Fernandez showed him to his cot and introduced him to the rest of the squad. He joked nonstop with the others who relaxed and went back to play-

---

Coño—Shit
Pana—Bro'
Vaya! Hermano—Wow! Brother

ing cards. Perez went to his cot and began unpacking his gear. Fernandez sat down at one end. "Watch yourself, Perez. They're allies but right at the edge. A wrong word, even a look gets you wasted. You're in our tent, so you'll be marked as one of us. I look like them, you don't, but remember who your friends are. The non-coms and officers are Blancos and we Trigueños and Spics are expendable. You got to follow direct orders, but remember we're just numbers. Obey orders during the day but always keep you head down. Night," Fernandez said, "is mad time and the game changes."

Perez looked at him and Fernandez met his eyes coolly. "This camp is a killing ground and no one can be trusted."

"Not even you, Carnal?"

Fernandez laughed. "Rank and power rule; all we Rainbows got is each other. You're from the streets?"

"My family lived in East Los, but we moved when I was young. You?"

"Spanish Harlem is my turf. Or was. I got to clear this place."

"How much time?"

"Coño, Pana. We don't count time here. Four months is a tour at this post, but I don't know nobody who made it that long. Only two tickets out: medevacked or bagged in plastic. The brass gave us a one-way ride. I hope you messed up that sergeant good."

"I hit him."

"Mano a mano, right? You looked him in the face and went for his throat. Coño, we got smarter ways," Fernandez said, and patted a grenade on his utility belt. "Always carry ten magazines plus the one in your weapon. Four grenades minimum. Never stay still in the open because of the incoming and snipers. Most people get zapped because they let down their guard a moment. Too long at the shitter, an uncovered match on post. We got to stay alive and tell our brothers."

"You ordered me to report to you, Sergeant," Hartman said, as he stood at attention in front of Talbot.

"You hear all right, at least. There are a couple of things I have to cover and now is as good a time as any. I see that you put in a request to be Kirsch's

---

Blancos — whites

Trigueños — people of mixed race

Carnal — homeboy

Mano a mano — one on one

driver and birddog on those so-called medical missions he makes to the villages surrounding us. You know no one else wants the job?"

"I know that, Sergeant," Hartman said, braced at attention.

"I have to order men to go with him. No one ever volunteers. The rest of the men feel it's a waste of time. No one knows who the enemy is in this hell hole. Chances are that most of the people Kirsch treats are the enemy. We've heard that those two-faced slants save the medicine that Kirsch passes out and give it to the sappers."

"I heard the others say that, Sergeant."

Talbot's eyes bore into Hartman's face. "What do you think?"

"I've seen their dead with our supplies. They could have taken medicine from our dead, from pilfered stock. I've seen our medicine on the black market . . ."

"I'm not talking about pills," Talbot cut him off. "I'm talking about Kirsch."

"I've been with Kirsch in the villages. He treats women and children."

"Kirsch treats mainly women and children because their men are in the hills lining up their rockets on us," Talbot said, his voice rising.

Hartman said nothing.

"He should question his loyalties, Hartman. You too. You've got to stand with us or the medic." Talbot waited for a reaction, but Hartman remained silent. "You know, Corporal, that Delta was hit from that village four miles away from this camp. If I had my way, I would have leveled that dung pile."

Hartman kept his face expressionless, but Talbot thought that the corporal's eyes looked at him strangely, as if he were seeing someone else.

"Their soldiers know how to force us into mistakes," Hartman finally said. "If that village is leveled, we lose anyone who sides with us. If it was in enemy hands, they would not risk attacking us from there. They could have hit Delta from other places."

"Kirsch gives those gooks too much credit," replied Talbot. "They hit us from Four-Miles because they know we couldn't retaliate. Too many of his women and kids in it. If we're hit again with rockets, that village will be incinerated. If we find anything alive, we will relocate it where those gooks can't get at us. You still want to work for Kirsch after I told you what's going on? I can cancel your request."

"No!" Hartman answered, too quick in Talbot's judgment.

"Your choice: live with it! I'm attaching you to Kirsch today. I'm even pulling you off our roster and watch list. You can carry the sea lawyer's medicines for him. Maybe you can ship over with the Navy."

Talbot's eyes locked onto Hartman's face. "What makes a man from a line company up north volunteer for duty with a medic? Quit hiding. Admit what's on your mind."

Hartman's face remained empty, except for his eyes which regarded Talbot as if Hartman were trying to make something out in the dark. "Am I dismissed, Sergeant?" the corporal asked in a level tone of voice.

"One more thing," Talbot said. "I want you to move in with Priest and Isaacs and the others. Change huts right now."

"Yes, Sergeant." Hartman did an about face and left.

I'll find you out Hartman, Talbot thought. It's just a matter of time.

"Don't be pissed," Point told Hartman. "Those sappers were cutting the wire. You kill or die."

"You set me up, Point. I don't kill wounded."

"Dibbs doesn't take prisoners, wounded or not. If they can talk, he loads them in a chopper. High up, he interrogates them and no matter what, he drops them. The combat pinwheel." Point rotated his fingers around each other, whistled like incoming and went, "whap."

"You know why this war is lost?" Point asked, throwing Hartman off balance. "The enemy knows about Dibbs. In a firefight, when wounded, they pull the pin on a grenade and lay down on the weapon. Whoever moves them gets blown up. If Dibbs takes them alive, and drops them at altitude, they don't scream—don't give him satisfaction . . ."

"Pull some sick stunt like that again, Point, and I'll push the button on you," Hartman told him.

"See," Point said, and his eyes glittered. "It was good I made you off them. Now you understand. Home ends at the wire, and no one goes back. States or combat—nothing's real except the killing. The enemy has a cause. We have technology. Got to kill them all."

Hartman was so tired he fell asleep after dark, even with Point on the loose.

Rotting burlap and damp earth—a musty, sweaty odor permeated the underground bunker. Thinking was a reptile's sense of smell. Tiered sandbags heaved in sync with the blasts and concussion from mortar, rocket and howitzer. In the emplacement, the dust from the close calls scoured his lungs.

Close, Perez' legs jerked in spasms and dirt clods tattooed the plywood floor. Again—timbers rattling and the wheezy soil. He forced the air out of his lungs in deep breaths so that he would not make a sound. Maria, back home you said my silence was killing me and that I was burying myself in books. Outside, death shrieked like *la llorona,* the woman of legend who wailed for her lost children.

"Why can't you admit that you're Mexican?" she had asked at college. Maria made Perez question his identity.

"I have lived in the United States all my life. I am not a citizen of Mexico. But I know I'm not an Anglo," he answered her and held out his arm next to hers. His *compañera* challenged his thinking about who he was.

Perez felt the gritty dust on his arms from the incoming and told himself, I am neither Mexican nor Anglo, neither Catholic nor Protestant, neither Spaniard nor Indian. I am as if suspended between different worlds, between the blast and aftershock, between one shell and the following round.

"Who are your people?" she once flared as they struggled to understand one another at the beginning of their relationship. "Don't talk in abstractions. Forget Western philosophy and the isolated self. No one lives solo. You're *sangre* and *hueso,* blood and bone, and you live only with people who are like you."

Mestizo-mestizaje: he was the mix of Spanish conquistador and Mesoamerican Indian—neither the one nor the other but a synthesis he had to create. Not Hispanic, as if Europe were better. Not Mexican-American, which had the facile inflection of the Melting Pot. Give me your tired . . . a new people. White is American. He was Chicano. Stay alive. His name was the point in the shrill incoming.

Chicanos marched on city hall during Perez' junior year to protest against the politicians who gerrymandered communities. Maria challenged him to act. Together, they joined with other university students who stormed the Board of Education and shouted down Dick and Jane—the White-way right-way teachers. They demanded textbooks that allowed children to learn about their history and culture in the Spanish language they used in their homes and which made them citizens of a hemisphere.

---

compañera– girlfriend

Another group picketed finance companies that red-lined the barrios. The wagons were drawn in a circle around the Indians. Perez watched his compatriots. Years of failed promises were over.

"Have you always known who you are?" he asked her once in baffled rage. He had not found answers in books.

She talked about her migrant background and working in the fields, about small rural towns and her traditional Catholic upbringing. Being Chicana didn't fit what sociologists know.

"Our backgrounds are unique," Maria agreed with Perez. "We have to stand for ourselves."

"I learned two lessons from my background: hard work and silence." Finally, Perez could say I to her. "My parents didn't have time. Even as kids, their hands were calloused. They never talked much about roots or how they saw the world. Long hours and low wages meant a home and education, and they watched their children grow without the sense of being buried alive on the bottom."

She hugged him close with surprising strength. He was angry for feeling like a sell-out, angry with his parents for their narrowed lives.

After meeting Talbot, Perez understood why he learned to keep silent. Once he let himself feel, Perez could shoot to kill.

Talbot. Spic, half-breed, dumb Mexican—constant insults and contempt. Perez' fist in that sergeant's sneering face. The blow was payment for his father. The ditch at work caved in and left him in a coma for two days. Three vertebrae fractured when the earthen wall at the construction site collapsed. He would walk but never be the same.

His father's face was ashen in the glaring hospital light. Bruised, scraped and flecked with crusty blood—he drifted in and out of consciousness and spoke both in English and Spanish. Perez' father rarely spoke Spanish, because English got hired. But because of Maria, Perez was able to understand. "Trabajo," his father said, "estoy listo." Or he would reach for a pocket and declare, "I have my papers; I'm not illegal." The nurses had to restrain him so that he would not tear out his tubing.

Even injured, his father was trying to make a home. A country he had helped build for fifty years wanted papers.

When the bombardment slackened and Fernandez checked the bunker with a battle lamp, he found Perez beating his fists against rotting sacks.

Trabajo . . . estoy listo—I'm ready to work

Two helicopters clattered over the dispensary and veered off toward the mountains. As they turned, their camouflaged bodies blended with the dark heights and disappeared. Only the rotors remained visible, blurs of light. Even these traces sometimes vanished, like paired images that cancel each other out.

Kirsch swept and mopped the dispensary with disinfectant. The stocks of new supplies and medicine were double checked, sorted and stored. There was nothing left to do except wait for sick-call. Kirsch went to his makeshift desk and chose a pencil from a number he kept sharpened. A lined regulation tablet was almost full of entries: the worn pages were held together by a clipboard. Sometimes pages wrote themselves. Whose hand? Kirsch wondered. Unsent letters or memos: to whomever this concerns.

In a rear-guard camp during a guerilla war, day-to-day life becomes ennui broken by sudden terror. Everything comes down to one thought, surviving a tour of duty. Troops greet each other with a constant refrain: only two hundred, only eighty-three, only so many more days to go. "I'm getting short, I'll be home soon." There is nothing to discuss except an escape. Hours measure nothing: light and dark are two sides of waiting. Time leaches any thoughts except returning home.

"We soldiers move from day to night over and again, chanting our litanies of escape." Talking to yourself again, Kirsch. The medic looked around the dispensary uneasily.

Time contracts to boredom and fear. Each one of the men I know, Priest, Isaacs, even Lieck, deals with them in his own way. After a matter of months even these constants blur. Perhaps to survive, soldiers go numb. Fear becomes a fatalistic sort of joking about death. What do you call your top sergeant in civilian clothes? The Grim Reaper. Terror is a paralysis of the spirit. The attack we fear will surely come. We have not been rocketed or mortared in months. No sense of relief because our number is up.

If we are lucky, no one will be killed, just maimed or medevacked. Terror is like dying. Almost better to accept the belief that if your number is up, then it's up. Letting fate be a death sentence stops the wheels. For every day in garrison spared from attack, there is a night. The dark belongs to the unseen enemy who is a master of surprise. At war how can a man be bored? Tedious routine makes life contract. If a soldier repeats useless tasks all day long, time becomes like the heat. Even the threat of death can be diminished by repetition.

Modern technology refashioned into tools of war is inescapable. Our trucks are weapons of transportation. Assembly line new, these vehicles are more than freight carriers. Machine guns are welded onto their cabs and boxes of belted ammunition are bolted into place beside the guns. The devastating efficiency of our machines makes itself part of the battlefield.

The country spews out goods that are shipped to this war. We march and counter-march, leaving our wreckage strewn about the countryside. The factories produce day and night. Everyone has work. The armies are resupplied and the destruction continues. Destruction and production seem the same.

Technology takes war out of the trenches, but does not make us human. The electricity in our plain but efficient dwellings, the water we pipe in from reservoirs in the foothills make dying hideous and absurd. Asleep in our plywood huts, or as we shave with blades honed to surgical sharpness, we can die. For all our so-called technological advances, we can die as did those who bludgeoned each other to death with rough clubs. We kill at a distance with the concussion from rockets or artillery, disembowel men with the shrapnel from sophisticated mines or mortars.

If we lived in trenches with no light or running water, then there might be less contradiction between our skills and what use we make of our hands. In this encampment ringed with barbed wire, the disparity between the best of our hopes and guerilla warfare is too obvious. Splitters of the atom, we cannot escape the oldest of evils.

6 / PEDRO B. ANCHONDO

Lonely Vietnam

Friday evening
Saturday morning
Sunday afternoon
qué importa! . . .
every day here
is patrol day
the only reality
is loneliness
I see the families
working together
in the rice paddies
and my heart shrinks
mi familia!—mi familia!
mi papá, mi mamá
y mis carnales
and their laughter
all of us together
working in our yards
far away dreams . . .
a bullet zooms
a buddy falls and
he is gone . . .

---

qué importa—what difference does it make?
mi familia—my family
mis carnales—my brothers

7 / LEROY V. QUINTANA

From *Interrogations*

Armed Forces Recruitment Day, Albuquerque High School, 1962

After the Navy,
the Air Force, and
the Army
Sgt. Castillo,
the Marine Corps
recruiter,
got a standing ovation
when he walked up
to the microphone
and said proudly
that unlike
the rest, all
he could promise
was a pack,
a rifle, and
a damned hard time.
Except for that,
he was the
biggest
of liars.

Lesson

He had been a bomber pilot in his war
the year I was born

and now he was accompanying me to mine
as far as Seattle.
From there, his vacation in Alaska to hunt bear.
He had known fear
and the fear of being afraid that first time
under fire.
One thing, he kindly told me, you will come to know
when that time comes.
You think you will be the only one,
but always,
there will be someone who is so much more afraid.

First Encounter

You have stopped for a break, stand up
to put your gear on and hear shots
see the flash of the muzzles.
You have been followed.
The whiteness of the branches
that have been cut along the way
tells you you're on a new trail,
but the sergeant is a stateside G.I.:
barracks inspections, rules and regs.
You are probably surrounded.
There are five others beside you.
You are twenty-three.
You look quickly around you:
the sky, the trees.
You're far from home.
You know now that your life
is no longer yours.

Eddie

After all the shit out in the boonies he got KP
and after a while flung away trays,

and scrub brush, and without a word
grabbed his M-16, a bandoleer,
fired up the First Sergeant,
walked out to the perimeter,
fired until his company added one more gook
to its body count,
only this one's name was Eddie.

Seen on a T-Shirt Superimposed on a Map of Viet Nam, Albuquerque, Summer, 1980

Participant
Southeast Asia
War Games
1968–1969
Second Place

8 / Daniel Cano

Somewhere Outside Duc Pho

The night we heard that our good friend Jesse Peña was missing, we decided
to get a search party together and check the bars in Duc Pho, an old city in
Vietnam's central highlands. We were in the rear area for a short rest before
beginning the next operation, and we knew that under stress, sometimes guys
who reached the limit and could not go on another day ended up AWOL, lost
in the delirium of booze and chaos. But our orders came through and we were
restricted to base camp, forced to disband our posse.

Two days later a long line of double-propped Chinook helicopters with
105 howitzers and nets full of ammunition dangling beneath them choppered
us into the mountains, about a half hour outside our base camp. They lifted
us to the top of a mountain that was scattered with light vegetation. Below
and all around us, the jungle landscape was immense. Mountain ranges
stretched in every direction.

We began knocking down trees, clearing away brush, unloading tools,
equipment, packs, and ammunition. On our bare shoulders we lugged 55-
pound projectiles into the ammo dump . . . long lines of shirtless men, bodies shining with sweat. The sledgehammers clanged against metal stakes and
echoed as the gun crews dug in their howitzers. We filled and stacked hundreds of sandbags, which formed long crooked walls, some semi-circular,
others round or rectangular—all protecting the battery just like the walls of
a castle. And above the shouting voices, the striking metal, and the popping
smoke grenades roared the engines of the helicopters as they landed, dropped
their cargo, and quickly lifted away.

Once the battery was settled in, I took up my position on the outpost.
There were three of us. We dug a four-foot deep bunker for ourselves and
stacked three rows of sandbags around the front and sides, protection from
incoming rounds and something we didn't like to think about: human assaults
on our position.

One night, after a week of wind and cold, a trip flare erupted, lighting up the jungle in front of us. We waited, then saw a shadow move across the perimeter. Instinctively we threw hand grenades and set off the claymores. Later, from another outpost, a machine gun burst into a steady stream of fire. The howitzers exploded, sending bright lights into the sky. I gripped my rifle tightly and watched the shadowy treeline as the flares descended and a cold silence filled the air. As always the flares burned out. Once the darkness hit, again the world rumbled around us.

An explosion sent a blast of light across our field of vision, the ground vibrated, my ears buzzed . . . and moments later, my left arm felt warm. I slid my fingers over the wet skin and touched a hole of punctured flesh, just below the shoulder. I told the others that I was wounded, and they got on the field telephone and called for a medic. The firing stopped. The jungle reverted back to an eerie blackness. Doc Langley, the battery medic, walked me back to our small infirmary and gave me some antibiotics, bandaged my left arm, and told me to get some sleep.

The next morning I was choppered to the field hospital at Pleiku. Doc Langley, who was also a good friend, went with me to take care of the paperwork and refill his supply of Darvon. The doctors sewed me up and I slept the whole day.

When I woke up, Doc Langley was sitting on my bunk. I caught most of his talk, even though I felt dizzy from the anesthetic. He told me that Jesse Peña had been spotted. Some men from the Tiger Force, a reconnaissance outfit, had been on a listening post in the jungle. They'd been observing a squad of Vietcong. As the enemy moved along the trail, there, right in the middle of the VC column, they saw Peña, or a chubby Mexican-looking guy in American fatigues. The Tigers claimed that Peña carried an M-16 and walked right along with the VC squad, not like he was a prisoner but like he was a part of them.

When Doc Langley left, I sat up in my bunk. There was no way I could believe that Peña was in the jungle with the VC. It was just too ridiculous, and I knew that none of our friends would believe it either. I started to think about Peña and the last time any of the guys or I had seen him.

Peña was part of a small group of friends. There were about ten of us when everybody showed up, but usually five or six regulars. Since most of us were assigned to different units of the 101st Airborne Division, we'd split up during the operations, but always get back together when we were in the rear area. Each night, we would meet at an isolated spot somewhere in the brigade area—behind a sandbag wall or trash dump—for what we called our sessions. We would drink beer, joke, and talk about hometowns and friends.

Peña, who could hold our attention for what seemed like hours, hadn't said much that last night he was with us. He'd been a bit removed, sitting slightly in the shadows, and he refused to drink any beer. Still, he had smiled a lot, as if nothing was wrong, and had eaten a couple of cans of peaches and just watched and listened. Someone had asked if he was all right, and he'd just answered, "Yeah, I'm o.k." While it was still early in the evening, he got up and said that he was tired—carrying the radio during the last operation had kicked his ass. He straightened his fingers into a mock salute, touched the tip of his cap, and said, "Time to go."

"So early? How come?" Little Rod had asked.

"I'm getting short . . . only three months. Gotta save all my energy so when I get back home, I'll have everything ready for you guys. Sabes?" said Jesse, his words confusing us.

"Come on, have a beer," Little Rod persisted.

"Can't, gotta keep my mind clear. Me voy."

Jesse turned, walked into the darkness of the brigade area, and that was the last we saw of him.

Jesse Peña was short, rotund, and always smiling, like one of those happy little Buddha statues. Although overweight, he was handsome. There was a childlike quality about him, a certain innocence and purity that made him immediately likeable. Two large dimples, one on each chubby cheek, brought a glow to his face.

After each operation, we'd look forward to our sessions, so we could hear more of his jokes and stories. His humor wasn't slapstick or silly, but intelligent, and always with a point or moral. Sometimes he'd reminisce about family and friends back home in Texas, like his cousin Bernie who was so much against the war that he had traveled down to Eagle's Pass, Texas, pretended to be a bracero, and was picked up by the U.S. immigration. According to Jesse, Bernie, who was American and fluent in English, spoke only Spanish to the INS agents. He was deported and went to live with relatives in Piedras Negras. All this, Peña said, just to beat the draft. In this way, Bernie could say that he hadn't dodged the draft; it was the U.S. that had rejected him.

Sabes?—You dig?
Me voy—I'm leaving

His stories led to questions and analyses, and all of us participated, pulling out every piece of information and insight that we could. Peña always seemed to have the right answers, but he was never overly egotistical. Always he came across as sincere and gracious.

I envied his ability to switch from English to Spanish in midsentence. His words moved with a natural musical rhythm, a blend of talk-laugh, where even tragic stories took on an element of lightness. He didn't present himself as an intellectual. His speech had a sophistication that didn't come with schooling but with breeding. Someplace in his family's background of poverty, there must have been an honest appreciation of language.

And he loved his Texas. To hear him talk, one would think that San Antonio was San Francisco, New York, or Paris. In his mind, San Anto', as he called it, had culture and personality. When it came to music, no one could come close to the talents of Willie Nelson or Little Joe y La Familia. Those of us from California didn't even know who they were. He'd play their music on his little tape recorder and we'd laugh and call him a goddamn cowboy, a redneck Mexican out of step with the times, and then we'd slip into arguing about our states and which was best, and how the city was better than the country . . . and on and on until we'd drained ourselves.

I placed my hands behind my head and looked at the wounded men around me. I didn't really see them, though, because I was thinking too much about Jesse Peña. It didn't make sense that he had suddenly shown up on his unit's duty roster as missing. Why would he go AWOL?

Three weeks later, the operation ended, the scab on my arm had hardened, and we were all back at our front area base camp. I wasn't the only one who'd heard the rumor. All of the guys knew about it. Big Rod, who was about six inches taller than Little Rod, knew some guys in the Tiger Force who confirmed the sighting.

Feeling superstitious about the whole thing, we decided to move the location of our next session. Two of the guys found an isolated spot near the edge of the brigade area. On one side it was separated from the rest of the brigade by a decaying sandbag wall about four feet high. Many of the bags were torn, but the heat and moisture of the tropical valley air had hardened the sand as if it were cement. Empty wooden ammo boxes, some broken and black with mildew, were scattered around the area. Twenty-five yards to our front was the jungle—not as thick as the field, but dense enough to hide someone or something. As the night moved in, the foliage darkened and the only protection from the wilderness beyond was a gun tower manned by two fellow paratroopers.

It didn't take long before the guys, and some interested new ones, started arriving. We discussed the possibilities that Jesse was either kidnapped or had deserted. Kidnap seemed impossible because our base camp was a fortress: guards securing the perimeter in gun towers, M.P.'s patrolling in gun Jeeps, units posting watches throughout the night; it just didn't seem possible. Besides, I argued, what interest would the VC have in a PFC radio operator from San Antonio, who only cared about getting home to his wife and child?

Alex Martínez, a surly Californian from the San Fernando Valley, stuck to the argument that Peña had just gone AWOL. "Old Peña split, man—just got tired of the shit. He's probably shacked up with some old lady downtown. Tiger Force probably saw some fat gook dressed in fatigues and thought it was him, man. He'll be back. Give him a few days."

We kicked the idea around. It wasn't absurd. We were reminded of Michael Oberson, a cook who had gone AWOL, changed his name, and lived with a Vietnamese waitress in Saigon for fourteen months. He'd gotten himself a job with an American insurance company and a nice apartment in the Cholon district. He finally turned himself in, and while he waited for his court martial, he was assigned to our unit. We remembered how he had laughed when he told us that the U.S. government subsidized a portion of the salaries of all the employees who worked for the insurance company. "So," he would say, "Uncle Sam was paying me to stay AWOL. How could I give it up?"

Danny Ríos argued that Jesse was too short. Nobody went AWOL with only three months left. It didn't make sense, any of it. Besides, he reminded us, Peña was so committed to his wife that he wouldn't even look at other women. Although he admitted he'd seen a change in Peña's personality over the past couple of months. Like everybody else, Danny took it as a mood swing. He shook his head, more confused than anything else.

Big Rod said that he suspected more. "I've been thinking, you know," Big Rod began. "Not too long ago Peña told me something was wrong . . . inside. I asked him like if it was his old lady or kid, but he said no, it wasn't like that. He said it was more of a feeling, like something that grabs at your stomach and twists and twists and doesn't let go. Not too much a pain, you know, more like a chunk of metal glued to your stomach, something that hangs and pulls until it feels like your insides are falling, and he said it wouldn't go away. Every day he woke up feeling like that."

After a few hours, many of the newer guys went back to their units. The night thickened and the five of us who were Peña's closest friends remained.

We sat in a circle. In the middle was a used C-ration can filled with lighted heat tablets that gave some relief from the darkness of the jungle—a darkness that loomed silently around us. Every once in a while, we heard the whispers of the perimeter guards who were positioned in the jungle . . . human alarms against a possible attack.

Little Rod, who was from Brownsville, Texas—"Right down in the corner of the goddamn country," he once told us—pulled out his Camels, slowly tapped the bottom of the pack, and placed a cigarette to his lips. He sat on an empty wood ammo crate and leaned back against the sandbag wall. After a long silence, Little Rod leaned over, stuck his cigarette into the heat tablet, and sucked on the tobacco until the tip swelled in an orange glow.

"I seen him start to change," said Little Rod, whose English was heavily accented. He wore his cap down low on his forehead so that the shadow from the brim buried his eyes.

"When Peña volunteered to carry the radio, I told him not to do it. He never saw much action—not until he started humping that radio. I saw how he kept laughing, real nervous, when he came to the sessions, but I saw that he was trying to hide it. I could tell, man, that he was scared, too, something in his eyes. He tried to not show it . . . but I seen it. I seen it."

"Sure he was scared, man," responded level-headed Danny Ríos, a Northern Californian who always tried to find a balance in every situation . . . a cause for every effect . . . a good reason for every tragedy. He wore his cap high on his head, like a star baseball player, so that his whole face was visible. He continued: "Peña didn't know what he was getting himself into. He said he wanted to see some action, said he was tired of filling sandbags and carrying ammo. Yep, he got his transfer all right, and I think he hated it out in the bush. That's Charlie's country. That's his backyard. You go messing around out there and you best be scared. Common sense, man . . . common sense."

Little Rod didn't turn to face Danny. He spoke, his back against the dirty sandbags and his voice came out of the darkness: a somber tone exploring, probing, "It ain't what I mean. Peña's a nice kinda guy, you know? He got his vieja and kid. Every time the priest comes out to the bush, Peña goes to com-

---

vieja— old lady

munion. Something bad had to of happen to him. Maybe he learned that God ain't out there. Maybe he learned that God ain't here either. The first time he carried that radio was when his platoon went in to help out C Company. You remember, C Company got ambushed . . . bodies tore up into thousands of pieces. Peña smelt the burnt meat, bodies that belonged to his friends. He saw those dead, nasty eyes."

"So what are you saying?" argued Alex. "You believe it was Peña the Tiger Force saw out there, that Peña is out there fighting with the Cong, that death is going to make him run off with the gooks? It don't make sense, man, no sense at all."

Little Rod continued, "I remember one time his squad come in from the bush, must a been right after his transfer; he's carrying that radio. Remember, Ríos? You was there. We was set up someplace outside of Tuy Hoa."

"Rain come down in chorros. Everything was like a sponge. Peña come out of that jungle into our battery area . . . his eyes big . . . like two big ol' hard boiled eggs. That ain't a regular scared. He's soaked, dirty, smelly, and he's talkin' a hundred miles an hour. You had to slow him down. Hundred miles an hour, ese. That ain't regular scared. Something happen to Peña, man. I seen it. That ain't no shit; I seen it."

"Little Rod's right. Peña was panicked. His face was stretched, his skin white . . . cold, like a ghost." Danny Ríos confirmed Rod's words. "He talked like a machine gun and moved with quick jerks. I felt sorry for him. His lieutenant let him stay with us a couple of hours. We made him some hot chocolate and warmed him up. He just kept talking, man. He couldn't stop. Two hours later, when his squad moved out, Peña went. No questions asked, didn't complain, didn't fight it; just like the other guys in the squad. He walked back into the bush like a zombie, and that jungle, with rain still coming down, swallowed him right up. They said they had to find cover before dark. Little Rod's right. That wasn't no regular scared. Hell, made me thank God I was in the artillery. But it's just common sense, man. Put a dude in a situation like that and . . . hey."

"Then it's still not logical. If he's scared," I asked, "why's he going to take off with the Cong? He wouldn't even know how to find them. And if he did, they'd probably shoot him first. Alex is right, man. It doesn't make sense."

---

chorros— torrents
ese— dude

"Yup. Don't fucking sound like Peña to me," Alex said, the light shining against his square jaw and pitted skin. "He's probably in town right now, hung over and wanting to come back."

Finally, Big Rod, who was like a brother to Peña, went through jump school with him, and had met his family while they were both on leave in San Antonio, spoke up, his voice more serious than I'd ever heard: "I think he went. I think he took off into that jungle and went with them. I don't know how he did it, why, or where he went, but he's out there looking for something . . . maybe looking for us . . . maybe looking for himself. Remember his last words, 'I'll have everything ready for you guys.' He was trying to tell us something."

The battery commanders from A and B batteries called each of us in to find out what they could. It was clear that they thought Jesse was AWOL and somewhere in Duc Pho. That's what most of the guys in the brigade thought, too. Jesse would come back, get court martialed, and that would be the end of it. But Jesse had never been in trouble before. He was the one who kept us out of trouble, making sure we'd get back to camp after a crazy day in town or calming us down after a run-in with an NCO or officer.

A month passed before a new rumor started. We were still operating somewhere outside of Duc Pho. A squad of grunts had made contact with a group of VC. They swore that a guy who looked like a Mexican, wearing GI camouflaged fatigues, had been walking point for the communists. It was no mistaken identity. One of the guys said he stared right into the pointman's eyes and that the Mexican just looked at him and smiled. Guns and grenades started going off, but Peña and his squad slipped back into the jungle.

Everybody in the brigade was talking about it. The guys who saw Jesse swore that it was "a Mexican-American" they'd seen out there. "The guy looked me right in the eyes. He coulda' shot me if he wanted. I was froze shit-less" were the words of one grunt. It was strange how the words flew and the story built, but then, after a short time, the story transformed itself into a legend.

The story of an American leading a Vietcong squad was not uncommon. Everyone had heard it one time or another during his tour. Usually, the American was blond, tall, and thin. No one who told the story had ever seen the guy. The story was always distanced by two or three narrators, and it was more of a fable or myth, our own type of antiwar protest, I guess. What made this thing about Jesse so different was that the guys reporting it claimed personally to have seen him. Still, not many guys really believed it, except Big Rod, Little Rod, and the grunts who said they'd seen Jesse.

"Things are so crazy 'round this place guys'll make up anything fer 'musement," said Josh Spenser, an Oklahoman, who added, "I just don't know, man. I just don't know."

Two weeks passed before the next sighting. "Saw Peña, man." The guys who were now reporting the sightings started using his name, as if they personally knew him. One evening, when we were in the front area base camp, Big Rod, Little Rod, Alex, and I walked across the brigade area to talk to one of the soldiers who said he'd seen Jesse.

At first he didn't believe we were Jesse's friends. The guy didn't trust anybody because, as he put it, guys were saying that he was making the whole thing up, but after we explained our relationship to Jesse, he began to talk.

"It's the shits, man. Captain tol' me he didn't want me spreadin' no rumors," his voice lowered, "but I saw 'em. Big as shit, I saw."

The guy's name was Conklin. He seemed wired, like he was high on speed, sincere . . . yet nervous. He told us his story like someone who had been trying to convince people that he'd seen a UFO. Conklin said that he and his squad were on an ambush. They had the whole thing set up by nightfall: claymores out, good cover, M-16s, grenades, and an M-60 at the ready. He said that it was quiet out there, no noise, no animal sounds, nothing. But, as he told it, the VC never showed.

Since there had been no contact, the choppers came out to pick them up the next morning. He described how he bent down low and made his way out to retrieve the claymores. He disconnected the cap, and squatting down low, started to wrap the wire around the curved, green device. As he wrapped, he kept his eyes on the trail, looking both ways and also checking the jungle to his front. And then he saw Peña. Just like that, Conklin said, using Jesse's last name.

"Peña," pronouncing it Peenya, "was down in the bush, a Thompson submachine gun pointed right at me. I was gonna reach for my rifle but he just nods, cool-like, slow . . . and I know he means for me to not go for it so's I jes' set there and stare at him, and all he does is stare back. I couldn't talk, man. I couldn't yell. It was like . . . like one of them nightmares where you feel suffocated and can't nobody help you. Then he moves back, real slow-like, still squatting, like gooks do, an' then I see two other gooks, one on each side of him. He stands up and the gooks stand up and they move backward into the brush, just like that, fuckin'-A, man, and he's gone."

"What's he look like?" asked Alex.

"Got on gook clothes, man. Pajamas—a black top and black bottoms, cut off just above the knees . . . light complexion, 'bout like you," he says pointing to Big Rod. "I guess he's close to 5'7" or 8", not too tall . . . probably 145 or 150 pounds."

"Peña's closer to 175, maybe 180," Alex tells Conklin.

"Not no more he ain't. Guy I saw wasn't no 180. And when he smiled, he made me feel O.K., you know. Even though I was scared and he could'a blown a hole through me, still . . . made me feel like . . . O.K. Maybe had something to do with those dimples. Big mothers . . . one on each cheek."

Big Rod and I looked at each other.

"Kinda made him look like a kid. But he wasn't bullshitting, man. It wasn't no joke. If I'd a gone for my weapon, he'd a blowed my ass clean away. I can't figure it out, man. Gone, just like that . . . disappeared with those gooks right into the jungle. And nobody else seen it, only me."

Three months had passed since Jesse disappeared. His ETS date came and went. Maybe we expected a miracle, as if Jesse was going to walk into the base camp, say "hi," and tell us about his days with the VC as he packed his bags and prepared to catch a hop to Cam Ranh Bay where he'd DEROS home. But nothing. It was just another day; besides, by this time we were in Phan Rang, our rear area base camp, and a long way from where Peña had last been seen.

That night, the night of Peña's ETS, we held a "session," more of a funeral, over by the training course, which was at the perimeter of the brigade area. Even some of the nonbelievers showed up.

We met in front of the mess hall, one of many in the brigade area. It was located on a hill at the east end of the base camp, where we could look out over the entire airborne complex.

The sun had descended and the work day completed. We could see GIs slowly walking the dirt roads, some going to the Enlisted Men's or Officers' Clubs, others to the USO, and still others strolling as if they were out for an evening in some country town. In an hour or so it would be dark and carefully rationed lights would bring a different life to the area. There would be drinking and card games, laughter and yells, tales about families and girlfriends, stories of heroics in the field with a few guys displaying the macabre trophies. Some guys would listen to records in their tents and wonder what their buddies back home were doing. At the USO, they'd be talking to the donut dollies, playing Monopoly, Scrabble, dominoes, and other games, while in their minds they'd be making love to the American women who sat at the opposite side of the gameboards.

We turned away and headed toward the obstacle course. A range of jungle-covered mountains formed the camp's eastern perimeter.

We followed a dirt trail down a hill and gathered in a clearing that was used for a map reading course. It was off-limits at night so we had to be quiet.

As the two Rods and I approached, we saw that Alex and Danny, with C-ration cans and heat tablets, had designed a church-like atmosphere. The small blue flames, much like candles, were spread out in a circle to our front, lifting the darkness so that our faces were barely recognizable. The jungle surrounded us with a heaviness that leaned more toward enigma than fear. After a short while, the shuffling of feet along the trail stopped, the whispering voices were silent, and about twenty of us sat on logs formed into a semi-circle.

Big Rod said that there would be no drinking, not yet, anyway. Doc Langley handed him a stack of joints. Big Rod passed them around and said to light up. Not everyone liked to smoke, but this night they all breathed in the stinging herb. It didn't take long for the weed to take effect. The jungle moved in closer. The trees came down over our heads like thick spider webs and the plants weighed against our backs. The joints moved around the circle until the air and smoke mingled into a kind of anesthetized gas.

Big Rod pulled a paper from his pocket, unfolded it, and began to read. It was from Margaret, Peña's wife. The army had told her that Jesse was listed as AWOL because it couldn't be determined when he officially had been lost. In her letter, which made Big Rod pause many times as he read, she wanted to know what happened to her husband. She trusted that Rod would tell her the truth since it seemed nobody else would. Was Jesse dead? That's what she really wanted to know.

"Please answer soon," were her last words. Rod wanted to know how he should respond, then, frustrated, he gave me the letter. He said that since I was the one with some college, I should answer.

Johnny Sabia, an infantryman from Sevilla, New Mexico, and a guy who didn't come around much, said that we shouldn't be moping but that we should be celebrating. "Write her," he said to me. "Tell her the truth. Her old man split. The dude's the only one with any balls. I don't know how, but this guy Peña understands that everything here means nothing. I've never met the guy, but I've been thinking about him and I've heard the stories. Everybody's talking about him. I heard that Peña lives in San Antonio, in some rat hole that he can't afford to buy because the bank won't lend him the money. I heard that in the summer when it hits a hundred, him and his neighbors fry like goddamn chickens because they can't afford air conditioning. So now they send him here to fight for his country! What a joke, man."

None of us ever talked about it. Peña never talked about it. Sabia was the first one who raised the issue. All we wanted to do was fight the war, get to the rear area, drink, joke, and never think about why we were here or what the truth was about our lives back home.

An argument started. Someone said that whatever we have it's better than what other people have. Even if we work in the fields in the states, it's better than working the fields in Mexico. An angry voice said, "Bullshit! We don't live in Mexico. We live in the U.S. Our parents worked to make the U.S. what it is; our fathers fought and died in WWII. We got rights just like anybody else."

Someone else wanted to know how come we get the worst duties. Whether it's pulling the shittiest hours on guard duty or going into dangerous situations, if there's a Chicano around, he's the one who gets it.

"Because we don't say shit, man. Whatever they want to push on us, we just take it. Like pendejos . . . we do whatever nobody else wants to do. We don't want to be crybabies. Well, maybe we should start crying."

"That's right," someone else said. "Gonzales got himself shot up because nobody else wanted to take their turn at the point. He walked the point for his squad almost every operation. What good did it do? He's dead now. Pobre Gonzales, man; talk about poor, he showed me a picture of his family who lived in someplace called Livingston, in Califas. His house looked like a damn chicken coop."

Then Alex stood up. He told how he was raised in the middle-class San Fernando Valley and remembered teachers who insulted him in front of his Anglo classmates, but only now, tonight, did he understand that it was because he was Mexican. Lamely, he said, "It never hit me. I just thought I was

---

pendejos– dumb shits
Pobre– Poor

the only fuck-up in that school. There were a lot of white dudes who screwed up, but I don't ever remember the teachers jumping on them like they jumped on me."

Johnny Sabia talked some more, about tennis clubs built over fields where the townspeople of Sevilla had once grown corn and vegetables, about schoolhouses with holes in the roofs, streets still unpaved in 1967, primitive electrical systems for lighting. And he and others went on and on until they worked themselves into a fury.

Someone pulled out the beer. As the alcohol hit, the voices got louder and belligerent. Before long, the whiskey bottles started to make the rounds and nobody was talking about Peña any longer. Everyone talked about their friends back home, their girlfriends, or good places to find prostitutes in Phan Rang. The session was over. Somebody kicked out the heat tabs, and the jungle, once again, distanced itself from us.

We marched over to the Enlisted Men's Club, toasted Jesse Peña several times, honoring him and wishing him well, and drank until they threw us out. Then we staggered along the roads, falling into ditches, staring at the stars splattered against the sky, and vomiting as we worked our way back to our units. We finally found our bunks and sank into a dizzying sleep.

The next morning when we woke up, most of us were hungover. We went through our usual routines, cleaning weapons and resupplying our units. A few days later, we flew out in C-130 transport planes to the next operation, somewhere outside of Chu Lai. There were a few rumors that Peña was still traveling with the VC, but no one would swear to the sightings. His memory became painful for those of us who knew him. When I left Vietnam, the new guys joining the Division heard about the Mexican who ran off to join the VC, and they kept the story alive, building on Peña's adventures. One squad reported that they saw his dead body after the ambush of a VC unit, but nobody believed that story either.

9 / DANIEL CANO

From *Shifting Loyalties*

Esprit de Corps (David Almas)

David Almas was tired of sitting in Raymond's bedroom. It was Friday night, almost 11:00 P.M. David hadn't wanted to steal the hubcaps, had said it was stupid. The other two thought it was stupid, too, but they were bored. They wanted to do something.

"Anyways," Kenny had argued earlier that evening, "ain't that what people say Chicanos do, steal hubcaps?"

"Shit, that went out in the 50's," Raymond said.

"Well, then let's do it just to see what it's like."

"Dumb, man," David said. "Nobody even uses hubcaps anymore. Everybody's got chrome rims."

"Fuck it. I'm doing it. I saw some spinners on a chopped Oldsmobile over at that used car lot on Pico and Steward," said Kenny.

"Man, the guys from Santa Monica catch us and they'll 'jack us up,'" Raymond said, cracking his knuckles then pushing himself from the wall.

"It'll take us five minutes. In and out, quick, clean. We'll be back here in no time," Kenny said.

"What do you think?" Raymond said, turning to David.

"Stupid, but what the hell. You guys go, then I'm game."

The whole thing took about a half hour. A ten-minute ride to the car lot, sneaking around in the dark, each guy pulling off a hubcap. They jumped back into the car and were back at Raymond's mom's apartment, where they sat around flirting with Raymond's older sisters until the girls' boyfriends picked them up.

"So . . . this is it, our Friday night?" said David, taking the hubcap from Kenny, flipping it over twice, and tossing it into a corner where it banged against the other hubcaps. "Let's go to Carole's party. We can get Julian to buy us a six-pack. There's probably all kinds of people gonna be there."

"No way!" Raymond answered, looking at the four hubcaps then scanning his narrow, windowless room where the single bed and a three-drawer dresser barely fit.

"Raymond's afraid Carmen's gonna be there," said Kenny, as if Raymond wasn't in the room.

"So let her be there, man," David said. "Show her you're glad to be free of her. Put on your Jimmy Cagney face."

"I can't, man. I never felt like this before, you know," said Raymond.

Carmen was an Italian who ran with Chicanas. She looked like a model, thin and shapely, light-brown hair, hazel eyes.

Raymond and David argued.

Kenny picked up the front page of the *Los Angeles Herald Examiner*. He read the captions under the photographs. His lips moved slowly.

"Well, if you want her back," said David, "you can't let her know how much it hurts. You gotta go in there and make her jealous; let her see you dancing with other girls. Shit, forget Carmen. Barbara's crazy about your ass, has been for years. So is Helen . . . and Alice."

"I'd rather stay here."

"Man, when you get in your moods, Raymond, you're like an . . . an old man. This is bunk," David said. "We can't stay cooped up here all night."

"You're my friends! Aren't you?" said Raymond. "You're supposed to be here with me. We do everything together."

Kenny held the newspaper where they could see it.

"Check out this shit, man," Kenny said.

The newspaper's hazy black and white photograph showed a line of Marines lying in a prone position, hands holding onto their helmets, as if a strong wind was blowing. Smoke clouds hung over their heads. Thick brush surrounded them. Their rifles lay at their sides.

"Man . . ." David said.

"That ain't shit. We can go over there and kick some ass. I swear to God. You won't catch me hiding my head like that," said Raymond.

David read the article out loud. The Marines were operating around Da Nang. They'd run into an ambush and were pinned down. The reporter wrote that each year the Viet Cong were gaining strength and becoming more confident, hitting American troops in daylight.

"Yeah, let us in and we'll clean up that shit in no time," Kenny said.

They hadn't talked about the war before or about the military. They'd never discussed politics or much else, other than girls, parties, alcohol, and cars.

"The Marines are tough bastards, tougher than all them other units," Kenny said.

"They ain't nothing compared to the Airborne," said David. "My old man was a paratrooper. Nobody's badder than them."

"Ain't no way," said Raymond. "The Marines, man, bad dudes."

They argued for an hour. David knew some facts, like the 82nd and 101st jumping behind German lines on D-Day, the first Americans to make contact. He told them about the standoff at Bastogne, the New Year's Day jump in Belgium, and how many Chicanos from Los Angeles were in the Screaming Eagles, gave their lives for the country. Kenny and Raymond argued more from emotion than from anything concrete or factual. They talked about war movies, *The Sands of Iwo Jima* and *Guadalcanal Diary*.

The three decided to join. Just like that. Why not? They were all eighteen. David had graduated from high school and was enrolled in community college. Raymond and Kenny had quit school in the eleventh grade. One was driving a delivery truck and the other was moving furniture. For each, it was their third or fourth job since leaving high school.

"All right, let's do it," Raymond said, his chin jutting out.

"Yeah . . . Monday we go down to the recruiting office together, just to check it out. Me and Raymond'll go talk to the Marines and you do your paratrooper thing. We'll go to Vietnam and clean that shit up in no time."

The next week, they talked again. David had read all the Army literature. He found out everything about going Airborne. The photographs in the colorful brochures showed guys leaping from planes, filling the skies with parachutes. The recruiter explained how David would go to basic training, probably to Texas, then travel to AIT, either in Louisiana, maybe Kansas or Oklahoma and then to Jump School at Fort Benning, Georgia. None of them had ever been more than 200 miles from home. It all sounded romantic, like it was a dream.

The three settled on a date. They wouldn't tell anybody about it, not even their parents, and surprise everybody.

"Man, wait'll Carmen sees me in my dress blues," Raymond said, running his hand through his dark, wavy hair. "She'll come begging me to take her back."

"Shit yes," said Kenny. "And when I walk down the street with my uniform, man, the broads'll be fighting over me."

"I don't care about all that. I just got to get away, see what it's all about," said David.

He had already signed all the papers. His mom and dad were sitting on the couch, watching television. His sisters were in the den and his little brother was in bed.

"Hi, *m'ijo*. Where were you?" his mother asked.

"At Raymond's."

"How's Bertha?" she said, referring to Raymond's mother.

"Fine . . . I need to tell you something."

His dad looked up from the television.

His mom's words came out slowly. "What is it?"

He looked at the two of them, opened his mouth, hesitated, turned away and said, almost whispering, "I joined the Army." He looked back at them.

No one spoke.

"What?" his dad asked.

"I went to the Army recruiter and joined. I'm going Airborne."

David's dad rose from the couch. He put his newspaper down and stepped around the glass-top coffee table. He moved towards David and stopped a few feet away.

His mother's face dropped, as if all the muscles had lost their power. She looked up at David, confused and dazed.

"Why?" his dad asked.

"I want to go Airborne, like you. It's time for me to do something on my own. You joined when you were seventeen. You told me all those stories about paratroopers at Bastogne and Normandy, about the Screaming Eagles and the All-Americans, you know, the 82nd."

David's father wasn't sure what to say.

His mother sat still. She looked away from her son to the television. The actors flickered around like caricatures, their movements silly, uncertain. The light from the screen flashed against the wall, changing from dark to bright, like a strobe light. From the den, David's youngest sister yelled, "Mama! Sally's teasing me again and she won't stop." His mother stood, walked to the television and turned it off.

---

m'ijo— my boy

"Why didn't you ask us?" she said.

"I wanted to make my own decision."

"There's a war going on. Those boys, every day more of them are dying. We have a right to know if you're thinking about doing something like that," she said.

"I'm sorry, Ma. It's something I had to do."

"You've never even mentioned the Army. What about college?" his dad said.

"When I get out, I can get the G.I. Bill. They'll pay for all my college."

His parents looked at each other. Then his mother turned to David. "I wish you would have talked to us. I wish you would have said something first."

She chewed the inside of her lip and moved back to the couch. His father returned to the couch and sat next to her. David stood there, hands at his sides.

"I just thought, you know . . . I want to be on my own. It's something I've always wanted."

"You could be killed," said his dad.

"I'll be all right. I know it."

"You don't know nothing."

"*M'ijo,* I wish you would have said something, at least talked to us," said his mom.

"It's something I want to do, something I need to do."

"You don't know what you need," said his father.

"*You* joined!"

"Times were different. We had nothing. You got everything."

"I want to be like you."

They didn't answer. His dad got up, walked to the television and turned it on again. He stared at the screen.

"Are you hungry? There's some food in the refrigerator. You can warm it up."

"No, thanks, Ma. I stopped at the Nu-way and had a chili dog."

"When do you go?" his dad asked.

"A couple of months, after the fall semester."

His father nodded, his eyes on the television.

David waited for them to speak. Nobody said a word.

He walked past the television, said excuse me, and went to his room. He threw his coat over a chair and turned on his radio. Some guy was singing,

"How does it feel . . . to be all alone, with no direction home, like a rolling stone?"

David lay back in his bed and listened, wondering if maybe he had made a mistake. His decision had been so natural. The Army . . . just another step in growing up. His dad and uncles had done it. They'd fought in the big war. At family parties they laughed about it, joked about guys they'd served with. Now it was his turn. The voice on the radio sang, "You used to laugh about, everybody that was hanging 'round . . . now you don't laugh so loud, now you don't seem so proud, about having to be scrounging your next meal."

On the morning of April 25th, David's mother drove him to the recruitment station on Spring Street in downtown Los Angeles. His dad had to work and couldn't get off. He woke David up before leaving for work, shook his hand, and wished him luck.

The tall buildings cast dark shadows over the streets. Horns honked as David's mother stopped to let him off.

"I'll park in that lot over there and meet you in the building," she said, and pointed to a brick structure where a crowd of men stood on the sidewalk.

"No, Mom. Go home. I'll be here all day taking a physical and getting my papers. They'll take us to the airport from here."

"But *m'ijo.*"

"You can't, Mom."

"I . . ."

The horns honked behind her. One car sped past, tires screeching.

"I'll be okay. I'll call you later."

"But, where are they taking you?"

"I don't know. I'll get my orders here."

"David." Her eyes filled with tears. She reached out and he took her hand.

"Bye, Mama. I love you."

He closed the door and walked quickly down the sidewalk. She watched him. He stood at the fringes of the crowd. She turned away for a moment. When she looked again, he'd blended in with the other boys. She stepped lightly on the accelerator and turned on Hill Street, got onto Olympic, and went home the slow way, rather than taking the new freeway back to Santa Monica.

David found Raymond, who was leaning against the building, hands in his pockets. He was wearing pressed khakis, a white t-shirt and a Pendleton, unbuttoned. Although there were a lot of guys standing on the sidewalk, few of them talked.

"Shit, man. I thought you changed your mind," Raymond said.

"I told you I was gonna do it," said David. "Where's Kenny?"

"I don't know. I called him all last night and his mom said he was out."

"Out? Shit."

"Maybe he went over to Lucy's house."

"He should've been here by now."

They stood next to the locked glass doors. They heard the lock jingling. The doors flew open and a Marine, stripes all over his sleeves, crewcut hair, looked at Raymond and bellowed, "Tuck that shirttail into your trousers, mister."

Raymond looked at him.

The Marine bellowed, "Now! Now, not tomorrow!"

Raymond quickly unbuttoned his shirt and tucked it into his waist.

"And the rest of you . . . do as I say."

They followed him inside the building, and for six hours they walked through various rooms, signing papers, removing their clothes, walking through lines of doctors, signing more papers. But mostly they waited in long lines, waited for the word to enter, to exit, to move, to walk, to stop, to stand straight and not slouch, and the bellowing echoed through the cold halls, strong, hoarse voices, commanding, and cursing.

They broke for lunch and were marched to a diner where they all ate in different shifts. After lunch they marched back to the induction center and stood in front of the building as dark green buses pulled to the curb.

"How many of you suckers joined?" hollered a Marine sergeant, talking to all of the new recruits.

David, Raymond, and about one-third of the crowd raised their hands.

"All right then, ya' all move to one side, next to those buses."

They did as they were told.

The sergeant called for all who had joined the Marines to get onto the first three buses. Those who joined the Army were ordered to board the last three buses. David shook Raymond's sweaty hand.

"I think we fucked up, *ese*," Raymond said, looking around nervously.

---

ese— dude

David wouldn't admit to anything. "We're in now, too late. Eight weeks and I'll see you back home. We get a leave after Basic."

"Yeah, okay. Be cool."

"You, too."

As he moved towards his bus, Raymond turned to David one last time. "Fucking Kenny, man. He didn't show. Fucker."

"Get yer ass on that bus and stop using that profane language around civilians. You hearing me!" a sergeant yelled, rushing up and putting his nose to Raymond.

"Yeah, I hear."

"Bullshit! Nobody says 'yeah' to me. 'Yes, sergeant!' that's all I wanna hear come out of your filthy mouth. 'Yes, sergeant!' nothing else."

Raymond lowered his eyes.

"Are you understanding me, spic?"

"Yes, sergeant," Raymond said, his voice monotone.

"What did you say? I can't hear you."

"Yes, sergeant!" Raymond yelled loudly, his voice cracking.

David boarded the last bus. His heart pounded. None of the recruits said a word.

"Open up them windows, pussies. It's like a furnace in here," said an Army sergeant.

David opened his window and the smoggy, downtown air, mixed with gas fumes, entered. He looked at the hundred or so men still standing on the sidewalk. In front of them was a Marine sergeant who said, "So, you didn't have the guts to join my Corps. That right?"

The draftees looked around at one another not knowing what to say.

"Sergeant Wilson," the Marine said to an Army NCO, "did these men join your Army?"

"No, sergeant! They waited for us to come and get their sorry asses. They're scum, maggots, got no guts."

"Line it up, ladies. Gimme one straight row, right here in front of me."

They scooted around until they stood in one long line stretching down the sidewalk.

"Draftees, are you?" said the sergeant.

None of them spoke.

"Think you're gonna get some cushy Army job, do you? Well, I got news for you gentlemen. When Uncle Sam drafts you, your ass is his and he puts you where he damn well pleases. So NOW! From my left, starting with the number 1 . . . sound off!"

Silence.

The sergeant swiped the cap from his head, crunched it in his hand, and ran down the sidewalk to the first man in line.

He spoke softly, as if choking, the veins pulsating in his neck, his eyes bulging. "Did you hear me, young man?"

"Uh, yes, sergeant."

"Well!" came the burst from the sergeant's lungs. "Call out! Damn it. Say ONE. Scream it out like a man."

Down the row came the numbers, 1,2,3,4,5,6,7,8. . . .

When they finished, the sergeant smiled. "Good. Very good. Now, all even numbers take one step forward."

Half of the men, about fifty or so, moved to the front.

"Sons, welcome to the United States Marine Corps."

A sound, something like a stunted sigh, came from the men who stepped forward. They turned and looked at one another.

"Board that bus right there," said the sergeant as a bus came up the street and pulled to the curb.

"The rest of you ladies jump onto the last three buses with the other Army dogfaces and say a prayer to your god that you didn't pick an even number."

The men rushed towards the bus and scrambled up the steps. David rubbed his palms over his thighs. He breathed deeply and fell back into the seat. He looked at the man next to him. The guy was staring straight towards the front, like a mannequin, no movement, not even a blink of an eye.

The sidewalk was clear. The glass doors of the induction center closed. A few men in military uniform, both Marine and Army, stood inside the lobby. The buses pulled away from the curb, smoke from the exhausts billowing into the air, the engines whining. David whispered the Act of Contrition as the bus sped toward the L.A. Airport.

10 / Francisco Javier Munguía M.

From *A Mexican in Vietnam*

They were telling him something he already knew: that the war in Viet Nam was a bloody war and that there was a high probability that he would die or come back handicapped for the rest of his life. Why was he going? The United States was not his country and Asians weren't threatening either Mexico or the U.S. It was a stupid war freely inherited from the French in order to erase the embarrassing defeat they had suffered. Besides, he was Catholic and the priest at the sanctuary of Guadalupe, when they spoke after Mass last Sunday, had told him that one can go to war because of duty or because of conviction, and either way it wouldn't be a sin to kill. But if he wasn't convinced of the goals or couldn't accept responsibility, killing could be a heavy load for his conscience. He suggested options but the message was very clear. Everyone said, even in the U.S., that it was an unjust and undesirable war. Besides, now he believed he could avoid it by deserting and staying in Mexico.

Joe's uncles and aunts exerted so much pressure that they were in regular phone contact with his parents in order to convince them that he should remain living in Guadalajara in his Uncle Miguel's house. His mother had told him in tears and with resentment against the American system that he should stay in Guadalajara because she feared for his well-being and for his life if he were to go to Viet Nam. His father told him that he should listen to his conscience, that he shouldn't worry about the family: they were already together in the U.S. and he was old enough to make his own decisions. He didn't suggest what path to take but he let him know that he and his mother would be pleased if he were to stay in Guadalajara.

Until that moment Joe had not realized that for him to live in the United States, the system was asking that he pay a high price. He had already struggled and suffered numerous jobs during his and his family's immigration, and now he probably would have to give his life for that idea. Was it worth it?

Definitely not. Joe had gone to the U.S. driven by circumstances; he had demonstrated initiative, an ability to work, to apply himself intelligently in his studies. He could study in Guadalajara, get a college degree, and then pay back his uncle and aunt the money they had agreed to put up. His aunt and uncle seemed to be doing well financially and they only had three children, all of them students. Manolo was at the university already. The thought of staying was becoming more appealing. His decision was the obligatory topic in all conversations, especially with Veronica and her friends who were all openly anti-American. They described with a clarity and logic he had never heard before the exploitation of Mexicans and other minorities in the U.S. Besides, they saw the war in Viet Nam as an unjust and senseless war.

With only twenty-four hours left of his leave, Joe had decided to desert. The day before he had celebrated his twenty-first birthday with a cake in his aunt and uncle's house. Then he had gone to the movies with Veronica. The film was a piece of fluff, *Lovers Can Learn* with Troy Donahue and Suzanne Pleshette. A saccharine movie, but one that fit well with his age and newfound love. He really was falling for Veronica and she for him. Her kisses were warm and her behavior, although sensual, had a purity about it to which he was unaccustomed. Suddenly, he remembered Rosie and decided to break up with her.

During his first year in the army he had a girlfriend in San Fernando, Rosie, and a lover, Jan, the sister of Steve McManon and a prostitute in the making. She slept with anyone and enjoyed it, and she made him enjoy it, but he couldn't take her seriously as a girlfriend. The funny thing was that Jan had insisted that they get married before he went to Viet Nam even more than Rosie had.

He had had three or four other meaningless sexual encounters, but his feelings for Veronica were different. His cousin was the perfect girl with whom to have a long and pure relationship and eventually marry. He turned to look at her and smiled; she squeezed his hand and put her head on his shoulder.

December 4, 1966, was supposedly his last day of leave. He had to be at Fort Ord, California, on the 5th before 6 P.M. There, they would put him on a plane for Wichita, Kansas, and the next day he would leave for Viet Nam with the advance deployment of the Ninth Division. At least, that's what the orders he had in his suitcase said. That day passed like all previous ones, quickly and enjoyably. After being with Veronica, he returned to his uncle's house at 9 P.M., ate dinner, and went to bed.

But he didn't sleep, just thought about the problem he had. Apparently, he was convinced that he would desert and stay in Mexico, but deep inside he wasn't sure. Everything he had done and suffered up until then would be in vain if he stayed. More than anything, he had one thing clear: he had never run away from a problem. The decision to desert could mean reprisals against his family or could cause trouble for his younger brothers. In a couple of years, one of them would surely take his place, and if anything happened to one of them, he would never forgive himself. He also considered how he would not be able to return to the U.S. without risking jail or deportation. What did it matter that it was someone else's war, unjust, and that he was just cannon fodder? Many would survive and he could be one of them. He had always trusted his fate, and now he was thinking about avoiding the most decisive test of his life. Besides, he was trained to survive and he was a good soldier. He remembered the last conversation he had with Captain Summers, when he gave him his orders for Viet Nam:

"The waiting is finally over, Joe," he had said with a smile. "We're all going to Viet Nam. I've had doubts about granting you this leave since you've mentioned several times that you might desert and you never miss a chance to voice your hatred of the army and this 'dog's life,' as you call it. But your actions belie your words. You've been a good soldier, disciplined and skilled. You were one of the first to earn promotion to corporal. Why are you still doubting yourself?"

"I hate the army and everything it represents," Joe responded with authority. "But I learned a long time ago that it's no good to be a bad soldier or you'll always have a boot in your face. It's better to lead and give orders than to be ordered around and punished."

"But," the captain continued, "are you sure you won't desert? The paperwork and explanations for declaring someone a deserter are a pain and it will show up on my record."

"Don't worry captain, I'm not going to desert . . ." Captain Summers had no idea how close I was to causing him a major headache, Joe thought. Although this was the least of his problems. He also remembered some of the things the first sergeant had said when they parted company:

"Soldiers!" he had shouted, "the adventure you are embarking on is not a game. Some of you will die, as it must be in every war, but the majority of you will survive and will have one of the most important experiences in the life of a man. Look around and I'm sure each one of you is thinking: I will come back. Maybe the others won't, but I will. Well, nobody knows that now, but it's for sure that some of you will come back in a pine box. You've gone through a tough and demanding training program, the best in the world. You've learned all the techniques of war that we can teach you in simulated conditions. The rest you'll learn in your first combat experience."

And then Lieutenant Payne: "Keep your spirits up, men. Don't let the sergeant get you down. He's a sentimental old man. We're all going to Viet Nam to fight bravely and it doesn't matter how many die or who dies. Destiny will decide that."

"Destiny will decide that," Joe told himself assuredly, "and I can't run from my destiny." Suddenly, he knew that he could not desert and that he wanted to go to Viet Nam to try his luck. He got up and looked at the clock: it was three-thirty in the morning. He got in the shower. The noise would wake everyone, but it was his habit to rise early and so they wouldn't get up. He would leave a note for his Uncle Miguel, explaining why he left.

At four in the morning he hit the street with his duffel bag over his shoulder to hail a cab. He walked a block toward Hidalgo Avenue and saw a taxi. He asked to be taken to the airport.

His ticket to Los Angeles had expired the day before, but he would see what was available. He smiled, remembering the look of surprise on his uncle's face when he had bumped into him as he left. No explanation needed; he understood. These things are better understood among men. He thanked him for his hospitality and the offer and asked him to speak with Veronica. He would write to her when he could. His uncle gave him a big hug and wished him luck. When he moved away, he saw that his uncle's eyes were full of tears, but his smile was positive.

At eight-thirty in the morning, he left for a three-hour flight to L.A. on Mexicana Airlines. His uncle had called his parents and the whole family was there to greet him and say good-bye. He had not considered going to Viet Nam without saying good-bye to his family, and he thanked his Uncle Miguel for notifying them.

Before boarding the small commuter plane that would take him to Monterey, California, he went into a public bathroom and put on the uniform he had not worn for fifteen days. He felt very comfortable in it. It looked good on him, and he thought it suited his character. The shadows of doubt vanished and, relieved, he walked confidently toward the plane. Joe was ready.

Translation by George Mariscal

11 / Roy Benavidez

From *Medal of Honor: A Vietnam Warrior's Story*

Dress Code Black

The only chance we had to relax and be ourselves was back at Tam Ky, where there was a good-sized American compound. It was called the "Payne Compound" and was named after a U.S. Marine adviser who had been killed a few months earlier. Quite a few Americans were in Vietnam then, and a lot of them weren't in uniform. They were agricultural advisers, political consultants, industrial observers, and communications technicians. They were CIA, and they were running the show.

I'm a soldier. I follow orders. It just seemed strange to know that our senior officers were following CIA orders. Our battle plan was obviously political, not military.

Payne Compound was the only place where you could get some real news and hear what was going on outside of your little sector. It was a clearinghouse for information and a stopping-off point for guys coming into the interior. The conversation and camaraderie there kept us all sane. It kept everything in perspective, except, of course, when we heard news of something like what President Lyndon B. Johnson had said in a speech at Johns Hopkins University.

He had said that the goal of the United States in Vietnam was to allow the South Vietnamese "to guide their country in their own way." Some of us who had witnessed some of their "ways" wondered if that was such a good idea.

Tam Ky is located about twenty miles east of the Black Virgin mountain range. The famous north-south route known as the Ho Chi Minh trail wound through those mountains. While we were building up the strength of our advisers in the south, the North Vietnamese were using the trail to build up their troop strength in the south to match it. This buildup was what a lot of the talk at the compound was about in those days.

One day, out of pure frustration, I decided to use some of that information in an attempt to finally do the job I was sent there for. "Captain Lewis," I said, "everybody knows those guys are building up troops over in the mountains. How about I take a few of our CIDG's or Saigon Cowboys over there and get the straight of it?" (CIDG's were members of the Civilian Irregular Defense Group, hired by the American troops for information and scouting purposes.)

"What are you talking about, Roy?" he said. "Our orders are to observe and advise the local troops, not go looking for trouble."

"Come on, *Die Uy,* you know what our duty's like. Take a walk in the brush till someone pops a cap at us. Then we go find the closest village and sit around while our troops try to torture someone into admitting they're VC. Cap, they trained me to gather intelligence; let me do my job."

I nagged him like a CIDG, or hired cowboy, who wanted an ice-cream cone. It worked. He passed the suggestion on up to Division and they filtered their go-ahead back down through Tran, the intelligence officer. Right after that was when the guys got killed on their way to church. Real interesting coincidence.

A few days later LaChance and I led our hand-picked squad out of camp, west toward the mountains. We were all dressed in black pajamas and those little conical hats peasants wear. South Vietnamese troops were known for not ranging too far from their fortified compounds. By the first night we were well into what we considered enemy territory and we needed to blend in. We carried a mix of U.S. and Russian weapons and looked like a bunch of VC on patrol.

By the second day out we were up in the low mountains. We walked along in a steady drizzle surrounded by clouds of mosquitoes. It seemed all uphill now. We fought the rock and the mud and the stinking jungle as we moved farther into enemy territory. Every second we expected to run into a bunch of VC or NVA regulars. The tension mounted as the hours crawled slowly by.

By the third day we had come across several old VC camps. Some looked like they had just been abandoned. We had hand-picked our squad but still didn't really trust any of them. With Tran in on the planning of this mission, we didn't know if we might be walking into a trap.

On the fourth day out it was more of the same. We were all beat from the climb into the mountains and edgy from the tension. Around late morning we took a break and I went out to scout around.

One second I was cutting through the vines, the next I was sliding on my back downhill. I dug in my heels and grabbed for the trees as I slid past them, finally catching one of the trunks and stopping. I looked up and could see I was only ten or fifteen feet down off the ledge of the cliff. When I looked down I froze. The rest of the way down wasn't as steep. At the bottom of the hill, about three hundred yards away, camped along a riverbed, were between eight hundred and a thousand men.

I just lay there sweating while the insects chewed on me. After a few minutes of panic I realized that the troops below hadn't spotted me, and I slowly crawled back up the hill. I'd crawl a few feet, then look down, then crawl a few more. By the time I made it back to camp I thought I'd been gone an hour. LaChance said it had been only about ten minutes. I filled them in on what I had seen, and we went back and cut out a good observation post along the edge of the cliff.

At first glance it had looked like VC camped down there. When we got our field glasses on them we could tell the difference real quick. Uncle Ho Chi Minh, the Communist dictator of North Vietnam, had been telling the world that the civil war in South Vietnam was just that, a civil war between the South Vietnamese troops and the Vietcong rebels. The only outsiders, he said, were the American advisers.

To keep the lie alive Ho Chi Minh's troops would follow the trail out of North Vietnam into Laos and Cambodia rather than entering South Vietnam directly. In Laos or Cambodia they would change into the standard VC uniform of black pajamas and sandals cut from the rubber of old truck tires. All their personal things and all identification were left behind as they crossed from Laos or Cambodia back into South Vietnam. Even from three hundred yards away through the glasses you could see that their black pajamas were new and that the camp was run with a military precision that was not the ragtag VC style. This was a well-fed, well-equipped, well-disciplined North Vietnamese Army (NVA) battalion.

Now we needed more information. We had come a long way to find the North Vietnamese. The longer we stayed out, the shorter the odds were getting that we would make it back in one piece. We needed to make this "walk in the bush" worthwhile.

LaChance started joking with our squad about sending one of them down there to infiltrate when all of a sudden a kid by the name of Tho said "I go Sergeant" in his broken English. Tho was sixteen or seventeen, and he had become a favorite of the advisers. We had even talked of sending him back to the States for school. When he said he'd go to the camp we didn't know if it was bravery or the act of a traitor. Neither did the other ARVN soldiers with him. They knew they had traitors with them just as we did.

We swapped Tho's U.S.-made M-2 carbine for the Russian-made AK-47 that I was carrying, and within ten minutes we could see him walk past their sentries. They didn't have any better security than our ARVN troops did. Maybe it was a national trait. Before Tho walked out of camp I had a talk with him. I said, "Tho, if I ever prove you're a traitor, I'll cut your throat personally."

Every second we were sitting there we were waiting for the NVA troops to come pouring up that mountain like a mess of ants at a picnic.

While we were waiting, Clarence started joking with me. "Hey, Roy, if they come a-running up this here hill you gonna wait for Tho or hightail it for home?" He loved using his cowboy movie Texas slang with me. I probably sounded that way to him.

Then he got serious. "Roy, if they do come up after us, what do you think our odds are of getting out?" I didn't have time to answer. Through the glasses I could see one of them separate from the camp and start working his way up the hill about a hundred yards to our right. Pretty soon I could make out that it was Tho and that he was alone. LaChance kept an eye on the camp while I went out to meet him.

He was like a little kid who had been given a new toy. He couldn't stop laughing and grinning. He had accomplished his mission without creating suspicion, and we were there to prove it.

When we debriefed him we really didn't get too much more than we already knew. He could tell they were NVA from their accents and what they were saying. They assumed he was from one of the small VC groups they were controlling. He told us that they were real proud of themselves. They were talking about how all the South Vietnamese troops were afraid of them and how the American advisers were scared to come out at night.

LaChance started joking around about how he was mad and told our boys to lock and load. We were going down there and give 'em a fight. Our boys thought he was serious and almost started home without us. It became obvious Tho was one of the standouts—although just a kid, he was a brave man compared to many of his countrymen.

From a pure military standpoint Tho didn't get much we could use. It was one of those acts of pure bravery that convinced us that we didn't understand these people and that we had to be careful about generalizing about them.

In two days we made it back to base camp. Captain Lewis was just starting to get nervous when we came trotting back through the gates. He was beginning to realize how much flak he'd have to take if he lost half of his advisers at one time, and so he was real glad to see us.

We were debriefed both by our own officers and by some U.S. "civilians" who were just "hanging around" when we got back. To tell you the truth, I never did find out if our information made any difference. In the months that followed I never heard a thing about any action in the area we had scouted. But I was just a grunt. I did my job.

Every time I thought I was getting a handle on what was going on and why, something else would pop up and convince me I knew no more than a flea on the backside of a dog. Wherever that hound decided to go, I was going along for the ride.

All our maps had the whole country divided into rough geometric sectors. You would use the topographical highlights of the area you were in to identify where you were, then cross-reference onto the map grids to put your location into perspective.

One day, we were out on patrol and I was on point. Now, point was the most dangerous spot to be in. You were the first in and the last out, and if the point man got killed it served as a warning to the rest of the patrol.

It was my own big mouth that had gotten me there. A few days before, I had been jacking with the ARVN colonel about my being an Indian. I guess he had seen too many reruns of the Lone Ranger and figured "Tonto" was the guy he wanted out there scouting on his patrols.

I know that this was my last mission out of Tam Ky. The problem is, I don't remember it. I've tried to find out about it since then but the military files are sealed. Even after all this time, it is still considered classified information.

All that I've been told is that a squad of marines found a body near a jungle trail. No location, just a jungle trail.

The guy looked dead. He was dressed in black pajamas and Ho Chi Minh sandals. There was a Russian AK-47 near the body. They assumed the body was booby-trapped so they were real careful flipping it over. They needed to search the body. It looked like another dead VC who had stepped on a land mine. They found a set of dog tags sewn into the lapel of the pajamas. They cut them out.

BENAVIDEZ, SGT RP.

Yeah, they thought. That face could be Mexican, not Oriental. The corpsman found a weak pulse and they evacuated me. That's all I've been told, and to this day, that is all I know.

Dress Code White

Brooke Army Medical Center
Beach Pavilion
Fort Sam Houston
San Antonio, Texas

White.

The world is white, the people are white, the floor is white, the ceiling is white, everything is white.

White is the first thing I remember. The first thing I could put a word to. A word, finally words. Maybe it's been words I've been hearing. I don't know yet, I think white is all I know for now.

"Benavidez, how you doin' today? Time to go back."

"Doc, y'all got things messed up here, these pegs don't fit in those holes."

"Hey, Sarge, welcome to the real world, you wanna talk a little? Nurse, have Sergeant Benavidez brought into my office."

Over two months earlier I had been medevacked in from Vietnam. The year was 1966, and war wounds and trauma cases were still a new thing here. I was in the first wave of the flood to follow.

The only real external wound was a big X, like a brand, on my butt. The X rays showed the real damage. The best they could figure out was that I had stepped on a land mine. The mine, or a pretty big flat piece of it, had come flying out of the ground with thousands of pounds of pressure and hit me square in the butt end. It just didn't explode like it should and blow me and my butt into a thousand pieces.

What it did do was twist and telescope my spine like a corkscrew. Bone and cartilage were shattered, but the cord looked intact. The doctors said that they knew that I would never walk again. My brain had been rattled so violently in my skull that they never expected me to regain my senses either.

In two months of sitting there and staring at those blocks that covered the ceiling, this was the first responsive remark that I had made.

"Maybe he got lucky again," the doctor mused as Benavidez was being wheeled into his office.

"Sergeant, tell me your name."

"I don't care about my damn name. How do you expect me to do my job when you don't give me the right pegs for those holes?"

The sarge was back, and the doctor knew it. When he started to smile I got madder. "And why's everything white around here? What is this place, a damn hospital or something?"

By this time, the doctor was outright laughing and I was getting madder and madder. If I could have gotten out of that chair I would have done something about it, too. The more the doctor laughed, the madder I got, and the madder I got, the more memories began to come back to me.

Within hours everything had come back. No, not everything. To this day I can't tell you exactly what happened on that jungle trail. Why on this particular day I was dressed in Vietcong black pajamas is still a mystery to me. Where I was going and what my mission was are still drifting around in that fog. But, finally, I did know who I was, and where I was.

I knew, too, that it was my wife, Lala, who had been driving a hundred and fifty miles every weekend to sit and talk to a wooden Indian. And to tell you the truth, I wasn't real happy about any of the things I was remembering.

At first I was glad to be alive. I was glad to be home and to have Lala with me. Whenever I did begin to feel unhappy, I would tell myself to look around the ward. I'd try to feel blessed. At least I got all of my pieces still attached, I told myself. The kid next to me left a leg in 'Nam. The soldier next to him left two, and the GI across the aisle had two burned stumps where his hands used to be. I guess I am one blessed man, I would think for a while.

Soon, though, I would begin to have negative thoughts. The people back in El Campo would say I had been blessed. That lucky "Mezikin" boy, they'd probably say.

If I had to go home to recuperate, I imagined the comments of the biased residents of my town: "Look at that boy just sitting on that porch in that chair. That boy ain't got a care in the world. Only problem he got is if the mail comes late. We're working for that boy's welfare check. Bet he shot himself in the foot just so he could get that check. Heck, they're all the same, even too lazy to steal. Except from the gov'ment."

My thoughts were wild in many ways. If I could just figure out what happened, I would think, if I knew what happened, I know I could fix it. Man, I can't live like this. They shoulda just left me there, they shoulda just let me die. This is worse than dying. If my legs were gone, man, that's one thing, I mean, all right, they're gone, it's over, you live in the chair and you make the best of it. You go on. But they're not gone.

Man, those doctors are crazy. I'm not stupid, they said the spinal cord's not broken, just "traumatized." I know they can fix me, they just won't. I heard them talking about me. I know they're getting ready to discharge me on a total disability. I heard them saying there's nothing they can do for me. I just don't believe it.

I've spent eleven years in the army. This is my life. I've got respect here, I've got pride, and I'm good at what I do. What in God's name do they expect me to do? Quit a loser?

"Sergeant, you've got some visitors, let's get you into that chair."

The chair, the damned chair. For the rest of my life someone is gonna have to help me into the chair.

Rogelio, my brother, took the chair from the orderly and pushed me to the dayroom. He or my cousin Leo and his wife, Margaret, drove Lala up to San Antonio from El Campo every weekend. The dayroom where we sat and talked looked out over the parade ground at Fort Sam Houston. Actually, I sat and they talked, and talked, and talked. They talked about home and the family. Some relative had been ill. We had another new nephew. Someone had gotten married. Through it all, I wanted to scream. Down below, out the window, I could see the soldiers marching, and running, and walking, and standing. I just wanted to scream. "Help me, God, don't leave me like this, please, God, help me."

My memories of those days are still a little foggy. I kept going in and out of the fog, absorbed by my own problems. Only later did I realize that seeing me like that had to be a living hell for Lala. First the telegram telling her that I had been injured, how badly she didn't know. Then the wait until I was back in Texas. She never talked about it, but she must have gone through a nightmare of her own before I was returned and she learned that I was in one piece, one broken piece, but alive.

Our marriage, like our courtship, was more traditional than the marriages of today. In the 1990s, everybody's liberated, marriages are equal partnerships, and everybody's got a vote.

But that's not the way we were raised. Our arrangements were very formal, and our roles were fairly well defined. Lala was the wife; she took care of the house, and she would take care of the children when they were born. I was the husband; I earned the living and made the family decisions. Sounds simple, but it's a lot more complicated than that.

At the time that I was injured, we had no children, but Lala's life was all tied up in the woman's work of our big, extended Latin family. The men talked to the men and the women talked to the women. With me gone all the time it was not much of a life for her. But that's the way it was. For her to complain about it would have been unthinkable. I could have been the town drunk and she would have kept her grief to herself.

The women did have their ways of getting through to the men, but that open discussion that is taken for granted today just didn't exist in our culture then. At least for the women it didn't.

It was a long time before I began to wonder how Lala felt those first few weeks when I was really out in left field. I didn't even know who she was. Heck, I didn't even know who I was yet. When I began coming out of it, I'm sure I made life even worse for her. For a while, I didn't want to talk. I didn't want to listen. All I cared about were those two dead stumps hanging off the end of that chair. Everything else went in one ear and out the other. I really loved Lala for making that trip up to see me so many times, but I couldn't show it. I was so wrapped up in my problems I just couldn't realize anybody else existed. I was too busy holding my own personal "pity party."

When I finally did want to talk, all I wanted to talk about was what my life had become. My life was the bed and the chair. The days were broken up with little diversions like Lala's visits and therapy. The staff called it therapy. Most of it was made up of teaching me how to live in the bed and the chair. Suddenly, I realized they really believed the bed and the chair would be my way of life. They were convinced, but I wasn't.

Counting ceiling tiles was a big part of my day. I could see 327 of those little buggers from my bed. Every day, it was the same number.

One thing kept me going. I had always been religious. My belief had begun when I was a little kid. Just looking around in the big church taught me something about faith. I knew even then that there was something bigger than I was, bigger even than the adults I knew. I knew then, too, that God listens, even when nobody else listens or cares. From the time I was a child and I lost my parents I have always believed that.

Hispanic life was strongly tied to the Church when I was growing up. It still is today, and wherever in the world I was, I maintained my ties to the Church. I believe in Jesus Christ. I am a Christian.

While I was in the hospital, I spent a great deal of time in the little chapel, which was usually empty. When the doctors didn't listen, and the therapists didn't listen, and when Lala just couldn't listen anymore, I had someone to talk to. My faith grew stronger each day. Somehow I just knew that it was not my destiny to sit in a chair the rest of my life.

I began to believe that my life had been spared for some purpose. I remembered the first time I had awakened after getting blown up by the mine. I was staring into the eyes of a priest. I let out a scream that disturbed the entire ward. The priest was looking at me with a solemn expression on his face, and I thought he was giving me the last rites. He probably was until I started yelling. I demonstrated loudly that I was not ready to quit this life yet.

Sitting alone in the hospital chapel, I examined my beliefs. I came to believe that I was living proof that we have a loving Father. I began to look forward and to try to envision my future once more.

A New Enemy

The doctors had made up their minds. The army had no use for me. Like a misfired round from a 105-mm howitzer, I was useless to them. But they did have to dispose of me carefully. Sounds cold. It is cold, and it needs to be that way. When the business is death and destruction and their aftermath, the attitude toward the individual soldier must be cold.

My inability to soldier properly could cost other men their lives.

If a soldier is out in the field and there are casualties, he has to make decisions. If he doesn't think that he can save one man, he is trained to hit him with some morphine, if he can spare it, so the injured man will die without so much pain. Then he will go work on the guys he may be able to save. The same rules applied here. When the doctors first looked at my X rays they made decisions. The fact that I didn't like them didn't mean a whole lot to them.

The way I looked at it I had two goals that I had to reach. The first was to stall, buy some time so that they wouldn't discharge me immediately. I needed time. Things were moving too fast. My life was out of my control, and I was out of the loop.

The second goal was to walk again. To achieve that, I needed the time.

The doctors and nurses did care about me and their other patients, but, by necessity, they thought of us more as pieces of military equipment than as men. As a piece of machinery, I had to be removed from the rolls as a sergeant in the 82nd Airborne. A good inventory of equipment is necessary in the military. As a man, I would be discharged with a full disability pension and put into the Veterans Administration system of care. I had to slow down that process until I could convince somebody, anybody, in that hospital that I could recover and go back into the inventory again.

I tried begging. They were human, and it worked for a little while. But the decision had been made before I even got back to the real world. It almost had been chiseled in stone before I became able to argue my case. Every week, the staff would meet and discuss the status of the patients, and it was getting pretty hard for anybody to justify the reason that my papers hadn't been processed for discharge yet.

So, I prayed a lot. I also started to do the only thing that had ever gotten me anywhere in my whole life. I put my head down and I went to work.

During the night I used my arms and I rolled myself out of bed. The floor seemed as far away as the red clay at Fort Bragg had seemed when I had jumped from the tower. I hit with a crunch.

The guys in the ward heard me fall and started yelling for the nurses. "Shut up, you guys," I groaned. "This is my therapy, leave me alone."

The first night, I didn't even make the wall before Mrs. Smith, a black nurse, came in and chewed me out as only an army nurse can do. She got the orderlies to get me back into bed. From that moment on I just marked time during the days and worked on building up my arms and shoulders so I could work on my therapy program at night.

The next night I made it to the wall and dragged myself around so that I was sitting against the wall. That's where the nurses found me. I got my butt chewed out again and was thrown back into my prison cell, the bed.

Before my next try, I had the guy next to me move his nightstand over so both stands were between our beds. That night I crawled all the way to the wall and managed to use my arms on the two nightstands to finally pull myself erect against it. My two hands were flat on top of the nightstands and I was just sort of hanging there. I tried to put weight on my legs and a burning pain shot through my back that felt like I'd been stabbed with a red-hot knife. I collapsed against the wall and slid to the floor. That's where the nurses found me that time.

Night after night, I bailed out of bed, crawled for the wall at the head of my bed, and pulled myself up. I pushed the nightstands ahead with my arms, pressed my feet against the cold tile floor, and dragged my dead body along until my arms were under me again. Then I'd start all over again. Finally, I was moving about two tiles at a time.

Mrs. Smith and Mrs. Rainey, another nurse on the ward, stayed on me for a while, but eventually they came to ignore me. They could either ignore me or tie me up. They were too full of humanity to tie me up, so they ignored me. They'd ask me if I needed help; if I said no, they'd just shake their heads, walk on, and leave me alone.

I had learned that if I got knocked down, I had to get up and keep fighting until I knocked my opponent down and he didn't get up. Every night, I got knocked down. Every night I got back up again.

For the guys in my ward, my nightly performance became the best show in town. In fact, it was about the only show in the ward at night. As soon as I rolled toward the floor, I heard them start placing their bets.

"Hey, look at that Mexican. I'll bet you a beer he falls."

"I'll bet you a drink he falls."

At first, not much money or beer changed hands after the nightly betting. I did fall at first. I fell down so many times that nobody was willing to bet that I would stay upright. Finally, I stood braced against the wall with my hands lifted six inches above those two nightstands. After that the betting got pretty even again that I would someday walk out of there.

The pain was like nothing I could have ever dreamed about. Every night it would suck the sweat and tears from my body and my soul. Every day I would go back to that little chapel and sit alone and restore my soul. I went through all the stages of blaming God, accusing, doubting, and arguing, but he never deserted me. He'd never let me leave that chapel until I was ready to try again. After chapel, I went to physical therapy to try to restore the rest of my body for my nightly battle.

Finally, I could stand. In unbearable pain, I could lock my dead limbs under me and they would hold my weight. The next step was moving. Night after night I would work my toes until I could move them. Then I worked on my ankles. Finally, I could angle the toes in one direction, then slide the heels along behind them and slowly shuffle along the wall. I did this myself, at night, alone except for the hoots and cheers of the guys betting on my success or my failure.

I feared the psychological pain I suffered during the day more than I dreaded my nightly therapy. I feared the trip in the chair to a doctor's office where he would tell me my papers had been processed and that I was history as far as the army was concerned. Every time they came to get me for therapy I was wound up like a spring.

"Where am I going, am I going to therapy? Do I have a visitor?" I'd whine.

"Yeah, Roy, I'm taking you to therapy again, just relax, you're going to therapy."

In therapy I'd sit with the guys with no legs, or the true paraplegics, and learn how to live in the chair. I was not a good student. I wouldn't give in to the chair. At night I was beginning to win my battle, and I wasn't going to let the therapists convince me that it was a lost cause.

When Lala came to visit me on weekends, I sometimes treated her coldly. When I was wheeled into the dayroom and I saw her waiting, I felt as if the brightest light in my life had just been turned on, but by the time I reached her side, I became sullen and silent. Every time, after she had left I had an urge as strong as my urge to walk again. I wanted to kick myself for being so cold to her. Time and again, I froze up during her visits because I hated to have her see me in that chair. I didn't want her to begin to believe that I would be in it for the rest of our lives.

The doctors had informed Lala of their prognosis that I would never be able to walk, and I was afraid she would believe them. I didn't feel too evenly matched with them—a shell of a man strapped in a chair against doctors in starched white coats with the authority of X rays and five-dollar words.

Because of my fear and pain, I put my sweetheart, the only woman I had ever wanted to have as my wife, through plenty of anguish, and at a time when she should have been happy, for she was expecting our first child.

I was living in constant fear of being presented with my discharge papers. If that happened, I feared the future. I could not envision my life without the pride that I had developed during eleven years in the army. Without the army, I felt that I had no future. The army was my home, and my job, and my future. A wheelchair out on the porch in El Campo and a few dollars a month wasn't a good trade.

I compared my situation to that of a concert pianist whose hands had been amputated. Someone might say to him, "Here's a few dollars every month. You can listen to that music all you want. You just can't play it anymore. No, we don't want to hear about your problems, to us you're just a number, so move on so we can get to the next number."

I was bitter. I was a soldier, I knew the rules, I understood the reasons for them, but I was bitter and mean to anybody who would listen to me. Even to Lala.

One day I had that confrontation I had been dreading. Instead of coming to take me to therapy in the morning the staff just left me in the bed. Pretty soon I could see a big man with a clipboard coming toward me. He was a full-bird colonel and a staff officer, the head of orthopedics.

"Well, Sergeant," he said, "they tell me that you have been making some progress on your own."

"Yes, sir," was all that I could say.

"You know, son, no matter what you do, I don't believe that you will ever walk again. We're processing your discharge papers. I think it's time for you to get serious about your therapy and rehabilitation and get on with the rest of your life. You'll learn that you can live a long and productive life in the chair. Don't you agree, Sergeant?"

"No sir, no sir," I stammered. "I can walk, I'm starting to walk already." I threw the covers off my legs and rolled them off the bed. I wouldn't let him speak until I could show him. I stood against the bed and shuffled along the floor, with that horrible fire in my spine, for three steps, keeping one hand on the bed for balance.

The ward was strangely quiet but for the shuffling of my feet on the floor. My ward mates could not have been more focused had they been standing at attention in the presence of an officer, something that many of them would never be able to do again. My nurses, Mrs. Smith and Mrs. Rainey, stood alongside me for support.

"That's real good, son. We just don't believe that you'll ever regain enough use to be qualified for active duty again. We have no choice but to discharge you."

Man, at that point I had nothing to lose. "No, Colonel, you can't do that. I know General Westmoreland personally; I used to be his driver. I'm going to call him and tell him to get me out of here. I'm going to tell him to get me someplace with doctors that want to help me, not kick me out." The guys in the ward were piping up, too. What did they have to lose either?

"Give the guy a break."

"Come on, Colonel, listen to him."

"Don't kick him out yet. I've got two beers bet on his walk tonight."

"Yeah, Colonel, fix him up so he can go back and get zapped the next time." There was no shutting those guys up. They were fighters, too, and I had given them something to fight for.

The colonel snapped his file shut and marched out of there. He never said another word to me and I never saw another senior officer again. But they didn't discharge me. At some point discharge procedures were dropped. I never knew when, and I never knew why, but I suspected that my daily talks in the chapel had been the reason.

In May 1966, when I had been at Beach Pavilion for five months, I began to be given therapy to walk again. As I started to walk again I started to become a whole person once more. I couldn't wait for Lala to get back each time so that she could see the progress I was making each day. She was seeing the change in me, too, and our visits became more and more normal.

As I healed, I quit feeling so sorry for myself and really started looking around the ward. I realized that I had been selfish and self-centered. A lot of the guys who had been cheering me on would have felt lucky to be able to live in a wheelchair.

One guy had two burned stumps where his hands used to be. He was having to learn to live that way for the rest of his life. I told myself that I would remember to be grateful every time I picked up a phone, or a pencil. Or when I held somebody's hand, or brushed my teeth, or wiped my butt.

My buddies didn't want pity; all they needed was a little understanding. I vowed that I would try to make other people aware of how such men feel. I would say, "When you see that guy on the street don't pity him. He doesn't want that. Don't help him either. He's a man and just as proud of what he can do as you are. Just treat him like a man and try to understand. Try and understand that he got that way fighting for you and your way of life.

"Maybe it was ten thousand miles away, and maybe it was a stupid senseless war, but he was there. He didn't choose the time and place and the situation. When he was called, he served. And he sacrificed, without question, for you. If you've got a problem, blame the politicians who commanded him to go there. Better yet, blame yourself for electing those guys in the first place."

I looked around me and felt more and more blessed that I could walk. It hurt like hell, but I could walk.

Within a couple of months I was moving well enough to be declared fit for limited duty. I was in constant pain, but I wouldn't dare mention it or I figured they'd still want to discharge me.

Before the fourth of July, six months after I had been flown in, I walked out holding Lala's hand for support. The men in the ward cheered, but the orthopedist, who was there to see me off, complained, in reference to the betting that had gone on while I was trying to walk, "Sergeant, you've left me with a whole ward of alcoholics."

Lala and I went to El Campo to pack before going on to Fort Bragg, where I would be assigned to a desk job, the only one they figured I was fit enough for. The pain was still so bad that I was living in a Darvon fog. It was the only way that I could stand it.

I had crammed twelve to eighteen months of healing and therapy into six short months. I did it out of fear, and I was now paying the price.

12 / Everett Alvarez, Jr., with Anthony S. Pitch

From *Chained Eagle*

Anguish on the Home Front

Tipped off in advance by the networks, the family bunched expectantly around the TV in Chole and Lalo's home on Bohannon Drive, Santa Clara, to watch the film of the Hanoi parade. They were unprepared for the fury of the crowds and the physical threat to the Americans. They could barely distinguish Everett in the melee of flailing arms and kicking legs. Unwilling to watch him beaten yet unable to avert their eyes, the family watched transfixed.

It was the first live-action film they had seen of him in almost a year and a half, when NBC had shown clips from a propaganda movie prepared by North Vietnamese and Japanese photographers. Then they had seen Everett prodded along a road by an armed Vietnamese until he was later "interrogated" by a military officer. They could not have known that this was staged by the Vietnamese, not that Everett had lost his temper during the charade and tried to distance himself from the armed man in a pith helmet. Nevertheless, the family was cheered by Everett's photographic image because it showed him alert and uninjured.

Now, however, as they watched the throngs of crazed Vietnamese chanting and bashing the straggling line of captive pilots, their spirits plummeted. An ocean apart, they could only pray for his safety. Their delight in seeing him living and breathing was so brief that it left no feeling of joy. When the black and white clip was through, they were again left on the outside of their aviator's tomb of silence. Only this time their dread was heightened because of what they had just witnessed.

Two full years of waiting and hoping had gradually changed all of them. It was as if they had been seasoned by the years. They had steeped themselves in the history of that distant land, scouring the public libraries and seizing on any recommended book or magazine article. There was not much in print but it was enough to advance them far beyond their initial concept of Indochina as just another geographical blip somewhere in the East. Neither of Everett's parents was handicapped by their lack of formal education. The material had such compelling relevance. They turned the pages of Vietnamese history not so much out of curiosity as from a compulsion to learn. It taught them about the ancient land of their son's captivity and its strange natives who could so easily snuff out his young life. In time, their new knowledge gave them the confidence to articulate uncommon views. But they weren't ready yet to express them outside the home. Forever conscious of the boundaries between private license and public constraints, they dared not expose the family free-for-alls to the watchful and critical eye of the public.

Chole had always been the most curious about the broad sweep of historical events. Her romance with history began in childhood when she played among the ruins of a Christian mission at Lompoc, California. The faded glory of her surroundings made her think about her roots and her ancestors. Where did they come from? Why were some in her family light-complected and blue-eyed while others resembled burnished, copper-colored Aztecs? The more Chole researched the more she wanted to get out and see the legacy of Mexico in California. She took the initiative when Everett was still in high school and by the time of his capture had visited all but one of the twenty-one Christian missions.

Chole brought the same keen inquiry to her studies of Vietnamese history. Though eager to learn, she was a slow, plodding reader who dimmed her bedside lamp with a newspaper so her husband could sleep undisturbed while she held her book open late into the night. As she read about the millennium of subjugation by the Chinese, followed by a century of French colonial rule, she began to doubt the wisdom of the American presence in Vietnam. No people of another culture had ever triumphed permanently over the Vietnamese. How, then, did Americans believe they could influence or squelch what other empires, with closer links and historical ties had failed to do? The politicians said they were containing communism. They spoke of a domino theory: if South Vietnam fell then neighboring countries would follow suit. Chole began to ask herself why, if the battle was against communism, the fight was not taken to the heart of the conspiracy, to Russia itself. Why not hit the snake on the head? In the privacy of her own home, she even began to wonder how she would react if an enemy parachuted down in her backyard. She developed the idea that God had put the Vietnamese over there, in their own continent, in their own area, to live the way that was best for them. He had likewise given Americans their portion of the world. There was even something comparable in her mind between the poorly armed Mexicans who fought for their sovereignty against a much better equipped army, and the out-gunned Vietnamese who appeared night after night on her television screen. Force would never change them, so let them believe in whatever they wanted. And if they killed each other, well, so be it. That was their country. In the privacy of her own home, she began to wonder aloud whether America should not rather stay on its side of the world and manage its own affairs. It was a view she did not hold when her son was shot down and captured. But that had been two long years ago.

Lalo was a much more earthy observer. Not for him this muddling, slow process of arriving at a conclusion. He had always held that there were only two causes for all wars: economics and religion. Wasn't this the case in Vietnam? Hadn't Ike sent Cardinal Spellman over on some kind of mission? And hadn't the cardinal returned recommending Americans get involved there, otherwise all those Catholics were going to be overrun by communists? Clearly, thought Lalo, the cardinal really cared only about saving his religion. And economics? Why, the Vietnamese had manganese, didn't they? And America would go down the tubes if it didn't have the raw materials needed to keep its factories going. What angered him was why they had to go to war for these necessary resources. Why couldn't they apply a little bit of good old American ingenuity and build up a healthy trade relationship?

And yet Lalo felt it was the duty of citizens to support the government and respect the president's decisions. What a man said in the confines of his own home was his own business, but he'd better watch his tongue in public, particularly if, like himself, he worked in a defense-related industry, with a son serving in the military and the country at war.

So he kept his peace, whenever possible. It wasn't easy to avoid the mounting provocations as Everett's captivity stretched into a third year. Once, an ex-marine and World War II veteran Lalo worked with mouthed-off about how wrong he felt the war was, with all the bombing and killing. Lalo took exception and the two narrowly avoided getting into a fist-fight, the former marine eventually growling that he had fought for his country once before and would gladly go again if called, then storming off, not wanting to escalate this fruitless exchange of insults. The war was becoming a divisive issue at home for just about everyone. And Lalo found it increasingly difficult to stand aside from the ugly squabbling.

Two years back, he had assigned Delia the job of family spokesperson. A graduate in social work from San Jose State University, she articulated with ease what her parents struggled to express. In time, Delia inevitably assumed the mantle of leadership, tugging her reluctant family into a more confident role, unafraid to speak out and take issue with officialdom. Her abundant self-assurance and vigor were the very lifesaving qualities needed to pull the dejected family through its travail. With her dynamism they might somehow salvage Everett from the war without end.

But the transformation was slow even for her. She, too, had clung to the view that the military and the government must know best because they were in charge and had access to all the facts. In the beginning she was a staunch supporter of the war, so much so that when Everett was captured she had cursed her gender for disqualifying her from a combat role. But six months after his capture the bombing had begun, with the U.S. aerial armada blitzing Vietnamese targets. Delia knew then that it would be a long time before her brother came home. This was a hot war and Everett was trapped behind enemy lines.

Defense Department officials apologized for not being able to divulge the nature of ongoing secret negotiations and offered reassurances that they were doing their best. But even if this were true it did not assuage the family's frustrations and Delia, like the others, felt it increasingly hard to hold fast and keep faith with the bureaucrats.

Delia had long since canceled plans to enroll in the Peace Corps for community development work among Chile's poor. She had been scheduled to go at the end of 1964, but by then it was clear that Everett would not be coming home as soon as they expected. Now she worked full-time for the Santa Clara welfare department among the same underprivileged Spanish-speaking families she would have served in Chile. In the community's eyes she was the good Samaritan, an educated young woman who called on the elderly, brought hope to the unemployed and comfort to those in the throes of emotional breakdowns. While she checked their eligibility for financial assistance, applicants took note of how she always insisted upon every child remaining in school. As one of the country's handful of Hispanic female college graduates, Delia had become even more deeply attached to the community through volunteer calls on the schools. Her message never varied: they *must* continue their studies because education was the proven key to better jobs and advancement.

Familiar as she was with so many of these families, it became apparent how the war in Vietnam was spawning even more injustices against her ethnic group. A disproportionate number of its young men were being sent to fight in Vietnam. They all knew it was only because they lacked the educational opportunities to enroll in college, and earn an automatic deferment like countless young men across the country from more fortunate backgrounds.

Frustration about the course of the war grew more intense, and the bickering at home turned nastier. Delia felt the family should become more outspoken and take a stand publicly against the war. Her father would not hear of it, even though he agreed that the war had dragged on for long enough and there seemed to be no end in sight, nor hope of Everett's early repatriation. What they had all accepted as gospel in the early days of the war was now dismissed with varying degrees of anger and cynicism as false and misleading. They had been told they were at war to save democracy in South Vietnam. But television brought them images of South Vietnamese holy men burning themselves alive to protest government injustices. They had watched with dismay as one government coup followed another in Saigon's swirl of political intrigue, and how the corruption had spread to the South Vietnamese armed forces and to the civilian population. Why should America help prop up a regime that showed no signs of wanting to help itself? Delia and her parents began to ask themselves how the communists of the North could really be worse than their enemies in the South. At least the despots in the North were disciplined and dedicated. The family's doubts mounted as every day seemed to bring greater military escalation with nothing to show for it. The rain of bombs did not staunch the flow of men and material from North to South Vietnam. The enemy showed no sign of giving up nor any readiness to negotiate, even under the enormous pressure of more than 300,000 U.S. military personnel who had moved into Vietnam within two years of Everett's shootdown.

Vietnam consumed their lives. It was in the morning papers and on the portable transistors. In the evenings they saw it on television. And when the family sat down to relax the talk invariably turned to the war.

The tension was palpable and Madeleine, now in her teens, consciously kept out of the way. Much earlier, she had tried to discuss the routine concerns of a normal teenager with her mother but her father had snapped, "Be a good girl and don't make waves or cause any trouble. Your mother's going through enough tension." So Madeleine turned inward and grew up a quieter adolescent than she might have been, keeping her questions to herself and crying quietly in her room. She had trouble sleeping. There was no one at school to whom she could turn. Even her two best friends had no inkling of what was going on in Southeast Asia and how this had touched her so personally. She talked to them about boys and clothes and movies but never about Vietnam and Everett. Once she had tried but they had looked at her curiously, with blank faces. Their brothers were not involved, so they had no way of feeling her anguish. Her peers knew she was different because Madeleine's name was in the news so often, but they just had no way of relating to her loneliness. The other students didn't shun her but they did set her apart, in a way, because they were overprotective and condescending, giving her the feeling that they knew something was terribly wrong and that they were going to be especially nice to her. How she wished things could be normal like they used to be.

Desolation

. . . Even more popular were the entertainers among us, the raconteurs, the born storytellers who could recite the screenplays of movies they had seen. Such performances called for a delight in verbal dramatization, an inventive and imaginative mind, a flair for the telling line, an eye for vivid color and a gift for embellishment. Sometimes the "soundtrack" of these movies stretched over several days of telling, heightening the suspense and exerting a powerful hold over the audience.

I spun a yarn I had developed over the previous six years to pass the time. Set in the years encompassing the Civil War, it was the saga of an Hispanic boy, whose epic struggles seemed to reflect my own constant challenges, though the untitled story was in no way autobiographical. My hero was orphaned as a child in Texas when bandits slew his parents. He came to be raised by an Indian until, as a teenager, he was smart enough to fend for himself. He joined a wagon train to Missouri, worked as a stable hand, then journeyed to the East Coast where a Navy captain became his surrogate father. Together they sailed the seven seas while the old salt taught the boy to read and write, then got him an appointment to West Point. Both men fought with the Union troops though the old sailor fell in combat. Disgusted by the slaughter, the young man stashed his inheritance into saddle bags and rode back to the wild Southwest, where other men were quick to discriminate against his ethnic group, calling him Pancho and telling him he could not drink in their bars. Goaded and insulted, he killed many of his taunters in gunfights. Only when he moved down to Mexico did he find peace of mind through a cultural identity. He married the daughter of a large landowner but his bride died during a cholera epidemic. Devastated again, the young man rode north, signed up as a military scout, then met a beautiful woman who, like him, had experienced life's ups and downs by roaming far and wide. For the final chapter I envisaged the couple riding off to California to fulfill their dreams in the booming new frontierland. It was little more than the outline for a novel but it seemed to hold the attention of all who listened in. . . .

13 / Ignacio M. García

Unfinished Letter to Terry

Román looked out of the helicopter into the vast openness and the greenery that lay before him, several hundred feet down on the moving Earth. The helicopter was crowded, and he sat with legs hanging out. There was enough shoulder room to read a book or write a letter; Román had chosen the latter. His letter was almost finished, which was good, because he had struggled to write it to Terry. He had promised Huong he would do it, and he wanted to keep that promise before he went back to see her, to touch her, to caress her hair and beautiful face. In the letter, he had taken a long time to get to the point, first detailing the mission and some of his personal feelings before getting to Huong. Now that he had, he had not known how to conclude it.

He felt the gush of wind that flapped the loose sheets of paper in his small notebook. It was a beautiful day, not too hot and not too humid. It was like a Saturday morning back home, maybe around noon, after returning from a baseball or football game where he had given it his best; like going home to mom and her spicy food and delicious desserts. Home, the sanctuary, where he would spend the rest of the day seeing Wide World of Sports, and then getting ready for the church dance that night. Except now there would be no spicy food, no television, and no dance. Still, there would be Huong, and that was better than anything back home. Sorry mom, but that was the truth. He looked at the words on the first of the four pages of letter.

Dear Terry, If it looks like a chicken wrote this letter, it is because I am writing while riding on a trembling helicopter that is carrying too many people. (It was not a great beginning, but it was original) *We're returning from a secret mission,* (The censors? Who cares). *Although it looks more like we're running away from one. We do not look like we've had too much success, judging from the faces of the soldiers here. We took a terrific pounding and those here and in the other helicopters are lucky to have had a reprieve from the body bag. This was a mission designed to cripple the enemy before the*

Nixon withdrawals encouraged him to more audacious moves, but I think that, again, the American command has underestimated the enemy. At best, this mission may have served to extend the war only a few more days, while causing more grief to American and Vietnamese parents, wives, and children. While we did inflict heavy damage on the enemy, the main objective was not really accomplished.

If war was like a soccer game, where only the goals (the body count) were important, then the United States could leave Vietnam today and claim victory. We have killed so many of their men that it would take the North Vietnamese a century to catch up. Unfortunately for us, wars are not won by how many people you kill, but rather by how much you are willing to sacrifice and persist. And in persistence and sacrificial fervor, the North Vietnamese are centuries ahead. They've waged a continual war for over thirty years against the French and now us, and are probably ready to wage it against anyone else foolish enough to follow us.

This is a country with people that you can only wonder about and be amazed by. All the mystique that American movies show about the orient does not compare to the real mystique of the people, the scenery, the customs, and the atmosphere. Vietnamese are people of permanence, of heritage, and history. They have a link to the past that many Americans only dream about. Even our Mexican heritage does not have the same type of continuity about it. The historical essence of their lives is the thing that urges them on to live and wait for a better future, when everything around them is without hope. The difference in this war has been that Ho Chi Minh and his Communists have been able to transform that stoicness, that sense of destiny, into a will to win. While the South Vietnamese consider it obligatory to accept what destiny brings, the North Vietnamese are pushed on with the belief that destiny has promised a victory, and who are they to deny that destiny. Their lives if it's to precipitate the destined victory, are very little sacrifice. I do not believe in pre-destination, but it is hard not to consider it a possiblity when you are in this land. It seems that no matter how much you struggle, the outcome has been arbitrarily decided. You will fail in your fight to change it. As an American (a Chicano) I cannot altogether comprehend this and as a Mormon I shouldn't believe in it, but at least for now I do not dispute it.

In the mission we lost some good men. Some of them I knew only for a few days, but I learned to appreciate and respect them. There is a thing about war, and that is that emotions are felt at a more intense level, and expressed with a greater passion (I think I've told you this before), that knowing someone for a few days here is more revealing than knowing someone for a few months back in the states. One young man I met here and learned to like immediately was Ray Richardson, a kicker from Missouri, who had been in the country only five months, and already proven to be a good medic. He was a workhorse from the moment the mission began, outworking all of us without a complaint, and *without a semblance of fear. He was one of those rare individuals who knows what his job is, does it, and doesn't waste anybody's time philosophizing about it. He came on this mission to save lives and he did it without caring whether the injured were American, Vietnamese, or Cambodian. He hurt an ankle while assisting two Vietnamese soldiers and that, in the end, cost him his life. In the rush to get out from where we were surrounded, those who were slow got killed and he, unfortunately, was one of those left behind. He and nearly half our wounded did not make it out. It was such an ugly feeling knowing we were leaving them behind to be used as exhibits of "yankee imperialism." The only thing that we can be thankful for is that they will not have to face imprisonment or torture; all died fighting or from the movement to evacuate them.*

Two other medics, Mark Schiltzer and David Capistrano were injured, but they both survived. Amazingly, Cesar got out without a scratch. I'm grateful for that, because I do not think I could have lived through his death. He and I have become the best of friends and we have become so close that several times we both risked our necks to save each other. There are probably no good reasons why we're so close to each other, but we are.

As for myself, I received shrapnel wounds and will be sore for several weeks, but other than some small ugly scars there will be no physical consequences. Psychological scars will be another thing. In these few days of the mission I have seen enough killing to last a lifetime and then some. I have seen human bodies torn apart by bullets, shrapnel, bombs and bayonets, machine guns, and powerful rockets. The mangling of bodies has left little to the imagination. Split heads, decapitated bodies, gaping stomach holes, amputated limbs, and clean, but deadly, bullet holes. The first few hours I did not believe I would stand it and I vomited several times, but in the end I was lifting up shattered bodies and dumping them into body bags without too much emotion. I now shudder to think that I becamse so insensitive, so cold, so detached from pain, yet, it was that state of mind that made me able to function under those adverse conditions, so I could provide the kind of help that was needed to save lives. Still, there were some decisions—like choosing who should die and who should live—that will always haunt me. My emotions, my nerves, my whole psychological framework are in shambles. I could cry now for all the things I saw, but the tears will not come. My mind refuses to believe what it can remember, and so my feelings are in some sort of suspended animation.

Among the nearly 105 men that died (135 more were injured) there was one soldier whose death I will surely never forget. He was a young Vietnamese intelligence officer named Nguyen Cao, who was the co-commander of the mission. I only talked to him a couple of times, the last the night before he was killed, but I was impressed with him. He was the kind of patriot any country would be proud to have. He was one of the noble ones that still wanted to give his government a chance to mend its ways, win the war, and go on with the job of making this Vietnamese democracy work. His death underscores the waste of war, especially this kind of war, where there is nothing to win, nothing to tell our grandchildren about. Noble causes cannot be led with indecision, without purpose, nor can they be fought with unwilling draftees. If we lose this war, it is because the other side had the cause, notwithstanding the unnobleness of the Communist crusade.

This young Vietnamese, so full of life, so much in command of himself, was in love with a beautiful woman. I've told you about her on numerous occasions. Huong is her name. Unfortunately for the young captain she was not in love with him. (Román had not known how to introduce himself into the letter again without being too abrupt. Even without seeing her, Román felt embarrassed and guilty) She was in love with somebody else; that somebody is me. Neither one of us planned it this way, it just happened, and before we knew it, we were deeply in love with each other. She had made up her mind that she would not get involved with an American, and I never imagined myself courting anyone other than you. But things happened. Now as I wait to return to my compound I do not know what lies ahead for me or Huong, I am sure many trials and obstacles to our love, but I do know that I love her and that I want her to be my wife. It is not a physical fascination because I am away from home. In fact, our expressions of love have been kisses and holding hands. I have looked at the situation enough to know that I love her and coming home will not be the same if she does not come back with me, and therein lies a problem. We have yet to adequately discuss her leaving her country. There are also other things to be resolved.

It must be strange to you that I'm telling you all of this. It is not the kind of thing you tell a penpal of the opposite sex that has been as faithful as you have been. Your letters have been a greater help than even you have imagined, because despite my love for Huong, things have been difficult here, and sometimes your letters are the only hope that things are different somewhere else, and that my tour will end sometime and I will go back home to some semblance of sanity. The letters were particularly crucial during my first weeks in this country, when time seemed to move at a snail's pace and everything seemed so strange and foreign. I grew to love you in those times, and I can still say that I have a special love for you. I hope you understand what I am saying because . . .

That was where Román had stopped writing. He was not sure what he wanted to say, because he did not know how Terry would react to the letter. Always, Terry had been a listener, one who allowed him to pour out his soul, and in her letters she had been the careful meticulous informer of what was happening in the outside world. She had been reserved in expressing her personal feelings, and unlike him, she had refrained from philosophizing. Román did not know her as profoundly as she knew him. But what he did know about her he liked.

Román looked out toward the sunny sky and wondered how many more times, in the next several months, he would have to be coming from combat? How many more times would he have to see fighting and people dying before it was his time to go back home?

He felt a large hand fall on his shoulder. It was rough and warm; he did not have to look back to know it was Cesar's. "Can you believe we're alive, bato?" said Cesar in the best of his streettalk tone. "But I guess they can't kill a couple of cholos like us, eh, bato?"

"Aquí estamos, no?" said Román in kind. "But we're lucky, luckier than we can imagine. I remember you were the one who was complaining that we were going to die, and you're the one who came out of this without a scratch. I'm the God-fearing man and I got all scrapped and wounded." At that moment Román remembered the wounds on his shoulders and legs and he felt them sting. The sweat that rolled into the untended wounds burned like salt water.

"Hey, I said more prayers than you can imagine," said Cesar. "I haven't been so religious since I went to mass for five weeks in a row as a kid. I was madly in love with my catechism teacher."

"Back in there, when I was scared, sure that either I was going to get killed or I was going to kill someone because I did not know what I was doing, I thought a lot about myself and the things I learned when I was young."

"You mean the religious stuff?" Cesar leaned closer to Román.

"Yes. I think that for the last several months I've felt detached from what I grew up with. It seems that when they took me away from my church, they also took away the religion from me."

"I don't believe that. You're one of the most religious people I've ever met. And you do it without being preachy or without making people uncomfortable."

"I've made you uncomfortable. More than once you told me not to preach." Román turned toward Cesar for an answer.

"I'm a special case. I do so many things wrong that everything you say

---

bato – dude

cholos – tough guys

Aquí estamos, no – We're still here, right?

fits me. Also, remember, I was brought up in a real Catholic home, and I know that I'm not doing what I'm supposed to. My mother wouldn't believe you if you told her what I do here."

"She thinks you're a saint?"

"You know, *las jefitas,* they can't believe their sons do anything wrong."

"She's probably not the only one. There're many wounded soldiers out there," Román pointed at the other helicopters, "who probably feel the same way. You worked hard and saved a lot of lives."

"You didn't do so bad yourself. You took command of the situation. You kept control. You don't know how good it felt to have someone in command. It was easier to bandage wounded soldiers knowing that I didn't have to make the hard decisions. I didn't envy you, *bato,* but I was proud."

"Are you trying to embarrass me?" said Román, conscious that some of the other soldiers in the helicopter were listening. "I think it's time to check on the wounded." He looked at the notebook and knew he had to finish the letter, but for now it would have to wait. The soldiers needed him, and besides, he could not think of anything else to add. Maybe Huong would help him. It would be nice to see Huong.

"I'll help," said Cesar.

"You better."

---

las jefitas – mothers

14 / PATRICIO PAIZ

En memoria de Arturo Tijerina

This poem is dedicated to my good friend who was killed in South Viet Nam on the 10th of May 1968. His name was Arturo Tijerina. I hope I do you justice carnal y ¡que viva la memoria de Arturo!

No Mexicans or dogs,
from the Halls of Montezuma
to the shores of Tripoli.
The vineyards of Fresno, California
to the deadly sands of Africa
From the lettuce fields of Delano, California,
to the sandy beaches of Normandy,
from the beet fields of Tejas and Colorado,
to the oil fields of Oklahoma,
the packing houses in West Tejas to
the Arctic cold of Germany,
from the aircraft carriers of the Pacific,
to Iwo Jima.

I was there—I was at the Alamo,
the Civil War, my history has
been left out.
No Mexicans or dogs.
I have fed your hungry nation,
AMERICA,

---

carnal—bro'
¡que viva la memoria de Arturo!—Long live Arthur!

yo me acuerdo de tí.
I was in Korea, yes,
don't forget Korea,
Forty below O,
            I can't forget,
I won't forget,
            I remember,
                US 54404674
17,500 en Viet Nam, Basta Ya!
I remember the death march of Bataan,
in the big war,
            the Real War!
How dead can one person be?
I remember UFWOC,
the United Farmworkers of California
I remember César Chávez
and what he said, "God knows
that we are not Beasts of Burden.
We are not agricultural implements,
or rented slaves.
            WE ARE MEN!"
You have exploited me,
            you have taken advantage
of my extreme poverty.
I have processed your vegetables,
I have disposed of your garbage,
I have done so much,
            for so little.
I have been in the coal mines of Virginia
            and Kentucky, and even
            Ratón, Nuevo México.
I was there,
I have been there where no one else will go
            sheepherding in Wyoming,

---

yo me acuerdo de tí—I remember you
Basta Ya!—Enough!

la lechuga en Arizona,
el algodón en Mississippi,
el betabel en Tejas,
el campo en Hereford,
la Causa en California,
All this, and I can't even stare
Justicia in the face.
I am a stranger to your system
of Justice.
I am a majority in your jails and prisons.
I am a majority
WHY?
In drugs,
why?
is there no human decency?
I remember the Zoot Suit riots,
I remember Las Gorras Blancas de Nuevo México,
I remember Jacinto Treviño,
I remember Pancho Villa,
I remember Emiliano Zapata,
Benito Juárez,
I will never forget
LA CAUSA!
I am an Americano,
I was Americano before your Anglo race arrived,
I was American before America existed
I am Arturo Tijerina 5-10-68
I am César Chávez
I am Valentín de la Sierra
I am Reies López Tijerina
I am Emiliano Zapata
I am the Crusade for Justice

---

la lechuga — lettuce
el algodón — cotton
el betabel — beets
el campo — the fields
la Causa — the Cause (the United Farm Workers' organizing drive)

I am El Partido de La Raza Unida de
            Tejas, de Nuevo México
I am Chicanos Unidos Para Justicia
            de Las Vegas.
I am the Chicano Liberation Front.
Is there no other way?
Is violence the ONLY way?
César Chávez y Martin Luther King.
            No Violence.
Fasting y Brotherhood Awareness.
Amerikkka, I won't forget you.
La lechuga, el betabel,
the inhuman conditions
            that my brothers have endured.

Get It On

In the chilly hours of the morning.
several weeks of uncertainty
in a world made by Capitalists, I wait
to kill a yellow race . . . my enemy, so I've been told.
I must fight, but Why?
            for God,
                        for country,
                                    for peace.
Isn't fighting for peace
            like fucking
for virginity? If I ever leave this place . . .
I will fight not for peace
            but for WAR.
Ya basta cabrones.

Ya basta cabrones—Enough, you sons of bitches

15 / Juan Ramirez

From "History of a Chicano Vietnam Veteran"

I began to have difficulty with other members of the other platoons of our company. There was one platoon in particular that had two Chicano squad leaders and an Indian kid who was a fire team leader, who took my bush attitude as being cowardly and confronted me with it once while we were in the rear.

This was one of those days in the rear when it was more like a company picnic my dad used to drag us to. We had been provided with as much beer as we could drink. Everybody was drunk, these three guys especially. They started in on me because I wasn't drinking—something to do with my lack of masculinity. Then they asked what it was I thought I was doing disgracing our heritage in the Marine Corps with this "pussyfooting" around with the Vietnamese. Didn't I realize that *everyone* was the enemy? I said I didn't think they understood the difference, so it was a waste of time to explain. They boasted about how many kills they had and how many wounds they had incurred getting them and said I was a disgrace to the race. I tried walking away, but they kept after me, calling me names, trying to provoke me. The Indian kid persisted, challenging me to a fight. I was tempted because he was so drunk he could hardly stand up, but I thought better of it, figuring I would have to fight them all if I picked on the most vulnerable. Nothing much else happened, but the incident hurt me deeply because it came from my *carnales,* my own kind. It also served to confuse me more than I already was. Was I cowardly in choosing this situation? Was I a disgrace to my race?

I didn't know, but I started to show some serious problems. One day on day patrol after weeks of no contact with the enemy, our point man stopped our column, calling me up to the point. When I got there, he was crouched down and very nervous. His eyes were wide as they could be. He said he thought he saw a person sneaking down on the other side of a rice paddy dike, just out to our flank. We both watched for a while, then I saw a person bob up, then scurry along the dike a few more feet. It looked like the person was armed, because there seemed to be a long, narrow object on his back, slung the way a rifle can be carried.

We waited quietly. The figure bobbed and scurried another few feet. This time I yelled out for him to come out from behind the dike. He did not. So I sighted in with my rifle and waited for him to move again. We had called in as soon as we suspected it was the enemy. The radio was now squawking from our CP and asking what was going on, but we didn't reply. We were intent on the person behind the dike. As he bobbed this time, I had him dead in my sights. Then it was as if I could see every detail just by sighting in, and I could see that the person I was about to shoot was an old woman with a bundle tied to a stick she had slung over her back. I saw all this within a split second. I had already been squeezing the trigger, but could have stopped. But I didn't. Although I realized that this woman probably was not armed, I fired anyway. I was shocked by my own actions. Half of the squad were already circling around behind the dike as I had ordered them to. The CP heard the shots and became more frantic over the radio. I told the radioman to tell Peanuts we were okay and that I'd explain the shots when we got back in.

I had wounded the old woman very badly and probably would have killed her if it hadn't been for all the stuff she was carrying. Some of it was cooking utensils and small pots and pans. These articles saved her life, absorbing most of the impact of the round. The corpsman got very mad with me that I hadn't called in a medevac chopper sooner. I was so stunned that I couldn't perform my duties, so Peterson called it. The woman was evacuated. I assumed that she lived.

16 / CHARLEY TRUJILLO

From *Soldados: Chicanos in Viet Nam*

Frank Delgado [An Oral History]

We flew from Travis Air Force Base to Viet Nam with a stopover in Hawaii and the Philippines. The airport in Hawaii is real pretty, with the ocean and the breeze, the whole works. I thought to myself about what I had to go through in order to see a place like this. People who are well off can fly over there easily. But I couldn't understand why I had the chance to stop in Hawaii under these circumstances.

I was thinking about going AWOL there. But I thought, what am I going to do? Call up my mom and tell her to send me some money because I'm going to go AWOL? Just as much as she didn't want me to go to Nam, I think she would have worried just as much with me being AWOL. Besides, I think we had it better than the soldiers in WWII. In Viet Nam, the enemy did not have bombs and airplanes to attack us like in WWII. They didn't have R&R, and when they were killed, they were buried overseas, whereas the soldiers killed in Viet Nam were sent home to their parents for a funeral.

As we were getting off the plane at Tan Son Nhut Airport, other soldiers were going to take the same plane home to the States. There was this little, short *mayate* going up the stairs of the plane. He was drunker than a skunk. He was singing the Stevie Wonder song, *Uptight*. It was all right for him because he was going back home. That's when it really sunk in that I had a whole year to go over there. As we got off, we could see all sorts of flashes and bombs going off in the mountains. This was about two in the morning.

In AIT they trained us good. But in a way, didn't train us good enough because all they told us was the VC this and the VC that. So I thought that

---

mayate— black guy

we were just going to be fighting the VC. I had no idea about the North Viet-namese Army. Every time they would show us the VC they would be in black pajamas and cone-head straw hats. To me, anyone who wore that was a VC. They took us on a bus through Saigon on our way to Camp Alpha, and what were ninety percent of the people wearing? Black pajamas and straw hats. I thought to myself, *Hijole man!* The VC are all around us.

We finally got to Camp Alpha where they assigned us to tents. The first night I was in Nam there was shooting all night along the perimeter. It was especially frightening because we hadn't been issued any weapons. Finally the next morning came and we found out what all the noise was about. Every time that the guards would hear noise along the perimeter, they would start shooting. In the morning there were a bunch of monkeys caught in the wire, all shot up and dead. They made the mistake of tripping tripflare wires.

After two or three days, I was sent to Pleiku. I was assigned to head-quarters company. I thought that was pretty good. When they were giving out the assignments they asked us if anyone knew how to play a musical in-strument, or type. The guys that did were assigned as clerks or to the band, which was real good duty. I was put in a reconnaissance platoon.

From Pleiku I was sent to my unit which was out in the I Drang Valley. I was assigned to my squad and when night came along, I was real scared. Everything was getting deeper and deeper. Sergeant Lowry and a *gabacho* they called the colonel were together in the same position. Sergeant Lowry took the first watch, the colonel the second, and me the third. I had always thought that soldiers slept in foxholes, but we didn't. We would sleep behind the foxhole. We only got into them when we received fire. A little after I had laid down I began to smell something funny, something I hadn't ever smelled before. It was the sergeant and the colonel smoking grass. "Hey, you want some?" they asked me. "No, man," I told them.

Somehow I fell asleep. I don't know how I did it because I was so scared. For some reason I woke up at about two or three in the morning. I sat up and looked around and the sergeant and the colonel had gotten so loaded that they had gone and visited their friends and left me there asleep. Man! That really freaked me out. I didn't know what to think. I got my M-16 and jumped into the foxhole. All that was in my head was the VC. Did the VC come and take these guys without seeing me? The position next to me was about twenty

Hijole—Wow
gabacho—white guy

yards away and I couldn't see them. I started looking to the front and I couldn't see nothing. The moon was hitting the treeline ahead of me and then the wind started blowing. Pretty soon I actually started hallucinating, I could see people with rifles coming at me. I think now that God must've been with me because I actually pulled the trigger and my rifle wouldn't go off. It was good that it didn't go off because I would have made a bunch of noise and attracted attention to myself. It was bad that it jammed because if I had actually needed it, it wouldn't have gone off.

Pretty soon I hear some noises and here come the sergeant and the colonel. Oh! Lord, they were laughing. They were just having a blast. I was glad to see the next morning. This went on for a long time until I finally got used to it. Out in the field I never got loaded because I was so pumped up from being out there.

Everyday the lieutenant would give us the information that intelligence had given him. He would tell us where they thought the enemy was and that their morale was low. Now, how in the hell did intelligence know that their morale was low? Did they go out and take a survey or what? But at nineteen years old, we thought, they don't call them intelligence for nothing.

We did a lot of humping out in the Central Highlands. Those were mountains out there, not hills. It was about 120° in the day time and 50° at night. It was a hell of a drop. That was in the dry season, which wasn't too bad, but when the monsoon came, it came down. It would just rain and rain and rain.

About two or three weeks after I got to Nam, we were out on an observation post (OP), Sergeant Lowry, the *marijuano,* was with us. We were kind of like following him. Pretty soon Sergeant Lowry does a double take and gets on his stomach and starts firing. "They're over there. There are seven of them," he said. I looked over there and I couldn't see nothing. All I could see was just bush. I began to fire too, I was firing in the direction that Sergeant Lowry was. Pretty soon he stopped firing. So, me and the rest of the squad stopped too. When the rest of the platoon came to where we were at, hey, I still didn't see nobody. We didn't know what had happened. So, the whole platoon got on line and we threw a sweep down the mountain. We were shooting about fifty yards away. We went down slowly. *Hijole! Man!* I was just getting deeper and deeper into it, still keeping this positive attitude. As we were getting closer, I didn't know what was going to happen. That's when I stepped on a dead North Vietnamese soldier. That guy had been laying out in the sun for three or four days. The guy was bloated and purple all over, and the ants were eating out his eyes. His hair was stiff like straw. Man! That scared the hell out of me. When I looked down, I looked right into his face.

Later we figured out what happened. There had been a fire fight a week before and the North Vietnamese were trying to retrieve their dead. The reason they wanted to pick up their dead was because they believe that if you leave a dead person behind, that person will come back and haunt you for the rest of your life. They would even leave the wounded before they would a dead person.

I was lucky in that all of the time I was there we only ran into small parties of North Vietnamese. Some of the guys who been there longer than I had used to throw party on them. The first month I was there I didn't have any jungle boots. All I had was regular combat boots and I was slipping and falling all over the place.

On September 9th, exactly one month after I had gotten to Nam, we were given an assignment to check out a North Vietnamese camp. We had the coordinates and we found the camp about 11 a.m., but they weren't there. So we thought we would be slick and wait until they came back and ambush them. It started raining and pretty soon we started hearing howitzers going off over our heads. In training they had told us that as long as you heard the whistling sound it's no problem. It's when it stops whistling that it is going to hit where you're at. That's when I heard the whistling sound. Then it stopped and before I could hit the ground that thing went off. There was shit flying everywhere . . . limbs, trees, rocks, and all kinds of stuff.

Somebody must've messed up because it was our own artillery that was firing at us. I was on the ground when this *mayate,* Washington, kept grabbing me on my arm. "Hey! what's wrong with you," I told him. "You're hit on your arm," he said. I raised up my arm and blood was coming out of my sleeve. When I saw that, boom, the pain hit me. My arm became real heavy and it was burning and I could feel the shrapnel. The lieutenant called in and the firing finally stopped. I looked around and I knew I was lucky to be alive. The butt of my rifle was completely blown off, the bullets in the magazine were literally twisted. The gun was useless.

After the artillery stopped, the called in a dust-off and I was taken to a field hospital. Of the ten guys, I was the only one hit. When I got there they took care of the guys who were worse off than me first. I remember seeing all these guys on stretchers. They were all dead. There must've been ten to fifteen dead. Two guys would come, pick them up and take them inside a tent. I guess they were taking their guts out and stuff because I could hear them working away on them inside the tent. I went up and looked at the dead guys to see if I knew any of them. I didn't.

When they saw my wound, they didn't think it was that bad compared to other wounds. From the field hospital, I was sent to Pleiku which was about eight hours after I had been wounded. I still hadn't received any medical attention. They finally operated on me and removed a two inch piece of shrapnel. From there I was taken to the hospital in Qui Nhon.

When I got there, I had a big old bandage on my arm. It had dried up and gotten into the wound. He (doctor) said he wanted to see it, so what he did was just grab the bandage, pulled on it hard and took it off. Right about that time everything got real bright, like when somebody flashes a camera in your face. The doctor asked me, "Are you alright?" I'm still trying to be tough and answered, "Yea." There was an old nurse there, I don't even know why she was there because she was that old. She would call me sonny. She told the doctor that he shouldn't have done that. By then my arm was just bleeding. Then the doctor looked at my wound. He told me that it had a lot of debris and that somebody had done a poor job of cleaning it out. It had gotten infected.

After I left the doctor, I began to walk to a tent to lie down. As I was walking, everything started getting whiter and whiter and whiter. Everything was so bright that I couldn't keep my eyes open anymore. I just passed out from the pain. The old nurse came over and picked me up. I spent about twenty days at the hospital. I came down with malaria, too.

When I got back to my unit I received a letter from my brother Steve and he told me he was in Viet Nam. In the second letter he told me he was in Camp Halloway, which was about five miles from our base camp. When I got back to our base camp, I went over to see him. It was a trip seeing my *carnal* over there. Johnny Guzman from Corcoran was there with him. The day that I got to Nam they passed a regulation that two brothers couldn't be there at the same time. My *carnal* told me it would be better if I would get out of Nam because I was in the infantry and he was in rations breakdown which was a softer job. At this time I was still pumped and full of shit from basic and AIT. I was still trying to pull the macho bullshit, and I argued that I should stay because I had been there longer. We finally agreed that I should request a leave because my chances were higher of being killed or wounded than his

---

carnal– brother

were. The army dragged their feet and ended up taking four months to have me shipped out of Nam.

All of this time I had been lying to my mom. I had told her that I was a truck driver. I changed the story when I got wounded and had to change my address. I told her that I was helping construct a new hospital. I don't think she really believed that, but I think she wanted to believe it. I'm glad they didn't send a telegram home when I got wounded because I don't think she could have taken it. She didn't find out I was wounded until I got home and she saw me without my shirt on when I was combing my hair in the bathroom.

I got to see my brother about four times when I was over there. On January the 6th, 1967, I was asleep when someone woke me up and told me that we were getting mortared. We were up on a mountain and my brother's camp was about five below from us and we could see that they were getting hit harder than we were. The next morning the first thing I did was jump on a truck that was going to town, and from there I got another ride to Camp Halloway. Man! When I got there, there were trucks and buildings all blown up and burned. I finally found my *carnal*. He was alright. He and Johnny Guzman were still kind of scared. These guys were too much because they showed me some little parachutes that they had gotten from the illuminating sky flares. When they were getting hit, they were out in the open running to catch the parachutes for souvenirs. I told them that they were crazy and stupid. Then, they told me that they didn't have any bunkers. They didn't know how to build a bunker, and I showed them how to build one. It's funny because my brother Steve and I never got along as we were growing up. He had his friends and I had mine. We really didn't treat each other as *carnales* until we saw each other in Nam. We had our first beer together over there.

I was lucky in the sense that we always ran into little parties like six, seven or eight people. We were always about forty guys and right away the guys would throw party on them. I was always in the situation that when we did run into them, they'd run into the squad in front of us. By the time my squad got there, everything was over with. But I still wanted to feel what it was like shooting somebody.

Every time I'd walk the point, my *camarada,* Albert Ortiz, would walk behind me. He told me that if I got into trouble, I should just drop and he would

---

camarada– comrade

take care of it. He helped me out a lot, he taught me the ropes. Albert was a little *pachuquillo* from Rockhard, Texas. He told me that he got into the army because he got into so much trouble that the cops finally gave him a choice of either joining the army or going to jail.

It was the 24th of December when we were supposed to go in and see the Bob Hope show. Before we could leave, we had to find and clear a landing zone for the choppers so they could pick us up. They gave us the coordinates for one and we found it real quick. But before we could use it we had to secure it. We could see from a distance that there were two hootches on the side of a mountain. We got up to the hootches and checked them out.

By this time I was a squad leader. When we got the the first hootch we knocked down the door. All that was in there was a little bit of rice on the floor and a hammock. We turned around and went into the second hootch. There wasn't anything in there either. At this time, there were only about twenty-five of us because they had gotten a lot of our guys and put them in other platoons that had gotten wiped out. About the time we knocked the second door down, this new guy tapped me on the shoulder and told me that there was a gook in the other hootch. When he said that, I felt all the blood go to my feet. I turned around to the other hootch, which was only about four feet away. The hootch that was supposed to be empty, wasn't. There was a North Vietnamese soldier asleep in the hammock. He had been asleep, so it looked empty. When I turned around into the hootch, he and I looked eye to eye at about three feet from each other. I only had an M-79 grenade launcher so I couldn't shoot him. He looked down and I looked to where he was looking at. There were two grenades on the floor and he reached for them. About that time everybody opens up on the North Vietnamese.

I hit the floor because I couldn't shoot at him. It was too close. They must've shot that guy about two hundred times. Every inch of that hootch was covered with bullets. When the shooting stopped, the lieutenant, who had only been in country for about a month, went in and shot him one more time in the head. One of my *camaradas* picked the gook up, and when he did, I could see one side of his head with the brains hanging out. I can still see that brain, it was gray in color. I could hear his brains sizzling because of all the bullets that hit him. My *camarada* picked him up from the butt and the collar, and I knew exactly what he was going to do, *vatos locos,* you know. He got

---

pachuquillo — street-type
vatos locos — crazy dudes

that guy and he threw him at me. I jumped back and the gook landed about two feet in front of my feet. His brains just went all over my boots. Everybody just busted out laughing. They thought it was the funniest thing in the world.

When we finished laughing, someone suggested that we eat lunch. We started eating, and the platoon leader looked around and said, "Isn't anyone going to bury him or something?" Here you have this guy with his brains sizzling, and by this time, the ants had come around and began to eat on the guy. We began to laugh again. When I was laughing, I was thinking to myself, why in the hell am I laughing, this isn't funny. That's when I started realizing that I wasn't the same person that I was a year ago back in Corcoran. I realized that something had changed in me. I don't think it was for the better, it was for the worse! I hadn't been raised up that way, to be out killing. To find humor in death is when I started realizing I was living like an animal. And pretty soon, you started acting like one.

The platoon leader called up headquarters and informed them of our situation. That North Vietnamese we killed was suffering from malaria and was asleep when we checked out the hootch. He was incapacitated. The reason that North Vietnamese was shot so excessively was that we were full of hate and anger. They had told us that if we made contact we had to stay out in the field. It was the guy's fault that we had to stay out, so everybody threw party on him.

The next day we go back to camp and I'm still all gung ho about seeing Bob Hope. As soon as I walked into the hootch, one guy told me that I had missed a good show.

After a couple of days, we went back to the field and into Cambodia. I had seen a chopper get knocked down in Cambodia. We were half way up the side of a mountain and the chopper was level to us when it got hit. A rocket hit it and that thing just started burning up and fell. It took us about forty-five minutes to get to the chopper. By that time it was burned up and so was the crew. One guy apparently decided to jump out rather than burn to death. When he hit the treeline, he broke into pieces. We found one of his boots with his foot in it. He must of been a black guy because the skin was black.

When we were putting the remains into green body bags, I began to think. If we get hit and I get burned up, there is no way that my remains are going to get back to my parents. That really bothered me a lot. Something that also bothered me was when I saw people after they had been shot, especially our own, the ants would get there quickly and would begin to eat out the eyes. I remember seeing *vatos* with the mud going in their mouths. I used to think that if I got shot, I didn't want to lie out in the mud and have the ants eating on me.

Pulling Listening Post's (LP's) at night was by far the worst experience to go through. Every other night we pulled an LP. For an LP, three guys would go out about three hundred meters from the perimeter and listen for enemy movement. One evening right before nightfall, my team went out on one. We went out about three hundred meters until we came to a fork in the trail. We set up about thirty meters in front of the fork. I thought this would be the perfect place for an LP. It must've been about two in the morning when I started hearing all kinds of stuff. I woke up the other two guys and I told them that somebody was coming at us. I radioed in to the platoon leader and told him we had movement. The platoon leader was green, and instead of telling us to go on in, he told just to wait and see what was happening. Maybe my mind was playing tricks on me but it sounded like about thirty of them.

By this time they were almost on us. When they came near to the fork, I heard their leader give a command and they halted. It was too late to run back. Then I heard another command and they moved out on line. I thought this guy was going to pull a sweep on us. But instead he called another command and they got back on the trail and went on the trail to the right. I called in and told them we were coming back in. I didn't ask or anything. We just ran as fast as we could. *Hijo de su!* My heart was pounding real hard!

Two days later when we had to go on LP again, I told those in the foxholes to the left and right of us that we were only going about thirty meters ahead. From that day on I didn't go further than thirty meters out.

When I first started fighting the war, I really believed we had a just cause, fighting communism and all of this bullshit they tell you. But after being there awhile, everything changed for me. My main objective was to make it out of there alive. I didn't give a shit who won the war anymore. My whole world had just turned around because I could see a lot of shit that wasn't right. For example, when we went back to base camp, I'd see all the South Vietnamese soldiers in starch fatigues and waxed down trucks. There were several times that South Vietnamese units went with us and they were sorry soldiers. Once the shooting started, the only way we could keep them with us was to literally threaten to shoot them in the back if they ran—and we would have.

Another thing that made me think that way was that people in the United

---

Hijo de su! – Fucking A

States didn't care about us individually. I finally realized that we were being used. I read a couple of articles in the Stars and Stripes Newspaper that so many congressmen had gone to Viet Nam and gotten a firsthand idea of what was going on, and that everything was under control. Hey! I never saw no congressman out in the field. They probably went to Saigon and partied at a couple of nightclubs and came back to the States.

When I was going to college about a year after I got out of the army, I began to listen to what people were saying against the war. It started to dawn on me that I had indeed been used and I hadn't really known what I was doing. I felt angry because I had let that happen to me and that I had gone along with it.

At the same time I didn't have much of a choice. If I had refused to get drafted, what was I going to do? It would have been just as hard to refuse the draft as it was to go into the army. Where was I going to go? I had nowhere to go. That would have been real hard on my *jefitos*. If people like Jane Fonda had come earlier, there would have been less guys killed in Nam. I go along with what she did.

We were brainwashed into thinking that we had a noble cause, which I don't think we had. The Pentagon underestimated the North Vietnamese capacity, determinism and their willingness to sacrifice. I had a hell of a lot of respect for them because they knew what they were doing. They were tougher than we were because they didn't get their sundries packed. They didn't get regular mail. They didn't have choppers flying them around. They didn't get to go on R&R. Somebody underestimated them. There are some people who believe that the United States lost the war because the right strategy and tactics were not used. I don't believe that one bit. Anyone who says that was probably never in Nam. And if they were, they weren't in the type of situation to see that it was impossible to do. The only alternative was to use nuclear weapons, and that's no alternative at all.

I had a couple of friends, Jimmy Smith and Burgess, who went over there together so we thought we were all going home together. We agreed that when we got back to California, my sister from Watsonville was going to pick us up and take us to her place for a Mexican dinner because Jimmy Smith had never eaten Mexican food. I don't know what ever happened to Burgess, but Jimmy was killed about a month after I left. He got his head chopped off by

---

jefitos– parents

a helicopter blade. There were a lot of other guys I knew that got killed, and I don't think it was worth it. His wife had a baby while he was in Nam, and Jimmy never got to see that boy.

The day I was leaving Nam, I asked this guy I knew, Danny Rhodes from Lemoore CA, if he wanted me to go see his people and tell them that I was with him and that he was okay. He asked me to go and see his grandfather and grandmother to tell them he was okay. When I got home on leave, Frank Molano, my friend from basic, was home on leave from Panama. One day I asked him if he remembered Danny from basic training and if he wanted to take a drive to Lemoore to see Danny's grandparents. Frank asked me, "Didn't you read the paper? Danny got killed last week." The funeral was the next day, so Frank and I went to the funeral. I remember seeing the grandparents at the funeral, his parents were there, too, but he was raised by his grandparents. I regret that I didn't go up and tell them that I knew Danny in Nam. I didn't know what to say.

When I finally got home from Nam and to my own bed, I slept for something like eighteen hours. My mom finally woke me up because she got scared. When I got home, I was expecting something to blow up any minute. Noises like firecrackers would make me nervous. Sometimes something would remind me of something that happened in Viet Nam and I would tell my wife and son about it. Even though they've heard it before, they still listen to me. They've been real supportive.

17 / Charley Trujillo

From *Dogs from Illusion*

"There ain't no tamales in Viet Nam"

Wino is walking the point for the platoon up a well-used, steep trail. Ro-Ro is his backup man. When they reach the top of the mountain, they take a short break next to some large rocks. Smoking cigarettes, Wino and Ro-Ro watch the trail leading down the mountain. At the foot of the mountain is a meandering stream. Chuco comes up and joins Wino and Ro-Ro. "Tienes el bote de pintura?" (Do you have the can of paint?), Ro-Ro asks Chuco.

"Sí, aquí está," says Chuco as he reaches inside his rucksack and pulls out an army issue spray paint can and hands it to Ro-Ro. After shaking the can, he writes graffiti, Chicano style, on the rocks. The first thing he writes is: El Ro-Ro loco de Xicali y qué. Then he writes: Que chinguen sus madres los chinos (Slick Ro-Ro from Mexicali; the Chinese can fuck their mamas).

"Pásame el bote," asks Wino. Ro-Ro hands it to him and he writes, El Wino con mi ruca la Trucha PV, followed by: la raza no se raja (Wino with my girl Trucha for life; Mexicans don't back down).

"Como estás loco, Wino. Pásame el bote. It's my turn," says Chuco. Next to El Chuco de Califas, he writes Mao Tse-tung es joto y Ho Chi Minh es chavala" (Chuco from California; Mao Tse-tung is a queer and Ho Chi Minh is a sissy). "This will piss the gooks off," he says. After the break, the word is given to move down the mountain. Wino and Ro-Ro know that ambushes and enemy camps are frequent near streams and rivers, so they move slower than usual.

They reach the bottom of the mountain and cross the stream. Suddenly, the cracking of AK-47s burst out. Wino is killed by a bullet to the chest. His only reaction is a painless sigh, "Ah." Ro-Ro is shot in the belly and legs. He manages to drag himself forward, away from the stream. A fierce fire fight ensues. Chuco brings his M-60 machine gun up and begins to lay a solid base of fire.

Across the stream, Ro-Ro gathers himself and takes cover behind a log. In front of him is a tiny meadow. The enemy is well protected by a tree line ahead of them, and they are dug in too close to call in artillery or mortars on them. They sporadically shoot back at one another for a while.

At times, Ro-Ro is able to talk to the platoon. "Sácame de aquí. I'm losing a lot of blood y me duele un chingo" (Get me out of here; it hurts like hell).

"We can't get across, compa. Wait till it gets dark y luego te podemos ayudar. Don't worry, we can keep them from getting to you," shouts Chuco.

The fire fight slackens and the opponents are in a stalemate. Nightfall comes and Ro-Ro surmises as he sees the moon rise, Lo sabía, there's going to be a full moon tonight; that's as bad as daylight. "Chuco, ayúdame," he yells.

"Ahi te voy, compa," shouts Chuco as he attempts to cross the stream, but is deterred by bullets. "I can't get across compa, but we can see them if they try and get you."

"¿Qué le pasó al Wino?" (What happened to Wino?), he asks.

"Le dieron en la madre" (They killed him), replies Chuco.

"Ayúdame, Chuco; me duele un chingo," says Ro-Ro.

Again Chuco tries to reach Ro-Ro, but is stopped by bullets.

"Ayúdame Chuco, me duele un chingo," Ro-Ro says again with pain.

"Orale, no te agüites," just hang on; the choppers are going to come with more vatos to help us. When they get here, te vamos a dar some real good grifa, un buen tequila y unos tamales de aquellotas" (We're going to give you some real good weed, fine tequila, and excellent tamales).

"Ya ni la chingas, there ain't no tamales in Viet Nam!"

"Yes there are. I didn't show you but my jefita sent me some in a can. I still have them. Y también, acuérdate de las nalgotas de Nena que te esperan en Mexicali" (And also remember Nena's big butt that waits for you in Mexicali).

"Orale buey, cómo sabes que Nena has a big butt?" complains Ro-Ro.

"You've only shown us her picture a million times. No te apures, I won't let the gooks get to you, cuñado," Chuco reassures him as he lets out a burst of machine gun fire. "Ves. Why don't you sing a song, a song that will help."

"Sing a song, are you stupid? Who are you, Mitch Miller?"

"Come on, sing a song. One of your favorite ones."

"Qué será, será," Ro-Ro begins to sing.

"Párale ya, compa," interjects Chuco. "If you keep singing that shit, we're going to shoot you ourselves," Chuco tells him, as a humorous psychology ploy to lift Ro-Ro's spirits. "Canta algo that reminds you of the good times when you were a happy little chavalio."

"Sí. That's right. Me acuerdo when I was a chavalio and the gringa teacher used to give us cookies and milk y cantábamos, 'Jimmy . . . Jimmy . . . crack corn . . . and I don't care. Jimmy . . . crack corn . . . and I don't care.' Or sometimes . . . cantábamos, 'Zipp . . . edy do . . . da, Zipp . . . edy ay. My . . . oh . . . my, wh . . . at a won . . . der . . . ful day. Zipp . . . e . . . dy do . . . da. Zipp . . . e . . . dy ay,'" he sings slowly and sadly.

"Yeah, keep singing like that Ro-Ro. Tú eres chingón" (You're a bad dude).

"Chuco . . . Chuco, I'm losing a lot of sangre, carnal," he says with agony.

"No te agüites, sing another song."

"La cuca———ra . . . cha, la cuca . . . ra . . . cha, ya no pue . . . de ca . . . minar. La cuca———ra . . . cha, la cuca . . . ra . . . cha, ya no pue . . . deca . . . minar. Por . . . que . . . le . . . fal . . . ta . . . , por . . . que . . . le . . . fal . . . ta . . . mari . . . jua . . . na que fu . . . mar," finishes Ro-Ro with his eyes staring at eternity.   *Translation by Charley Trujillo*

Party on the Mountain

Dedicated to Charley Trujillo, author of *Soldados: Chicanos in Viet Nam,* and to every Chicano who ever served in The Nam. And a special thanks to Jim Bradley and Lise Engel for asking Charley to send me a copy of his book.

The 2nd Battalion, 1st Marines, had spent the Spring and Summer of 1967 fighting the little people in the Badlands west of Da Nang. We were tired, dirty, and shot up. Our rifle squads were at half-strength. We had survived the firefights in the rice paddies and the destruction of The Bridge. Doc Gallagher had been killed and Doc Cochran had been all fucked up by a mine. The Badlands were grim shit, man. All we wanted, we thought, was to get the fuck outta Dodge.

Naturally, in September, 1967, we got our wish. We got the Word: Headin' North. The lieutenant tried to make us feel better about it, telling us we were going to leave our pleasant little Tactical Area of Responsibility (TAOR) for the dubious honor of assisting the 3rd Marine Division keep the North Vietnamese Army from decivilizing and depopulating the DMZ.

We set up on our mountain west of Khe Sanh—just where I never did know, and did not very much care—and ran a few company-size patrols to get a feel for our new TAOR. The DMZ was death waiting to happen; no place to fuck around. Get stupid here, get killed here. But the Lifers didn't want us to get killed up here so quick, so they cut us some slack and gave us some down time.

My Bro, Luis Alejandro Parker, was sent on "R and R" soon after we went north, so he missed the impromptu party held one late afternoon by the battalion's Chicanos on our mountain. Who started it is lost to time and memory:

"Let's have a party, ese."

---

ese—dude

"Orale, pues."

"Dile a los otros, m'ijo."

One vato passed the word to some dude who passed it to somebody else. 2/1's Chicanos were going to have a party, down in the saddle that separated Hotel Company from Echo Company's hooches. One of us brought his guitar and canned tamales, another his tortillas-in-a-can (Rosarita; I have not found them since) sent to him by his mother, and someone else brought the hot sauce and refried beans.

We built small fires out of C-4 explosive on which to cook our chow and we sang our songs: "Ojos Verdes" and "Sabor a mí," the songs of our youth. We told each other about our "Girl Back in The World," our Baby-san. We swapped lies and war stories about chicks and cars and bars and growing up in San Anto, San Jo, East Los, El Paso, Fresno, Santa Fe and wherever else we came from. Even some cholo from Kansas City made an appearance.

We reminisced about Whittier Boulevard and the Plush Bunny, that most famous of all nightclubs in East L.A. and Saturday night dances at the National Guard armories in small Texas towns. We agreed on green-eyed Chicanas and disagreed on güeras, those light-skinned, blonde-haired Chicanas who stood out from the crowd. Yes, we agreed, the '57 Chevy was the coolest automobile ever built and Coors beer was highly prized.

We spoke of pumping gas and cotton fields and orange groves where most of us had worked at one time or another, agreeing that picking cotton or fruit was just like The Nam: it sucked. We cursed La Migra, the Border Patrol and its tactics (irony of ironies: one of us would survive Vietnam and later join the Border Patrol. Go figure.).

We slipped easily into the idiom of the barrio, calling each other carnal, or brother, camarada and ese. We ate our tortillas, refried beans and tamales and wondered, as we licked our fingers and wiped our hands on our trousers and shirts, what our jefitas would think of our table manners. No, we agreed, they would not like how we chowed-down at all.

¿Tienes hermanita? was followed by threats of dismemberment if any-

---

Orale, pues—Right on
Dile a los otros, m'ijo—Tell the others, son
cholo—guy
jefitas—mothers
¿Tienes hermanita?—Do you have a sister?

body put la movida on a little sister. All of us laughed at the age-old right of the older brother to protect his sisters. Individually, we were are aware of being . . . different. We were a minority. We spoke a minimum of three languages: Chicano, English, and Marine. Some of us, like me, even spoke Spanish. We spoke and understood Chicano; some of us could speak English with difficulty, but all of us understood—and spoke—Marine. We may not have understood high school English or everything that was said in las películas, the movies; we probably did not know how to write a check or fill out a job application. We all knew, however, about fields of fire, general orders, Claymore mines, vertical envelopment, squads on-line and the nomenclature of the M-16. We were, after all, professional fighting men.

We came out of the barrios, the cities and the rural countrysides. A couple of grunts at the party that night had lived their entire lives on the King Ranch, never once having been off the property. And, they vowed, once they returned to the ranch, they were never going to leave it again. We knew all about gang fights and being refused service in restaurants and being told to get out of town. We knew discrimination (although we did not know it by that term; we just thought it was the way of the Gabacho). We did not talk that night about why we were in The Nam. Cabula shuck and jive like that we left to the chaplain or the Navy doctors down in Da Nang. Serving in the Armed Forces of the United States was something we grew up knowing we were going to do, so we did it. De verdad, we looked forward to it.

We did, that night, ask each other why we decided to join the Marine Corps. Some of us enlisted in Uncle Sam's Misguided Children to avoid the draft, although I could never figure out that one. Some of us enlisted because the Marine Corps was a tough outfit, and we were tough vatos. Some of us signed up because it was a way out: of the barrio, of the towns we lived in, to see something different, go new places and meet new people.

As we talked and joked and laughed, the professionalism of Fighting Men showed through. Wary eyes kept a watch on the mouth of the draw that led up to our mountain. As guitars played and some of us sang of lost loves,

---

la movida— a move
Gabacho—white man
Cabula—bullshit
De verdad—really
vatos—dudes

others of us wiped down our M-14s, M-16s, and shotguns with carefully-kept cleaning rags. We noted with appreciation as a squad of Echo Company Grunts—mostly whites and Blacks—set up blocking forces on the ridges facing both sides of the draw. Our party would not be interrupted. We tipped our soft covers in salute; they flipped us the 'finger' and grinned. Acknowledged that night was the fact that none us could conceive of serving in Vietnam as anything other than a Marine. As Marines, we were all one color: Marine Corps Green. We left the problems of race to the non-hackers in the rear. In The Bush, all that mattered was that you carried your own weight.

One of us remarked on the reality, la realidad, that we were a minority twice: Chicano and Marine. We thought about that and nodded our heads at the rightness of the observation. After all, we reasoned, how many of us can be La Raza? Very few, we agreed. One of us, looking out into the darkening gloom that was the DMZ, remarked, "And the meek shall inherit the earth." Sandoval, a machine-gunner from Fox Company, looked up at his Bro' and said, "They will, ese. That's why God made Marines." He laughed at himself, at the situation in which he found himself. "He just wants to make sure the meek have their chance."

As the sun set, the music slowed and conversation became desultory. We lay on our backs and stared up at the night sky that covered Vietnam like a feral cloak. ¿Qué vas a hacer cuando regresas al Mundo? When I get back to The World? Man, I am going to shuck these duds and find me a güera, ese. That's what I'm going to do. "Not me, ese. I'm gonna find myself una india, jet-black hair past her ass and deep brown skin con ojos this big. ¡And she'll wear a short skirt up to here—asta 'quí! We all laughed. Exactly right, my man. Oye, dame otra tortilla.

It was a great party; and, so far as we knew, the only one of its kind ever to take place in The Nam. Take what shots we wanted at the Lifers, they cut us a hus and left us alone. To be Chicano and Marine was as good as it got; the best of every world. We had a fine time enjoying the camaraderie of fellow grunts and fellow Chicanos. Brothers all. We did not think about tomorrow or the day after. Vietnam would take care of itself and the Marine Corps would take care of us. For a few hours, we were very content.

Some days after that night, the First Marines mounted Operation Medina and got shot to pieces by the NVA inside the Hai Lang National Forest. It was

ojos— eyes

Oye, dame otra tortilla—Hey, give me another tortilla

a killer ambush. Hotel Company alone had 18 KIAs and I don't know how many wounded. Among the stacks of dead and wounded Marines were many of those Chicanos who had attended the party on the mountain.

Perez was killed.
Guerrero was wounded.
Rodríguez was wounded.
Sandoval was killed.
Sánchez was wounded.
Dennis "Doc" Gonzales escaped without a scratch, although his platoon
     suffered the most dead. Un milagro.
I was wounded.

I returned from Charlie Med, a few weeks later, to the stunned faces of my Bros. "Andábamos mortificados!" We were scared to death, ese. We heard you got killed. No, I said. But it was close, ese. It was very close. Parker returned to us from "R and R" in Hong Kong, regaling us with stories of malaria and British Army hospitals and the nurse he met. ¿Una güera, Parker? Yes, he said. He lit a cigarette and looked around our mountain. Where is everybody, he wondered. Nos mataron, ese. They killed us, Lou.

The war went on. We grieved for our friends and camaradas and opened a can of cold C-rations and chowed down. We brewed tins of coffee, saw to our gear and smoked a last cigarette. Then we saddled up because the Skipper said so and the Gunny said so and we humped one more mountain and then one more mountain after that. Sometime later, just before I rotated back to The World, back to the Land of the All-Night PX and olive-skinned chicanitas and cold beer, I was manning a hole just inside the perimeter. The night was cool and the sky was cloudless and black. Pitch black. Señor Carlos—Mr. NVA—was out there somewhere, and that cabrón was a stone pro. To doze off was to risk death or injury or—worse—dismemberment. About two in the morning, 0200, I heard it, soft at first, and then clear and low. Off in the distance, I swear I could hear the mournful tune of some guitarra in some faraway valley playing "Ojos Verdes." My face felt grimy and flinty as I wiped my hand across it. I wished for a cigarette, knowing that was impossible. Ghosts, I thought. That's all. Camaradas.

Un milagro— a miracle
cabrón— son of a bitch

Es el aire; nada más. It's just the wind, homeboy. Don' mean nothing.

No; however much I wanted it to go away, I could hear it still. I looked around, knowing no one could see me. Rational; that's what I had to be. Still . . . off in the distance . . . I strained to listen. It sounded like Sandoval . . . "Yo nunca olvidaré . . ."

Yo nunca olvidaré—I'll never forget

From "The Tortilla Mission"

It is hard to imagine how depressing it was to be in another part of the world so far removed from your own familiar surroundings. Ripped from your culture by the jet age. Not being able to get a taste of the foods, or smell the aroma, or hear the familiar echoes, the ones you were used to hearing even from the fetal position. Every waking hour of every day you tasted flavors that you were not accustomed to tasting. Sometimes I just felt like biting into my grandma's corn tortillas like I did after church on Sunday morning.

Everything was painted green in this place. The other soldiers who were from Mid-America stared at me in bewilderment. They can't believe that there actually are other cultures within theirs. "You almost look like us," some say, "but you talk funny." I reacted to sounds and voices that I never was used to hearing on a routine basis before. Black buddies with their distinct voices and loud music. I'm almost sure that here in Guatemala, Texas, there never has been a Black family for as long as folks can remember. At least not lived here permanently.

I really met and got to know my fellow African Americans in the military. All I really knew about them before was what I saw through that false prophet—the electronic media. And some misinformed stories by old viejos who had never really seen a Black person either. "You all go to sleep," I would tell them. "You guys are always talking and arguing in the middle of the night. About some pink Cadillac that you say you have at home, but don't. As if we got too much sleep around here as it is." They would answer with a barrage of pillows at the very least. "Boy if you weren't a cactus nigger yourself, I'd be on you like stink on manure." Jackson would yell back. He called the Mexican types cactus niggers. The Arabs, to him, were sand niggers; the na-

---

viejos— old men

tive Americans were prairie niggers; the anglos were real estate niggers. I asked him once what he meant by calling the gringos "real estate niggers." Jackson used to say that anglos were always making the rules. New laws and rules and treaties and documents wherever they went. And it just so happened that those laws always turned out in their favor. "Wherever they go they have managed to make themselves owners of all the real estate. Imperialists," Jackson pointed out. But the strange thing, Jackson explained, was that the rest of us niggers let them get away with it. "Amen," I said all enlightened. "But Charlie nigger doesn't seem like he's going to give up too much real estate to no one any time soon."

Reminds me of the thorn brush in South Texas where we have these nasty little leaf-cutting ants that live it up in the brush. When we bought real estate in their territory, we tried to make an oasis there because it was all desert. We planted all sorts of lush plants and trees. No sooner did the ants find out than they began attacking the new invading vegetation with a vengeance. It was more like a siege than a normal search for food. They could not possibly use as much as they destroyed by relentless cutting. It seemed they were trying to repel the foliage as much as harvest it. My father quickly waged the old chemical warfare trick on them. He dusted the entrance holes full of pesticides and that was the end of that. Three days later, they were back. This time they had moved their bases of operation, that is, the entrance of their tunnels, deeper into the more difficult thorn-brush thicket. But they had to come out farther and expose themselves more in order to raid the rich plants. Three- or four-lane highway paths were carved on their fast foot-trodden trail. We retaliated by raining fire from the sky on their shy little heads. We fired up the cactus burning torch and strafed the hordes as they marched in their uniformed army-like frenzy. I hate to admit it, but I kind of enjoyed the way their pesky little bodies crackled and popped in the merciless gulf of flame. I mean we were trying to plant this vegetation to make the desert bloom. And it was hard enough work without those little malcontents.

They could have learned a lesson on determination from us superior human beings. But no. They were back and this time spread out all over the place where the torch was rendered useless and expensive to operate. We could not believe the audacity of these contemptuous creepy crawlers. It was as if every time they retreated to their little tunnel headquarters, they would plan a counterattack on everything we did. I smeared a ring of tar and grease on the tree trunks to make them stick and keep the ants from climbing up. It almost worked, but soon they built bridges out of their own stuck bodies and other woody debris. My father made excursions into the brush to intercept them in their holes, so they in turn began to camouflage the openings with leaves and twigs. When I began to spot the cover of leaves and grass hiding the entrances, I swept the mulch and dusted them. They countered my countermeasure with an elementary but ingenious counter countermeasure. They began to dig their tunnel entrances one inch from the surface. When human activity trickled to a halt late at night, they would dig out and do what ants were invented to do. Cut leaves. We had to implement the scorched earth policy on them. We bulldozed the stubborn area until it looked as ugly as the surface of the moon. But at the end we were not sure who had won. The place looked worse than when we came to save it. We sort of had to destroy the place . . . to save it.

20 / Ralph Molina

Dos recuerdos (after Octavio I. Romano V.)

I

It is January, 1968, and the Viet Nam War is still raging.

After one year overseas, I return. We land in Oakland.

I get a pass and walk a street, any street. I stop at the first hamburger stand I encounter. I enter and order a big double cheeseburger.

For months and months and months and months I have dreamed of this moment.

Enjoy.

The place is full of soldiers. Apparently they had the same dream.

The soldier sitting next to me turns, and, with ketchup on his upper lip, he says, "Worth fighting for, huh?" There is a look of pure sarcasm on his face.

"Yeah," I reply. I don't know about my face, but I have a deep feeling of rage inside.

Tomorrow I leave for L.A., and home.

It is Spring of 1970.

Pam and I are on a date. She is Irish, red-haired. I am a Chicano GI on leave. We met at work at a bookstore before I was drafted. We talk a lot about the war, and should we get married. We are in a coffee shop on Atlantic Blvd., eating lunch. Two cops enter the restaurant.

All of a sudden Pam says, "Let's get out of here." I am surprised. We each still have a full plate of food in front of us. She insists.

When we are out on the street I ask, "Why leave now?"

"Didn't you hear those two cops behind us?"

"No. Why?"

"They were talking about hassling that spic with the redhead. They meant you."

Four months later, I am sent to fight communism overseas. In Viet Nam I read about the members of the Sheriff's Department and the LAPD who repeatedly attacked Chicanos and Chicanas in East Los Angeles.

21 / Ricardo Mario Amézquita

I Just Got Back from Vietnam, Baby

I

It reminds me
of a roller coaster construction.
I am one of the ten instructed
to climb the ladders,
stand in a single line
and face the crowd below.
Twenty-five people are near the curb.
They are waiting for the show to begin.
A fireman pulls a hose from the pumper.
He takes aim. The fluid arches over
our heads for a few seconds then falls
in the middle of the scaffold.
The nine seem calm
except for twitching fingers
and tapping feet.
Someone drops a lighted match.
The liquid ignites.
Three jump from the inferno.
They fall like effigies,
I am closest to the ladder
and descend.

II

Stranded from my company
I hack through the jungle
to find them.
In my path
is a white box
rectangular
and standing on end.
I stop to wipe
my machete on my fatigues
then continue to cut
the growth in the box.
I hear noise
and freeze within
the oblong frame.
They are North Vietnamese
in tan uniforms.
They pass.
In minutes I have
slashed through the box.

Upon reaching the plain
I observe a firefight beginning.
I cross a stream and see
four Bowie Knives laying
on a log. I pick them up.
As I turn, a rifle slug
grazes me above the clavicle.
I think I am dead
because I bleed so little.
It is hand to hand combat.
I throw the knives
and kill three.
We are out flanked
and the fight is soon over.

A French trader
and a platinum blonde
in a black sweater
are negotiating
for our custody.
He warns the NVA commander
that more American forces
will shortly be in the area.
The Frenchman agrees to hold us
in his supply house
until they return.

III

I have returned
to my former station
at a desert Air Force Base.
The squadron shop is open.
No one there except
Harry, the civilian.
I check the schedule.
First take-off time
is 1205.
It is about 1100.
They should be going through
here briefly.
The pilots are checking
their equipment.
They are wearing
street clothes instead
of flight-suits.
Only one pilot recognizes me.
The last time I saw him
he was a general.
Sgt. Brown enters
the shop and ignores me.

An airman basic, an airman first-class
and a staff sergeant have taken
over my duties. There is
nothing for me to do.

IV

It's a girl
She doesn't cry much.
Light-brown hair, dark eyes
dressed in pink.

22 / Saúl Sánchez

El entierro

Lots and lots of people went to the funeral that day. From the Catholic Church all the way to the Mexican cemetery this large group of men in soldiers' uniforms marched behind the hearse which crossed town very, very slow, and lots of other men who had been just standing there along the streets watching, and even other kids from school, started joining the ones who were marching behind the casket. For a long while almost all the downtown traffic came to a complete stop. The only cars moving were the ones on their way to the funeral and they were really moving along very slow keeping one right behind the other. There were so many cars that there was no more room for those coming last in line to park close to the cemetery. Many people had to leave their cars over in the Plant's parking lot and walk from there alongside the railroad tracks. Almost all the kids from school had been let out or we had gotten permission to come watch. You could even see people already on their way back and at the same time others were just arriving. Even Father, the priest from the church who had buried and blessed the body, had gotten mad because they said that after everything had been over with and all the people who had gone to the funeral had left the cemetery, there were footprints all over the other graves where the people had crowded together. Even later that afternoon long after it was all over with people were still arriving to take a look at the grave and to make the sign of the cross.

And it was all because people had heard that the soldier that they were just burying that day had been sent home from Viet Nam in a little plastic bag, and that it was for that reason that some Anglo soldiers, and one Negro, had been watching the casket ever since it had been placed on the train in San Francisco, California. They said that they were doing that so nobody would open it to see what was inside. But then others said no; said that all who died

---

El entierro—The burial

in combat had it done that way, they were escorted. But then why was it that all the while the casket was there in the funeral home the six soldiers who had been guarding it since it was put on the train in San Francisco spent the entire time guarding it? Why? Huh? Why? And then too with those big old rifles slung across their shoulders. They didn't dare leave it alone a single minute all the time they were there. Not until it had been buried and they had removed the American flag draped over it to give it to the Mother did they move away from it.

It was hard to tell if the Mother and the Father understood why or for what purpose they had given it to them. The flag, I mean. The Anglo soldier who folded it was saying something when he was handing it over to them but it didn't look like they understood at all what he was trying to tell them. I don't even think they knew how to say the "Hay plesha lichans." I bet you I know how to say it. Look, you want me to show you? "Hay plesha lichans tu di flac . . ."

23 / Luis Omar Salinas

Death in Vietnam

the ears of strangers
                            listen
fighting men tarnish the ground
        death has whispered
                            tales to the young
and now choir boys are ringing
                            bells
        another sacrifice for America
                    a Mexican
        comes home
his beloved country
        gives homage
and mothers sleep
                    in cardboard houses
        let all anguish be futile
tomorrow it will rain
and the hills of Viet Nam
resume
        the sacrifice is not over

24 / NORMA ELIA CANTÚ

From *Canícula: Snapshots of a Girlhood en la Frontera*

Tino

He did it at four. And again at nine. He stands to the side with his hand out as if pointing a gun or a rifle. Everyone else is crowded around me; the piñata in the shape of a birthday cake sways in the wind above our heads. Everyone's there: aunts, uncles, cousins, the neighbors, my madrina, everyone, even Mamagrande Lupita from Monterrey. I'm holding the stick decorated with red, blue, yellow tissue paper that we will use to break the piñata. And he's playing, even in the picture, at being a soldier. Only ten years later, 1968, he is a soldier, and it's not a game. And we are gathered again: tías, tíos, cousins, comadres, neighbors, everyone, even Mamagrande Lupita from Monterrey, and Papi's cousin Ricardo who's escorted the body home. We have all gathered around a flag-draped coffin. Tino's come home from Vietnam. My brother. The sound of the trumpet caresses our hearts and Mami's gentle sobbing sways in the cool wind of March.

Perpetuo Socorro

On the wall, the image of the Virgen de San Juan, a pale rose background, grayish black outline, shines like silver in the dark. Bueli lights candles when Tino is so sick el Doctor del Valle, the doctor in Laredo, Mexico, fears he will die. He's only three. The illness has taken over. But Papi cries in front of another image of our Lady. It's a calendar from Cristo Rey Church with the image of Nuestra Señora del Perpetuo Socorro. He prays, he weeps, hits the wall

---

Perpetuo Socorro—Perpetual Aid

with his fists, like he would hit the mesquite tree in the backyard with his head sixteen years later like a wounded animal, mourning, in pain, that morning when Tino's death came to our door. But the child Tino survives the illness; the injections, the medication, the prayers, the remedios—something works, and Papi frames the calendar image in gold leaf, builds the image a repisita—a shelf for candles. In 1968, in his pain, tears running down his face, he'll talk to the image, "For this, you spared my son," he'll take the image down from its place on the wall, cannot bear to see it, to be reminded. On the wall, a rectangle of nothing, the color of the wallpaper Mami had hung for Tío Moy's last visit three years ago, like new—lines of green fern leaves on dusty beige. The votive candle on the tiny shelf still burning to an empty space.

Nun's Habit [excerpt]

At one time Tino could've been swayed into the priesthood. They tried, Brother Joseph, Father Jones, through Boy Scout camp, through altar boy solidarity, through jobs offered during the summer—jobs that paid wages that Papi paid for. How angry he was when he found out. Sometimes I'm sure Papi wonders what would've happened if Tino had gone to the seminary in high school. Would he have graduated, not gone to war, not been killed? Papi's guilt must've been tremendous. Must be why he blamed me. I, the oldest, the one who spoke English, why didn't I talk to my brother? He usually listened to me. I could've told him not to enlist, to wait till he finished high school, at least. Maybe then something else would've happened. Then Tino comes to say good-bye, I leave my desk in the back office where I work eight-to-five, come up front, and I don't know what to say. "Write," I mumble as I hug him good-bye. Papi, doesn't understand, I'm not to blame. Neither is he, nor Mami. He wants to blame someone. Everyone. And when the purple heart and other medals come with Tino's things, he has them framed, hangs them next to the faded photo of an Army uniformed seventeen-year-old, dreamy eyed, thin-lipped brown face, wearing pride like a badge.

---

remedios—home remedies

25 / TOMÁS M. CALDERÓN

Untitled

with their rice fields   burned
children   slaughtered
they stood a   vigil
         this is where our pig
         sty was
         my child was playing
         then came the bombs
         my child was killed
         the pigs still live
         what does a child know
         here is her skirt
         take this to nixon
         and ask him
         what does a child know
and another comrade saying
         if they burn our fields
         we will replant them
         and if they burn them again
         we will replant them again
         we will replant them
         again and again and again
         until victory is ours
with their rice fields   burned
children   slaughtered
they stood a   vigil
and   won.

26 / CARMEN TAFOLLA

La siembra

Some seeds are white and full,
well-cultivated, stored carefully,
too expensive to be fed to chickens
or thrown far to land by themselves out in the field.

Some seeds are dark and durable,
soft and red on the inside,
and used loosely, farmers thinking
there's plenty more where they came from.

Sad that they're so carefully separated.
You know, the hybrid could be
quite good.
And freedom finds its own,
without effort,
some seeds traveling in the wind,
on their own,
above farmers' intentions.

Jungles are strange gardens.
Sometimes they are defoliated
so they can be watered down good
con toda esa lluvia roja,
with all that red rain.
And all the seeds become rare together,
and each one just as valuable.

La siembra—The sowing

Sometimes you don't see the result
for a long while
but it's always there.
The maverick, germinating years later,
always leaves its mark.

Who knows what new plants will give
salsa picante and corn pone seeds
on former front lines?
Will it be black-eyed peas? Spinach greens?
Or corn to make masa for tamales?

Strange red rain of seeds—tossed so loosely—
with farmers thinking they could afford
to lose a few
or even a lot.

The leaves will sprout South Texas,
New Mexico, Harlem, Georgia—
Chicano leaves and Black leaves—
all over Viet Nam.
The land will have been
well watered.

Los Corts [excerpt]

Sí, entre, entre.

Usted es la que trabaja con el Padre Rodríguez. Pos la casa es humilde, pero
es suya. Para servirle, Teófila Hernández de Soto. Soto, ese fue mi esposo. Sí,
el de ese retrato allá—cuando éramos jovencitos—recién casados—nomás
teníamos el Benny Chuniar y la Lupita. Uh—y la Lupita ya es grande—ya
hasta se casó su hijo. Ese es, sí, ese en el T.V.—cuando fue su graduation de
jaiskul. Y esa bebita ay en la mesita es mi nieta la más reciente, pero allí nomás
tenía los tres años, y ahora fíjate qua ya tiene los siete. Sí, tengo mucha familia—digo, de los hijos y los nietos—porque ya de primos y de hermanos
ya casi todos se han muerto. De hijos y de hijas tengo muchos, y nunca me

dejan sola. Todos se han casado menos mijo el menor, Rudy (Rodolfo le puse, como mi hermano.) Ese es, el que está de uniforme de soldao. Sí, fue para Vietnam, y gracias a Dios, me lo mandaron bueno y sano otra vez. Nomás que me lo llevaron de muy muchacho y muy simpático y siempre sonriendo, y ahora a veces se me pone medio triste y se mete a pelear. Me dice que es porque le hacen menos y le insultan. Y dice que a veces es porque es Mexicano. Y yo le digo que más antes, fue peor, y que su papá también tuvo que defenderse, ha sido así por mucho tiempo, que no se enoje. Pero no puede hallar trabajo, y, a veces, yo entiendo y yo también me enojo, pero nomás aquí adentro. Aquí adentrito, y no le dijo a nadien.

(Yes, come in, come in. You're the one who works with Father Rodriguez. Well, my house is humble, but you're welcome. Teófila Hernández de Soto, at your service. Soto, that was my husband's name. Yes, the one in that portrait there—when we were young—newlyweds—we just had Benny Chuniar and La Lupita. Uh—now La Lupita is grown up—her son is even married. That's him, yes, the one on the TV—from his high school graduation. And the one on the table of that little baby is my newest granddaughter, but she was only three then and now, just imagine, she's seven. Yes, I have a big family—I mean, children and grandchildren—because almost all of my cousins and siblings are dead. I have a lot of children and they never abandon me. They've all married except my youngest son, Rudy (I named him Rodolfo after my brother). That's him, the one in the soldier's uniform. Yes, he went to Vietnam, and thank God he came back to me safe and sound. It's just that when they took him he was a young boy, very friendly and always smiling, and now sometimes he gets very sad and gets into fights. He tells me that it's because people treat him as inferior and insult him. And he says that sometimes it's because he's Mexican. And I tell him that it was worse before and that his father had to defend himself too, that it's been that way for a long time, that he shouldn't get angry. But he can't find a job and sometimes I understand and I get angry too, but just here inside. Here, way inside, and I don't say a thing about it to anyone.) *Translation by George Mariscal*

27 / Mushroom Montoya

"Too many targets, too high a body count"

I still keep a letter that I wrote to my brother John on his 17th birthday under my keyboard as a "memento" of my loss of innocence. I wrote to him on my first day on the gun line. On our first strike and our first of too many targets, too high a body count. The letter starts off innocently enough, "Happy Birthday, John! Your being 17 makes me feel old. The USS Trippe killed her first VC today. Somebody's mother's child is dead and, unfortunately, I was part of that. It makes me sick just to think about it . . . I can't tell you much though 'cause Mom's ears and eyes would hurt . . . Take care of yourself. Mushroom."

What I couldn't let my mother's eyes read is that on our very first strike, our very first shot, I watched three young men running on the beach carrying a wooden box. We fired! Screams, blood, body parts! Two of the young men got up and started running. Bam! Shoot number two. No screams, just body parts. I was looking through the Big Eyes. The gunner jumped down from the gun ecstatic over the news of his "better than perfect" score. I stood there, still in shock over what I had just witnessed. I looked him in the eye, and yelled, "How can you be happy? You just killed three guys! and you don't know for sure who they really were. You just killed THREE guys!" His eyes went wild as he screamed back, "Damn you, Mushroom! They are NOT people! They are just targets! If they were people, I couldn't do my job? Fuck you! Why did you have to go and spoil a perfect hit on a moving target?"

Too many targets, too high a body count.

Now my first-born son is dead. "And somebody's father's child is dead." He died in uniform, returning from lunch to the reserve center in Albuquerque, New Mexico. I wonder if those three boys were returning from lunch so many years ago on the shores of Vietnam. Now I have a glimpse of the pain we caused to the mothers and fathers of those young boys that we killed in Vietnam. Every night, in Vietnam, I used to pray and ask God to let me wake up from this nightmare and be back home. This HAD to be a nightmare, it couldn't possibly be real. But each time I woke up, the "nightmare" was still going on. Later, in 1978, while watching the fireworks, someone shot off white flares. For a small eternity, I was back in Vietnam. I was terrified that night. I was afraid that 1978 was a dream and that I would wake up on the ship and it would still be 1972.

Too many targets, too high a body count. I was unable to watch and enjoy fireworks without the weight and fear associated with the war until I went to the Vietnam Memorial in 1992. The Memorial caused a healing through many tears. I had my younger son take a photo of me pointing at the place where my name should have been. Part of me died in Vietnam. Part of all of us who were there died. We lost our innocence. We lost our sanity. We are plagued with ghosts that haunt us. We are all wounded too deeply from too many targets, too high a body count.

Part 2 / ¡Raza sí, guerra no!

INTRODUCTION

It is a little-known fact outside the Southwest that Chicanas and Chicanos organized some of the largest anti-war demonstrations of the late 1960s and early '70s. At the high point of the anti-war mobilization, between 20,000 and 30,000 people rallied on August 29, 1970, in Laguna Park in East L.A. The protest began peacefully with participants carrying signs in Spanish and English: "Traiga a mis carnales ahora" ("Bring my homeboys home now"), "A mí me dieron una medalla y $10,000 por mi único hijo" ("They gave me a medal and $10,000 for my only son"), "U.S. out of Vietnam." In the police riot that ensued, three people died: Lyn Ward, Angel Diaz, and Rubén Salazar, an *L.A. Times* reporter who had returned from assignments in Saigon and Mexico City and was writing investigative pieces exposing police brutality in the Chicano/Mexicano community.

News of the August 29 demonstration spread slowly across the country. The East Coast press paid little attention to the event, in essence reproducing police accounts of the clash between Chicanos and authorities. The *New York Times,* for example, ran a short piece on August 30 stating that 7,000 people had attended the rally and "five hundred policemen and Sheriff's deputies tried to break up roaming gangs."[1] Mexican newspapers such as *El Excelsior* and *Novedades,* published editorials on "La rebelión de los Chicanos" in which they astutely noted the role played by government agitators. Coincidentally, President Nixon was in Los Angeles the evening of August 29, attending a fundraiser on the Westside. Two days later, he received a telegram from Herman Sillas, chairman of the California State Advisory Committee to the U.S. Civil Rights Commission, asking for a meeting to discuss recent events. Sillas never received a reply. During the week that followed, smaller civil disturbances broke out across Southern California in Riverside, Barstow, and Wilmington.

The development of the Chicano anti-war movement followed the trajectory of other anti-war activities across the nation in that it greatly increased in intensity in the presidential election year of 1968. Regional leaders such as

Rodolfo "Corky" Gonzales, founder of the Crusade for Justice in Denver, and Reies Tijerina, organizer of the New Mexico land movement, had declared their opposition to Johnson's policy in 1967, but the Mexican American community remained relatively quiet on the issue. The early Chicano-organized demonstrations were small; a protest in the Mission district of San Francisco on Thanksgiving Day 1967 drew only 150 marchers. Several months later, however, Chicano magazines and journals were reporting on draft resistance and refusals of induction. In both Spanish and English, young Chicanos were urged to oppose the draft:

> Carnales, the government that seeks to induct you into military service is the same one that allows and promotes discrimination in employment, low wages for farm workers, one-sided and prejudicial educational programs, urban redevelopment, and a thousand other oppressive conditions. And then, they ask you to go defend and perpetuate this system with your life. ¿Qué creen que somos? [What do they think we are?] ¿BURROS? Those Gabachos even ask you to impose this system of oppression upon the people of Vietnam, Santo Domingo, Bolivia, and many other countries, as well as upon our own people.
>
> Hermanos, the peoples of those countries ARE NOT our enemies. Our enemies are the racists and greedy GABACHOS, and their Tacos, who grow richer every day on the sweat, tears, yes, and on the blood of chicanos, blacks, and other minorities. OUR WAR FOR FREEDOM IS HERE not in Viet Nam.[2]

In some cases, the attempt to sustain a class-based analysis of the war faltered under the pressure of racial and ethnic antagonisms. In an article "Why the Gringo Doesn't Like to Be Drafted," one writer complained: "Today, almost everyone who gets drafted goes to Vietnam and the chances are very good that he will get shot or killed. This still brings approval from the gringo, especially since he himself does not like being killed in such a stupid war."[3]

As Christian Appy has shown, in *Working-Class War: American Combat Soldiers & Vietnam* (1993), poor and working-class whites served and died in disproportionate numbers during the war. But there was a perception in minority communities that blacks and Latinos were even less likely to obtain deferments and that soldiers of color were often given more dangerous assignments. In a long meditation on the Chicano Movement composed in 1971, *tejano* poet Abelardo "Lalo" Delgado asked Mexican Americans to glance at any college campus in order to understand who was dying in Southeast Asia. "Even the peace movement," he argued, "without realizing or wanting to, has produced a hardship on Chicanos, since the Anglo kid refuses to go and goes to Canada or Sweden, or merely gets lost in the country, forcing draft boards to dig deeper into the Chicano communities, for quotas must be met, one way or another. I'm sure you have heard it said that even on the battle ground, a reverse discrimination does exist, by placing Chicanos on the front lines and protecting the 'güeros' [white kids] in the safe zones."[4] Delgado pointed out that Chicanos had long viewed the armed services as an escape from poverty and limited opportunity, but that young Chicanos no longer felt that way: "'Hell no, we won't go!' goes double for Chicanos."

By the early 1970s, the rhetoric of the Movement had become increasingly radical. Incisive analyses of the political economy of the war in Viet Nam linked Chicano issues to a critique of U.S. imperialism and to liberation movements around the world. In Nephtalí de León's play ¡Chicanos!: The Living and the Dead!, for example, the martyred Rubén Salazar (in the character of Manuel) is juxtaposed to Ché Guevara, who had been assassinated in 1967. The Ché character criticizes the efforts of Cesar Chavez, suggesting that under Chavez's leadership the farmworker has moved only from being a slave to being a slave with a contract. With regard to Viet Nam, one character declares: "As to the war, hermanos . . . we will no longer be cannon fodder for the materialist capitalists who are getting rich off the blood of Aztlán. Yes, we are a brave people, but we'll melt the medals we have won to throw back at them, hermanos."[5] The play closes with a call for armed insurgency as an act of self-defense. Throughout the Southwest, revolutionary groups such as the Communist Collective of the Chicano Nation, based in Albuquerque, echoed that call.[6]

In 1972 Lea Ybarra and Nina Genera produced La batalla está aquí (The battle is here), a bilingual pamphlet calling for an end to Chicano participation in the war and offering "legal ways to stay out of the military." Together with fellow UC Berkeley students Fernando Genera and María Elena Ramírez, Ybarra and Genera had been trained in anti-draft counseling by the American Friends Service. By 1969 they were advising young Chicanos in high schools and colleges throughout Northern California. Ybarra, who had eighteen cousins who served in Southeast Asia, recalls performing anti-war skits and reciting Daniel Valdez's popular "Corrido de Ricardo Campos":

You are dead, Richard Campos, you are gone
You are dead, and I bid you good-bye
But now that you're gone, there's a doubt in my mind
What would have happened if you never would have died?

Would they treat you the same?
Or send you on your way with a medal stuck in your hand
Saying "Thank you, boy, thank you very much,
You have paid your debt to Uncle Sam."

Now should a man
Should he have to kill
In order to live
Like a human being
In this country?[7]

Ybarra and Genera's pamphlet contained several graphic photographs of maimed and wounded Vietnamese children and asked readers: "What can you do to keep Chicanos from going to Viet Nam and killing or mutilating beautiful children? We only lose our men and our honor and pride by participating in or promoting the killing of thousands of men, women, and children" (p. 5).[8]

The text included a complete explanation of deferments and strategies for avoiding the draft as well as, in the section written in Spanish, the "Letter to the North American People from Vietnamese Catholics":

Aquellos que los EEUU acusan de comunistas son, en realidad, nuestros hermanos y hermanas, nuestros parientes y nuestros amigos. Ellos son campesinos y obreros quienes sólo piden una cosa: poder ganarse el pan con el sudor de su frente en un país libre de tropas extranjeras. . . . Nosotros compartimos con ustedes la fe en Cristo y les pedimos que en nombre de la religión que compartimos nos ayuden a parar esta guerra cruel.

(p. 34)

(Those whom the U.S. accuses of being communists are, in reality, our brothers and sisters, our relatives and our friends. They are peasants and workers who only request one thing: to be able to earn their daily bread by the sweat of their brow in a country free of foreign troops. . . . We share with you our faith in Christ and we ask in the name of the religion we share that you help us stop this cruel war.)

This appeal to the Chicano community's Catholicism as a source for anti-war activism was ironic given the Church's hawkish stance. But by 1970 the Church hierarchy was increasingly losing its grip on its Chicano parishioners. Texts such as Luis Valdez's "Pensamiento serpentino" (Reading 36) consciously refashioned Christian values in order to demonstrate how they might serve as a source of strength for political action at home, the key examples being Cesar Chavez's activism and the Vietnamese resistance.

Despite the radicalization of some segments of Chicano communities, their dominant institutions were either openly or tacitly pro-war. The leadership of the Catholic Church, which had no individuals of Mexican descent in its North American hierarchy, was inattentive to political changes taking place among Mexican Americans. In 1970 Católicos por la Raza—the Los Angeles–based reform movement—demanded that the Church express public support for ongoing struggles such as the farmworkers' boycotts and the anti-war movement. Cardinal McIntyre stated that the Church would remain "neutral" on the issue of the war, and the local Church hierarchy claimed to lack sufficient funding to provide support for such projects, although it had recently financed an opulent new church, St. Basil's, on the Westside. The Church's unresponsiveness was met by the Christmas Eve 1969 demonstration at St. Basil's and police riot described in the opening chapter of Oscar Zeta Acosta's novel *Revolt of the Cockroach People* (1973). McIntyre compared the Chicano demonstrators to the "rabble" at the crucifixion of Christ who should be forgiven "for they know not what they do."

Other Church officials were less abstruse, red-baiting the demonstrators as well-organized "revolutionaries." Despite the Church's avowed neutrality on the issue of the war, Church patriarchs exerted subtle pressure on individual parishioners and members of the clergy to support U.S. foreign policy.[9] McIntyre maintained close ties with the Nixon White House; Acosta referred to the cardinal as "the holy man who encouraged presidents to drop fire on poor Cockroaches in far-off villages in Vietnam."[10] In time, however, progressive clergy broke with official dogma and worked with organizations such as the UFW or formed groups such as Clergy and Laymen Concerned About Vietnam. This latter group included Puerto Rican Bishop Antulio Parrilla, who openly defied McIntyre a few days after the Christmas Eve violence by celebrating Mass at a vacant lot adjacent to St. Basil's with members of Católicos por la Raza and the primarily Anglo-led Coalition of Concerned Catholics.

Father John Luce, an Episcopalian pastor who had been an associate of organizer Saul Alinsky in New York, was active in virtually every aspect of the Chicano Movement. Father Luce brought his politically engaged message to East L.A. in 1955 and by the late 1960s was supporting efforts such as the Brown Berets (a grass-roots self-defense community organization based in East L.A.), the high school walk-outs, the production of *La Raza* newspaper, and Moratorium Committee activities. His Church of the Epiphany in Lincoln Heights was a meeting place for the most progressive elements of the community, especially every January on Día de los Reyes (Day of the Magi), which was often transformed into a combined religious celebration and political meeting.[11] Working with Father Luce was a dedicated group of activists that included Eliezer Risco, a former teaching fellow of Cuban descent at Stanford University's Bolívar House and co-chair of the Stanford Committee for Peace in Vietnam. In the mid-1960s Risco made the acquaintance of Luis Valdez, who convinced him to go to Delano to work with the United Farm Workers. By 1967 Risco was producing *La Raza* newspaper from Father Luce's basement and participating in a summer VISTA youth program that included Brown Beret founder David Sánchez and future film producer Moctezuma Esparza.[12]

The VISTA program in Laredo, Texas, served as an organizing base for John Dauer, an American Friends Service Committee member who by 1969 was directing anti-draft counseling projects on San Antonio's Westside. Dauer had himself refused induction into the military, and he saw San Antonio's five military bases and ten draft boards as prime targets for anti-war actions. Working with students from the Mexican American Youth organization (MAYO), the Student Non-violent Coordinating Committee (SNCC), and volunteers from liberal Jewish groups such as Women for Peace, Dauer orchestrated demonstrations to draw attention to the disproportionate number of Chicanos dying in Viet Nam; he also staged candlelight vigils and invited Rosalío Muñoz to speak on the progress of the Chicano anti-war movement in California. After successfully lobbying for the inclusion of Chicanos and Chicanas on local draft boards, Dauer's group established an "Alternative Recruiting Office" in the same building that housed official military recruiters; local authorities soon convinced the landlord to evict the draft counselors.[13]

Individual Roman Catholic priests and nuns often sympathized with the anti-war resistance. At the final demonstration organized by the Moratorium Committee, on January 30, 1971, for example, several contingents of multi-ethnic protesters converged on East Los Angeles from across Southern California. As the march passed Our Lady of Solitude Catholic church (La

Soledad) on Brooklyn Avenue, one group approached the building. A report in the *L. A. Times* described the priest's response:

> As they entered, the pastor, the Rev. Joseph M. Gamm, C.M.F., was praying for the safety of those taking part in the demonstration. Father Gamm saw the marchers at the rear of his crowded church—most of them young Chicano men, with a few girls, a few Anglos, and a few blacks mixed in. They carried knapsacks and a few had signs. The pastor halted his service and called the young people forward to the front of the church where they knelt as he gave them a special blessing and said: "Even if you have to suffer, remember that Christ suffered great injustice and yet he prayed for those at whose hands he suffered. When he was unjustly treated by the authorities in his day, he said, 'Father, forgive them, for they know not what they do.' Regardless of whatever pain and hurt you may endure, you must remember what he said and not hate those who inflict it upon you." There were tears in the pastor's eyes as the young people filed from his church.[14]

That Father Gamm uttered the same words Cardinal McIntyre had used in condemning the St. Basil demonstrators highlights the contradictions within the Catholic clergy during the war. Father Gamm's likening of the marchers to Christ and the marchers' willingness to receive the priest's blessing underscore the deep-seated traditional values of some segments of the Chicano Movement.

The United Farm Workers union, despite the Teatro Campesino's explicitly anti-war plays, was also riddled with contradictions with regard to the war. Many of the UFW's supporters were drawn from other unions, such as the Seafarers, where hawkish attitudes prevailed, and some UFW members equated patriotism with a pro-war stance. But the UFW's college student volunteers tended to have radical views. Cesar Chavez recalled several tense moments from early in the Movement: "When we started the strike, many volunteers were in and out. Some of the volunteers were for ending the Vietnam war above all else, and that shocked the workers because they thought that was unpatriotic. Once, when there was a group more interested in ending the war, I let them have a session with the farm workers. After a real battle, the volunteers came to me astounded. 'But they support the war!' they said. 'How come?' I told them farm workers are ordinary people, not saints."[15] Only through a concerted effort to prioritize political goals were such conflicts provisionally resolved so that fragile coalitions could survive.

When the U.S. Department of Defense supported the growers by purchasing scab grapes and lettuce, the UFW knew it had common cause with those who opposed the war. As the anti-war movement became increasingly confrontational, however, Chavez distanced himself from its tactical decisions. In an interview in 1970, he expressed his concern: "The real paradox here is that the people who advocate peace in Vietnam advocate violence in this country. Inconceivable; I don't understand it."[16] Nevertheless, several months later Chavez wrote to organizers of the August 29 Moratorium: "It is now clear to me that the war in Vietnam is gutting the soul of our nation. Of course we know the war to be wrong and unjustifiable, but today we see that it has destroyed the moral fiber of the people."[17] After the murder of Rubén Salazar, who had covered the farmworkers' march in May of the previous year, the UFW's official newspaper, *El Malcriado,* began to take a more openly anti-war stance on its editorial page.

Not surprisingly, mainstream Mexican American politicians condemned not only the more radical Chicano groups on the left but most of the student organizations as well. Representative Henry Gonzalez (D-Tex.), for example, criticized groups such as the Brown Berets and MAYO from the floor of the House, claiming that their critique of the dominant order was without substance and simply an act of mimicry: "We have those who cry 'brown power' only because they have heard 'black power' and we have those who yell 'oink' or 'pig' at police, only because they have heard others use the term. We have those who wear beards and berets, not because they attach any meaning to it, but because they have seen it done elsewhere."[18] Generational and political differences seem to have prevented Representative Gonzalez from understanding the sincere and often coherent strategies of the young Chicano protesters. While Gonzalez was willing to call for reforms aimed at benefiting Americans of Mexican descent, segments of the growing Chicano anti-war movement were intent on restructuring the entire system that had produced disastrous conditions for poor people of color at home and the debacle of U.S. involvement in Viet Nam.

The war was also a contentious issue for the American GI Forum, the most influential Mexican American veterans' organization in the country. Founded in 1948 in Corpus Cristi, Texas, to work on the issues of veterans' medical care and benefits, the GI Forum throughout the early 1960s had supported almost every progressive cause affecting Latino communities and had been instrumental in the electoral successes of Democrats on both the local and national levels. The Viet Nam War, however, put the GI Forum in the awkward situation of choosing between an anti-war position, perceived by many Forum members to be an anti-troops position and therefore unacceptable, and a hawkish stance toward an increasingly unpopular enterprise.

As party stalwarts, a large majority of Forum members supported the Johnson administration's policies and only reluctantly detached themselves from Nixon's policy under pressure from returning Chicano veterans. When the executive board of the Mexican American Political Association (MAPA) proposed to condemn the war as early as 1966, GI Forum members were instrumental in blocking the initiative. The argument that to criticize Johnson's foreign policy was to criticize Chicano/Mexican GIs was persuasive and divided the membership of the Forum, MAPA, and similar organizations.[19] Finally, in June 1970, the California state chapter of the Forum approved a resolution opposing the war and supporting the National Chicano Moratorium Committee's events in August. At its twenty-third annual convention the following year, the national organization unanimously passed a resolution calling for U.S. withdrawal from Southeast Asia; the resolution had originated in the Viet Nam veteran–led Forum chapter of Colton, California.[20]

Within the military services, a growing GI resistance movement conducted various anti-war activities in Viet Nam, on bases in the United States and Europe, and on board naval vessels at sea. The participation of Chicano GIs in this movement has not been documented, but at least some Chicanos were involved through the many GI anti-war organizations in the Southwest that maintained close contact with local Chicano communities. At Fort Bliss, Texas, and at Camp Pendleton, California, for example, groups such as GIs for Peace and Movement for a Democratic Military (MDM) mounted large demonstrations in late 1969 and throughout 1970. From its inception, MDM was a multi-ethnic coalition. The anti-war newspaper *Right on Post,* published at Fort Ord, California, ran letters from the local Chicano community such as the following in which the author, identified as a "Chicana Sister," speaks of her husband who had died recently in Viet Nam:

> Not only did he die for nothing, but he fought and killed in the name of a government that has shamed and discriminated against our race for over two hundred years. This same government that robbed our land and kept us slaves to work his fields. The same government that won't allow our children to speak our language in his racist schools. The same government that denied us our rights as human beings.
>
> (*Right on Post,* August 1970)

Letters expressing similar sentiments from Chicano servicemen were published in various Movement journals (Readings 41 and 42). There, as elsewhere, opposition to the war was often linked to the need to address such historic problems as racism and police violence. The American Serviceman's Union, founded by Andrew Stapp in 1967, listed among its demands "the right of black- and brown-skinned servicemen and women to determine their own lives free from the oppression of any racist whites. No troops to be sent into black or Spanish-speaking communities" (*The Bond,* December 16, 1970). On June 4, 1969, Latino GIs participated in the revolt against military police brutality in the Fort Dix stockade; in November 1971, contingents of servicemen in the Houston area participated in both a local peace rally and a Chicano-led protest against police violence.[21]

The National Chicano Moratorium Committee

By 1967 the Mexican American community in Los Angeles had produced at least one organization publicly opposed to the war. The Comité por la paz, chaired by Gil García and composed of members of the East Los Angeles Peace Center, complemented the openly dovish position taken by Congressman Ed Roybal. In a community about to explode over a range of long-simmering issues such as police brutality and educational reform, the National Chicano Moratorium Committee (NCMC) took shape. Two of the key figures were Ramses Noriega, a UCLA student from Mexicali who had gained organizing experience with Cesar Chavez in the Coachella Valley, and Rosalío Muñoz, active in student reform at UCLA and elected student-body president in 1968 (with Noriega as campaign manager). Noriega was a member of the United Mexican American Students (UMAS), and he and Muñoz had been active in United Farm Workers' demonstrations as well as anti-draft counseling.

After a long and arduous soul searching, which included consulting with Chicano/a leaders up and down California, Muñoz decided to refuse induction into the U.S. military.[22] On September 16, 1969, taking as his model Emile Zola's "J'accuse," Muñoz spoke to a large gathering in downtown Los Angeles:

> Today, the sixteenth of September, the day of independence for all Mexican peoples, I declare my independence of the Selective Service System.

I accuse the government of the United States of America of genocide against the Mexican people. Specifically, I accuse the draft, the entire social, political, and economic system of the United States of America of creating a funnel which shoots Mexican youth into Viet Nam to be killed and to kill innocent men, women, and children.[23]

Muñoz and Noriega's activities coincided with the increasingly anti-war agenda of the Brown Berets, a community self-defense group with chapters throughout the Southwest. David Sánchez, prime minister of the Berets, had moved the organization toward an anti-war position in the summer of 1968. In the initial stages of the fledgling NCMC, he served as co-chair with Muñoz and contributed his extensive knowledge of grass-roots politics in L.A. The organizing efforts of Sánchez, Muñoz, and Noriega; women Berets such as Gloria Arellanes and Hilda Reyes; former *L.A. Times* reporter Roberto Elias; and established lobbying groups—including the Congress of Mexican American Unity (CMAU) and Jewish foundations from L.A.'s Westside— forged the Moratorium Committee into a potent political force. Its message was neither separatist nor ideologically Marxist: its first march and demonstration, on December 20, 1969, for example, was held at the Five Points monument in East L.A., honoring World War II veterans, and at Eugene Obregón Park, a site named after the Chicano Korean War Veteran. Among the issues that concerned the NCMC were the farmworkers' struggle, educational issues, police brutality, and international solidarity with third world peoples.[24] The first of several historic marches included representatives of the Mexican American Youth Organization (a Texas-based student group), the Welfare Rights Organization, chapters of the Movimiento Estudiantil Chicano de Aztlán (MEChA), Católicos por la Raza, the United Farm Workers, LUCHA (an organization of Chicano *pintos,* or former prison inmates), Brown Beret contingents from across California, students from all local campuses, and members of the Puerto Rican Young Lords (see Reading 45). Cesar Chavez sent a message of "100% support," and El Teatro Popular de la Vida y Muerte from Long Beach, California, performed an anti-war, anti-machismo play.

As a broad-based coalition, the Moratorium was fractured by tensions among its member organizations. At one point the leaders of the Brown Berets, for example, despite their earlier support, withdrew from the coalition and criticized alliances with what they labeled "communist-infiltrated" organizations like Students for a Democratic Society (SDS). Those more interested in cultural nationalism than in broad-based coalition-building worried that Chicano issues would be subordinated to other agendas such as those of the anti-war movement, the "Anglo" ideology of socialism, or "third world" internationalism. The NCMC also was attacked from the left by groups such as the Socialist Workers Party and the Progressive Labor Party for "retreating" after the events of August 29.

Throughout the period, the Chicano anti-war mobilizations were in uneasy juxtaposition to traditional manifestations of Mexican American patriotism. On January 31, 1970, for example, a "War Moratorium" was held in San Bernardino, California, by the local chapter of the American GI Forum. Calling the support-the-troops event "a day of remembrance for Chicano Dead in Viet Nam," organizers appropriated the term "moratorium" from the anti-war NCMC and even used the artwork that had adorned the poster announcing the NCMC's demonstration a month earlier. But the GI Forum rejected the language of the NCMC's poster, which had included phrases such as "The death pits of Viet Nam," "March Against Death," and "Bring all our Carnales home . . . alive!" Instead, the bilingual text in the advertisement for the San Bernardino event "honored" Chicano servicemen and included the following request:

> Necesitamos que haya una muestra de interés y patriotismo por parte de todos nuestros conciudadanos en esta junta, que será una demonstración de agradecimiento a nuestros hijos, nuestros hermanos y nuestros esposos que participan, participarán y que murieron en la guerra de Viet Nam. Demuestra su patriotismo y agradecimiento participando en persona.
>
> (*El Chicano,* San Bernardino, January 12, 1970)

> (We need for there to be a show of interest and patriotism by our fellow citizens at this gathering which will be a demonstration of gratitude for our sons, our brothers, and our husbands who are participating and will participate and who have died in the war in Viet Nam. Show your patriotism and thanks by attending in person.)

The rhetoric of sacrifice and duty in the GI Forum's message reminds us of how difficult it was for activists to express opposition to the war without being accused of being insensitive to Chicano GIs and their families.

At the same time, the Moratorium was the subject of harassment and infiltration by the LAPD and federal agencies. As police chief Ed Davis put it: "The American Revolution is not going to start in the city of Los Angeles." [25]

Across the country, near hysteria in official circles was exacerbated by several incidents during the spring and summer of 1970: On May 4 four students were killed and nine wounded by Ohio National Guardsmen called in to disperse an anti-war demonstration; on May 9 some 100,000 people attended a demonstration in Washington, D.C., to protest the Kent State massacre; on May 14 two students were killed and nine wounded at Jackson State College (Mississippi) by police officers in events seemingly unrelated to the anti-war movement; on August 24 a graduate student was killed when a bomb that had been planted by anti-war activists exploded in the Army Math Research Center at the University of Wisconsin at Madison.

Similar events in Los Angeles did not make national headlines, but they attracted the full attention of the LAPD. The day after the killings at Kent State, police attacked demonstrators at a rally at UCLA, and Chicano faculty and students were singled out for violent treatment; on August 8 the NCMC organized a march of five hundred people (known as "La Marcha de los Muertos") in protest of the police killing of two young Chicano brothers three weeks earlier. On August 12, two mess halls were firebombed at Fort Ord, California, reportedly the work of "Black radicals." According to most police informers, a top priority of law enforcement agencies was to disrupt coalitions between Chicano and African American organizations, fearing the formation of a broad-based movement, potentially global in nature, organized and led by poor people of color.[26]

L.A. Times reporter Rubén Salazar believed that President Nixon had taken an interest in the events in Los Angeles because they constituted the most serious anti-war activities to date by a working-class minority community. On the eve of the August 29 march, Salazar met with community leaders to warn them of police and FBI provocateurs who, according to his sources, were planning to incite a violent confrontation with demonstrators. Less than twenty-four hours later, Salazar was dead.[27] Police reports claimed that Salazar had been struck accidentally by a tear gas projectile and killed instantly as he sat at the bar in the Silver Dollar Cafe. Eyewitness accounts, however, suggested that Salazar and others were forced to remain in the cafe, that he survived the initial blow, and that he was found dead only after police had sealed off the building for five hours.

The murder of Rubén Salazar overshadowed the deaths of Lyn Ward, a fifteen-year-old Brown Beret, and Angel Diaz, a passing motorist. As a well-known television personality who had taken on an increasingly activist role in the community, Salazar came to be identified not so much with the issue of the war but with the problem of police brutality against Mexican Americans. Remembering Salazar, *tejano* poet Abelardo Delgado wrote: "Death came to one of the highest of our Chicano assets, a brother who spoke the truth so honestly and with such eloquence, Rubén Salazar, hombre maduro [a mature man] . . . victim of the white man's violence that he so well hides with his own concept of law." Nephtalí de León remembered: "Fue periodista—un hombre de letras quien sacudió la nación un día cuando gritó con orgullo ¡Chicano!" ("He was a journalist—a man of letters who one day shook the nation when he shouted with pride: Chicano!") Roberto Vargas wrote: "It seems . . . just the other day / 6 million Chicanos offered their cactus / And cried chale no we won't go / The Alamo is alive and falling / in L.A. Remember the Salazars / And Chente . . . (Chicano Power   Chicano Power)."[28] The deaths of three Chicanos on August 29, however, did not register with the national media the way the events at Kent State had. With the exception of Enrique López's article in *The Nation* (Reading 49), most of the commentaries appeared in small media outlets and were written by those who had known Salazar personally (Reading 48).[29]

After the tragic events of August 29, the traditional September 16 parade to celebrate Mexican Independence Day was canceled by its organizers, who cited the new city curfew and the fear of further violence. NCMC leaders, however, urged the organizers—the Comité Cívico Patriótico—to proceed with the parade and agreed to march as a separate contingent, although they did not support all the participating organizations. In perhaps one of the most surreal moments of the Chicano anti-war movement, Moratorium members marched in a parade that included Democratic politician Jesse Unruh, beauty queens, Mexican *charros* (cowboys), a U.S. Navy recruiters' float, and a Marine Corps color guard.[30] Around 7 P.M. violent clashes between police and demonstrators began along Atlantic Boulevard and at the East Los Angeles City College campus. Three people were wounded by gunshots, a hundred were injured, and sixty-eight were arrested. In response, U.S. Senator Alan Cranston (D-Calif.), with the assistance of Board of Education member Julian Nava, facilitated an unofficial meeting between local business leaders and Chicano/a spokespeople. From the point of view of local activists, the meeting accomplished nothing.

In the fall of 1970, Moratorium offices were repeatedly raided without warrants by the LAPD; workers were harassed and threatened at gunpoint. On November 14 three young volunteers—Antonio Uranda, Juan Reyes, and Roberto Flores—were beaten severely by police and charged with "felonious assault on a police officer." Such raids were often coordinated by government agents. One Chicano informant, Eustacio "Frank" Martínez, an agent of the Bureau of Alcohol, Tobacco, and Firearms, was known to have infiltrated five separate Chicano organizations including the Moratorium Committee and the Brown Berets.[31] His infiltration of the Moratorium Committee began with his accusing Rosalío Muñoz of being insufficiently radical and ended with the establishment of what in essence was a parallel committee. (After breaking ties with the Committee early in 1971, Martínez infiltrated La Casa del Carnalismo in order to gather information on the Chicano Liberation Front.)

Demonstrations early in 1971—on January 9 in downtown L.A. and January 31 on the Eastside—also turned violent, with numerous injuries and heavy property damage. The latter demonstration and march included clashes between Brown Berets and members of the Progressive Labor Party, and resulted in the death of Gustav Montag, a twenty-four-year-old Austrian student who had been attending East Los Angeles City College. Although sheriff's deputies denied having fired live rounds into the crowd, eyewitness accounts suggest they did and thus were likely responsible for Montag's death (see Reading 57). Three deputies were dismissed from the department for using excessive force.

Despite the increasingly repressive police tactics, Chicana/o youth remained committed to the cause. As eighteen-year-old Joey García, a member of the Santa Barbara–based Teatro de la Esperanza, wrote in a brief *acto* addressed to a police officer: "With a gun on your side / you walk so tall. / But I know you're afraid / 'cause you can't kill us all. / So just go away, until another day, / When we shall meet face to face / Once again, / At the moratorium."[32]

The mounting police-instigated violence also moved a large segment of older Mexican Americans, the parents and grandparents of the '60s generation, into the ranks of the Chicano Movement. Decades of repressed rage—the product of racism, redlining, job discrimination, and daily harassment directed against Mexicans in Los Angeles—now came to the surface, and Salazar was viewed as only the most recent of a long column of people of Mexican descent whose lives had been tragically cut short. As the poet Ricardo Sánchez put it: "Think of Rubén Salazar—whom we got to know . . . most importantly, debemos de pensar de otros chicanos muertos aún en guerras de gavachos peleando al otro lado del mar por causas que nomás enriquecen al gringo" ("we should think about other dead Chicanos, even now in white men's wars, fighting overseas for causes that only make the gringo rich").[33] In literature and art, the figure of Rubén Salazar continues to be an important icon of the Latino struggle for equality.

After the violence of January 30, 1971, traditional Mexican American organizations began speaking publicly against the Moratorium Committee. Anti-war demonstrations continued through 1972, but Moratorium leaders like Rosalío Muñoz (who was cleared of draft evasion charges that year) moved on to other issues, such as urban redevelopment and police brutality. As the issues of the draft and Viet Nam slowly receded, the Moratorium's potential for a wide-ranging critique of U.S. society remained unrealized. The legacy of Committee-organized events, however, continued to influence the next generation of Chicano/a writers and artists (Readings 54, 55, and 56).

The fate of the Moratorium Committee must be seen as part of the process by which progressive agendas, with their attendant analyses of the political economy, imperialism, and class relations, have been systematically sabotaged in minority communities, thereby opening up a space for uncontested ethnic nationalisms. Gerald Horne's work on the African American left is instructive on this issue: "The use of regressive nationalism as a tool against the Left is one of the oldest of elite tactics. Regressive nationalism serves to distance, for example, African Americans from potential allies. As blacks are mostly working-class, this translates into difficulties in building working-class organizations to resist the entreaties of capital. It can also be a barrier on campuses."[34] Socialist programs in the Mexican American community have faced the additional obstacles of persistent Cold War rhetoric, in which "socialist" equals "un-American," as well as the widely shared misconception that socialism means the end of upward mobility and the so-called American Dream. For an ethnic minority group struggling to fit in and survive economically, a poorly understood socialism poses more danger than promise, despite the fact that the group's situation is to a great extent a direct result of its exploitation as a source of inexpensive labor.

The importance of the "nationalist moment" in any minority movement is undeniable; to dismiss it as a mere symptom of "alienation," as was done by some Marxist thinkers during the Viet Nam era, is certainly counterproductive. Yet any movement that remains frozen within issues of ethnic pride and ethnic origins is condemned to marginality. The broader strategic question remains, Do those ideologies that appeal to large segments of the Chicano community—ethnic pride, indigenous origins, Aztlán (homeland)—in the long run serve the status quo?

The unfortunate dichotomy of "either Chicano or Marxist" split the Movement into two factions that continue to limit the range of Chicano politics and cultural criticism today. The National Moratorium Committee that appeared in Los Angeles during the early 1990s, for example, had a much narrower focus than its predecessor. What Horne calls "regressive nationalism" replaced a multiculural coalition devoted to diverse national and international issues. During a period of political retrenchment and economic downsizing, Spanish-speaking communities found it more difficult than ever to identify allies outside their own *familia* in order to formulate an inclusive definition of social justice. By the mid-1990s, ultra-nationalist groups such as the Chicano Mexicano Mexica Empowerment Committee proselytized for a "return" to indigenous origins and the "warrior" values of pre-Columbian Mexico.

Abajo con los machos

The structures of experience I have identified so far suggest a necessary linkage among diverse communities of color as well as a rethinking of the category "white" along economic and class lines. But because any interrogation of "whiteness" is both complex and traditionally taboo in official academic discourse, critical works on representations of the war have focused elsewhere, most notably on gender. The critique of masculinity and the connections between war, violence, and patriarchy are important to an understanding of what occurred in Viet Nam and its aftermath. But to read the war solely as a "masculine problem" is to simplify a complex series of issues. Literary critics who speak of "oedipal" and "preoedipal" phases pathologize individual GIs and deploy a form of soft psychoanalysis against soldiers of color, who are portrayed as being "pre-linguistic" or undersocialized. This kind of analysis comes dangerously close to reproducing traditional racist stereotypes and rhetoric.

Analyses that mistakenly identify violent behavior as an essential quality of "masculinity" or pretend to find its extreme forms within a particular ethnic group are reductionistic. A more productive strategy might be to expose the ways in which overtly patriarchal representations of women are the result of a heavily gendered language that permeated (and continues to saturate) the fabric of U.S. society. Notice, for example, the stereotypes of good woman/bad woman and manly/unmanly man in Lyndon Johnson's description of how the war had undermined his domestic programs:

I knew from the start that I was bound to be crucified either way I moved. If I left the woman I really loved—the Great Society—in order to get involved with that bitch of a war on the other side of the world, then I would lose everything at home. . . . [And if I abandoned the war], there would be Robert Kennedy out in front leading the fight against me, telling everyone that I had betrayed John Kennedy's commitment to South Vietnam. That I had let a democracy fall into the hands of the Communists. That I was a coward. An unmanly man. A man without a spine.[35]

For common infantrymen, especially for working-class GIs of color, the pressures to be a man were severe. As the narrator in Joe Rodríguez's *Oddsplayer* explains, in discussing the African American character Hendricks: "People told you who to be. Be a nigger. Be a soldier. Be a man. The brothers on the street wanted him one way. The Marines another. Everyone wanted a tough guy who asked no questions. If you were yourself, they called you weak" (p. 103). Here, the prescribed codes of masculine behavior, which permeate social and gender relations at every level of daily life, require a young man not to be himself.

A tentative analysis of Chicano masculinity and the uses to which it was being put by the U.S. military was undertaken during the late 1960s. In an exploratory meeting of the founders of the Raza Unida Party in November 1969, Corky Gonzales identified the link between one form of masculinity and military service:

We have to understand that liberation comes from self-determination, and to start to use the tools of nationalism to win over our barrio brothers, to win over the brothers who are still believing that machismo means getting a gun and going to kill a communist in Vietnam because they've been jived about the fact that they will be accepted as long as they go get themselves killed for the gringo captain.[36]

From inside Folsom State prison, Joseph Arellano published an essay on the "victims of machismo," the young Chicano men who too eagerly volunteered for service in Viet Nam. Arellano wanted his readers to understand that machismo contained both negative and positive characteristics:

MACHISMO—we all know it is a quality of manhood that runs deep in our culture. We see it all around us, in the courts and with authority figures, our men never asking for a break because it runs against our grain.

Machismo is expressed in our foot-stomping music, in our lusty folk songs, now in our vengeful grito of Viva Zapata! Viva la revolución! But perhaps it is also machismo that accounts for many of our brothers not returning from World War II, Korea—and now the war in Vietnam.

Let us look at machismo, both its good and bad points. Where should we use good judgement instead of machismo? When should we demand our rights?

Machismo can be used, and is being used against us by those who know that the macho in us will not say no to "special assignments," "patrol duty," and so forth—in other words, the infamous bogged-down war in Southeast Asia. They know how to spot machismo and put us up against larger forces that they themselves will not face.[37]

In addition to the claim that the U.S. government was consciously manipulating and exploiting aggressive forms of Latino masculinity, Arellano's most forceful assertion is his contrast of traditional machismo and "good judgement." With an ironic point of view and sarcastic ending, Ben Reyes's poem "Juan Carlos González" (Reading 39) makes a similar point. The community that sends young men off to die may not understand what those men have died for, but it knows they are real men. Within the Chicano community, the examination of violent forms of masculinity continued as a subterranean discourse throughout the 1970s and developed into a full-fledged critique in the 1980s. Chicana writers, in particular, analyzed the ways in which certain aspects of the Movimiento, especially narrow nationalism, had subjugated women to traditional forms of patriarchy. Once these themes were picked up by revisionist historians and academic "theorists" in the field of Chicano studies, however, the entire Movement was broadly painted as sexist and "essentialist," an approach that blurred diverse political stances and erased the internal debates on gender relations that had taken place in many organizations.

Historians and theorists have also ignored the Christian-Gandhian rejection of "warrior masculinity" mounted by Cesar Chavez: "I am convinced that the truest act of courage, the strongest act of manliness is to sacrifice ourselves for others in a totally non-violent struggle for justice. To be a man is to suffer for others. God help us to be men!"[38] Casting aside the traditional figures of Mexicano/Chicano masculinity—the inherited figures of the Aztec warrior, the revolutionary, the pachuco, and the cholo—Chavez advocated non-violent tactics and passive resistance in the face of violent Teamsters, hostile police, and grower-instigated assassination plots.

Male leaders predominated in Chicano activist groups of the late 1960s and early '70s, but leadership roles were also filled by women, the best known of whom were Dolores Huerta, Elizabeth Martinez, and Alicia Escalante. Women's organizations included the Comisión Femenil Mexicana, founded in Sacramento in 1970 "in order to terminate exclusion of female leadership"; the women Brown Berets; the Chicana Forum, founded by women in 1971 in Southern California in order to foster "an open discussion and communication of our own roles and men's roles, and to create political awareness"; and Mujeres por la Raza, whose conference in Houston in 1971 attracted hundreds of Chicana feminists. In 1971 Chicana anti-war activists met with North Vietnamese women in Vancouver.

Early Chicana feminist writers include Francisca Flores, Ana Nieto Gómez, Marta Cotera, and Enriqueta Longeaux y Vásquez.[39] In Movement periodicals Chicanas often wrote on the topic of women's rights. As early as 1969, articles such as Rosa Martinez's "Women Still Powerless" (*El Machete,* East Los Angeles City College, October 2, 1969) appeared in local newspapers. In April 1971 *Hijas de Cuauhtemoc,* a collection of poetry published in Long Beach, California, explicitly raised the issue of gender relations in the Movement. Sara Estrella wrote:

> Yo despierto los días
> llorando, llorando.
> Y hombre no sabes
> porque yo lloro.
> Es porque no me dejas
> ayudarte, ayudarte.
> ¿Por qué no me dejas?
> ¿Tienes miedo Chicano?
>
> (*Hijas de Cuauhtemoc* 1 [April 1971]:11)

> (I awake every day crying, crying. And you don't know why I cry.
> It's because I want to help you, help you. Why don't you let me?
> Are you afraid, Chicano?)

An unsigned poem in the same collection makes a more forceful point about the need for Chicano men to reflect on the harm inflicted by patriarchy and traditional gender roles:

Chicano, dices que naciste para ser libre
Yo también nací para ser libre, pero de qué me sirve
De tu libertad eres dueño y de mi libertad eres extraño.
Chicano, te quiero con todo el alma, pero me has hecho daño.

Através de los años en reina me has encarnado,
Y te lo juro, que de esta ilusión me he enamorado
Chicano te quiero con todo el alma, pero me has hecho daño.

Tus lisonjas la mente me han oscurecido
Porque ahora comprendo que en esclavitud me has tenido
Chicano te quiero con todo el alma, pero me has hecho daño.

Te has convencido que en mi cabeza no hay lugar para la inteligencia
El sentimiento que tengo, Chicano, es que te lo he creído por tu
     insistencia
Chicano te quiero con todo el alma, pero me has hecho daño.

Chicano, a pisotear tu machismo no vengo
Sino a que reconozcas que las buenas ideas las tengo
Chicano te quiero con todo el alma, pero me has hecho daño.

¡Quiero gritar mi coraje contra esta opresión!
Y aunque tu quieras o no, tomaré parte en la decisión
Chicano te quiero con todo el alma, pero me has hecho daño.

Ahora, Chicano, la mano te pido,
Que juntos a pelear por la causa aspiro.
Chicano, te quiero con todo el alma, pero ya no me harás daño.

(Chicano, you say you were born to be free. I too was born to be
free, but what good does it do me if you assert your freedom but
do not recognize mine. Chicano, I love you with all my heart, but
you have done me harm. Throughout the years you have turned
me into a queen, and I admit that I have fallen for that illusion.
Chicano . . . Your flattery has clouded my mind because now I understand you've kept me enslaved. Chicano . . . You're convinced
that there's no space in my head for intelligence. My feeling, Chicano, is that I have believed you because you insisted on it. Chicano . . . Chicano, I do not come to trample your machismo but

only to make you recognize that I have good ideas. Chicano . . .
I want to shout out in anger against this oppression! And whether
you approve or not, I will take part in the decisions. Chicano . . .
Now, Chicano, I ask that you give me your hand, for I hope to
struggle with you for the Cause. Chicano, I love you with all my
heart, but you will no longer do me harm.)

The shift in the final refrain signifies the end of the Chicana's complicity with
patriarchy. In asserting women's equality and willingness to participate fully
in the Movement, the contributors to *Hijas de Cuauhtemoc* initiated an important new stage in the development of Chicana feminism.

Among the Chicanas in key positions with the Moratorium Committee
in Los Angeles, Ramona Tovar and Irene Tovar were exemplary figures. The
Tovar sisters were born in the Boyle Heights section of East Los Angeles and
raised in the San Fernando Valley. By the late 1960s Irene Tovar was a member of the Urban Coalition and on the board of directors of the Chicano Legal Defense Fund, having been active in a variety of community causes including educational reform. At the time that the Moratorium Committee was
forming, both women were conducting anti-draft counseling for young Chicanos, and they eagerly joined Rosalío Muñoz and David Sánchez in their efforts. On the eve of August 29, Ramona was the chair of the San Fernando
chapter of the Moratorium Committee charged with housing the Texas dele-
gation; Irene organized the pre-march breakfast held in Las Palmas park. After the police riot, during which Ramona and many others were maced, Irene
was in charge of posting bail for those who had been arrested and she co-
chaired a press conference with Muñoz. Like many Moratorium members, the
Tovar sisters were harassed by the LAPD and arrested without cause.

Katarina Davis del Valle was also an important organizer. Raised in South
Central Los Angeles by a Mexican mother and an African American father,
she became involved in the United Farm Workers' struggle while in high
school and conducted draft counseling as a student at the University of Red-
lands. On moving to East L.A., she joined Gloria Chavez, Gloria Arellanes (a
former Brown Beret), and other women who were working out of Moratorium offices on Brooklyn Avenue. She attended the Denver Youth Conference
in March 1970 and was an organizer for the 1971 Vancouver meeting between
Chicanas and North Vietnamese women. During preparations for the August
29 protest, Davis del Valle received a telegram of support and congratula-
tions addressed to the Moratorium Committee from Ho Chi Minh and the

National Liberation Front.[40] The contributions of the Tovars, Davis del Valle, Arellanes, and other Chicanas have yet to be fully chronicled; they are owed a tremendous debt of gratitude for their efforts to achieve economic and social justice.

But there is no denying that the Movement was founded on patriarchal structures. *Con Safos* and other Movement journals published sexist materials, and the anti-war chapters of the GI Forum sponsored beauty contests; "Miss Aztlán" contests were staged as late as 1971 by MEChA chapters in Los Angeles. Despite Irene Tovar's experience as an organizer, she was rarely given official tasks beyond that of recording secretary. For her part, Katarina Davis del Valle recalls very little sexist behavior within Moratorium leadership circles; she was assigned important positions early on and was in charge of security for the August 29 demonstration. The Movement's masculinist structures must, of course, be understood in historical context and as products of an early if not altogether pre-feminist moment. Nevertheless, certain emerging structures of experience, visible by the mid-1970s, critiqued any social analysis that excluded issues of gender. The poet and critic Alurista, for example, who was one of the Movement figures most often singled out in the late 1980s and early '90s for having proposed a narrow vision of *carnalismo,* or masculinist codes, had spoken of a multifaceted cultural criticism as early as 1975:

> De modo que hay cuatro contradicciones verdaderamente, que podríamos denominar: de sexo, de raza, de clase y, digamos, la filosófica o cosmológica. . . . Y hay que voltear, hay que mover, hay que terminar la relación de dominación que existe entre el hombre y la mujer, entre las caras pálidas y los pueblos de color, entre aquellos pueblos que poseen para vivir y viven para poseer y aquellos que trabajan para vivir.[41]

> (So there are really four contradictions that we can delineate: gender, race, class, and, let's call it, the philosophical or cosmological. . . . And one must turn, one must move, one must end the relation of domination that exists between men and women, between the pale faces and peoples of color, between those nations that possess in order to live and live in order to possess and those that labor in order to live.)

Alurista's invocation of race, class, and gender prefigures the critical "holy trinity" of categories that in the early 1990s would come to characterize the hegemonic academic cultural studies model in the United States.

The dominant method for reading representations of the war through the category of gender is exemplified by the work of Susan Jeffords. The failure to win the war "demasculinized" American culture, she argues; postwar literary and cinematic representations "remasculinized" the culture. She writes: "In that 'separate culture' [of war], one that seems to strip away other forms of social relations such as class, race, ethnicity, sexuality, geographical background, age, and education, the laws that define relations of dominance can be foregrounded and tested, in balder and more simplistic terms than would apply within the larger society."[42] But the assumption that power relations in wartime will necessarily lead to a strengthening of patriarchy and racism is misguided. "Remasculinization" is never a simple return to an earlier state but is most often a complex renegotiation of gender, class, and ethnic identities. The contradictions made visible in moments of extreme fear or confusion may also generate dissenting points of view that pierce the screen of false consciousness and lay the groundwork for a political analysis, a political analysis that may be (and in many cases was) turned into praxis on the home front.

The process of demystifying traditional "warrior" forms of masculine behavior was especially important to returning Chicano veteran-writers. New Mexico poet Leroy Quintana, for example, ends his collection of poems on Viet Nam with "An Open Letter to President Bush" written during the Persian Gulf War:

Perhaps if you
knew how much,
how much
I wept,
these past months,
so full of rage, another war.
Perhaps if you
knew that our son
almost died in infancy, twice;
his mother and I do not want
him harmed; you cannot
have him, another war.
Perhaps if you
knew how much
I prayed all through Catholic school,
but never like that day,
the VC so close, we trembled

uncontrollably in the mud, another war,
Perhaps if you
had seen Cookie,
who carried a metal-covered Bible
next to his heart, break down
and cry unashamedly in the chopper,
at the end of that day, another war,
Perhaps if you
met my daughters;
one has long, elegant fingers,
a *lunar* [beauty mark] near her upper lip; the
other,
large dark eyes, sprawling eyelashes;
50,000 body bags ordered, another war,
Perhaps if you,
then perhaps
you might not
make war
seem so unbelievably easy.[43]

Quintana's response to George Bush's corporate-driven adventurism through the lens of his own Viet Nam experience, and with his children as intermediaries, captures the anger or rage that precedes any political action. In a poem written after the bombing of the U.S. Marine barracks in Lebanon in 1983, Trinidad Sánchez asks "Why do we not honor / those that believe / in justice and peace, / those that have refused / to go into foreign lands / to kill innocent people / because presidents and generals / pass the order?" (Reading 62).

In a study of how state managers around the world manipulate ethnic minorities through military service, Cynthia Enloe makes the following provocative suggestion:

When such groups discover upon demobilization that their political power is no greater than it was before conscription, they may be disillusioned. In effect, military service supplied these conscripts with state ethnic security maps of their own, meaning their own perceptions of the role of their group in the maintenance of the state. Their mistake was to believe that they were taking part in a nation-state process, that their maps and those of the authorities conscripting them were identical. One consequence of conscripts forming mental "maps" that are out of line with elite "maps" can be a post-war politicization of ethnic groups led by their respective veterans' organizations.[44]

This process of politicization serves as the underlying structure of many of the texts in this anthology. Upon realizing that governing groups did not consider them as equal partners in the nation-state or national community, Chicano and other minority veterans initiated a radical critique of state power and the oppressive forms of masculinity that had sent them to war in the first place. The kind of clarity with which Frank Delgado looks back at Viet Nam has been displayed recently by veterans of the Gulf War: "When I was going to college about a year after I got out of the army, I began to listen to what people were saying against the war. It started to dawn on me that I had indeed been used and I hadn't really known what I was doing. I felt angry because I had let that happen to me and that I had gone along with it."[45] Or, as one Chicano veteran said shortly after returning from Viet Nam: "I got trained in guerrilla fighting and I'm good at it. If there is ever fighting against the U.S. government in New Mexico, I'm going to be there and I don't care what it costs me."[46]

The increased political awareness of many Viet Nam veterans must be seen as one of the few positive things that can be learned from a war. Tim O'Brien's admonition—"Nothing can be learned from a war"—is only partially true. As Glenn Gray wrote in his meditation on World War II: "War reveals dimensions of human nature both above and below the acceptable standards of humanity."[47] In other words, much can be learned. But in most cases the price is simply too high.

Viet Nam Veteran

[Based on a real conversation, San Jose, Califas, 1968—Ed.]

*A youth with one leg missing hops on crutches toward
a group of men and they begin to talk:*

NACHO: Hey, Johnny, long time no see. Where have you been?

JOHNNY: Vietnam.

NACHO: Hey, I didn't know. That explains your leg?

JOHNNY: My lack of a leg.

NACHO: Yeah. Marines? Army?

JOHNNY: Army.

NACHO: But didn't you just go in? How long you been in?

JOHNNY: Yeah, man, I got drafted. Took sixteen weeks training, leave, shipped to Vietnam, and I got hit three months after I got there.

NACHO: Bullet?

JOHNNY: No. Mortars. A round landed right in the middle of five of us. Killed three of my buddies.

NACHO: Got you by surprise, or what?

JOHNNY: Yeah, right in the rice paddies. They were up on some hills real close by. They were North Vietnamese with uniforms and all. Just as good as us. They got us right in the open. They killed everybody in my company except five of us. All the survivors were wounded.

NACHO AND OTHER MEN IN THE GROUP: ¡Hijo! ¡Puta, mano! ¡Jesus!

¡Hijo! ¡Puta, mano! – Wow! Shit, bro'!

NACHO: Were there other Chicanos?

JOHNNY: Yeah, plenty. About sixteen.

NACHO: All dead now?

JOHNNY: Yeah.

TRINI: How many in the company?

JOHNNY: Oh, about a hundred.

NACHO: Why do you ask that, Trini?

TRINI: Oh, some Chicanos were passing out leaflets around here that said where Chicanos were 9% of the population in California and that 21% of the Vietnam dead were Chicanos. 1967, I think.

NACHO: Who was passing out those leaflets? Hippies?

TRINI: No. Chicanos were passing them out.

(ANOTHER MAN): They were decent people.

NACHO: Oh? Decent?

(OTHER MAN): Yes. They were respectable people like you and me.

NACHO: Yeah?

JOHNNY: I'm against the war in Vietnam, too.

NACHO: Yeah? I'll be. I guess it's true what the hippies are saying.

JOHNNY: (to Trini) You're pissed off about the 21%. You are pissed off, you don't like it do you, about Chicanos dying in Vietnam, I mean.

TRINI: I don't like it. Of course I don't like it.

JOHNNY: Well, that ain't nothing. There were about twenty-five Negros in that company I was in. All dead, except one. There were some Puerto Riqueños too, about four or five. About half of the company was Negros and Latins.

TRINI: ¡Qué gacho!

NACHO: Man alive!

OTHER: ¡Hijole! ¡Jesus! Wow, man!

¡Qué gacho! — Bummer!

29 / Rosalío Muñoz

Speech Refusing Induction

Today, the sixteenth of September, the day of independence for all Mexican peoples, I declare my independence of the Selective Service System.

I accuse the government of the United States of America of genocide against the Mexican people. Specifically, I accuse the draft, the entire social, political, and economic system of the United States of America of creating a funnel which shoots Mexican youth into Viet Nam to be killed and to kill innocent men, women, and children.

I accuse the education system of the United States of breaking down the family structure of the Mexican people. Robbing us of our language and culture has torn the youth away from our fathers, mothers, grandfathers, and grandmothers. Thus it is that I accuse the educational system of uneducating Chicano youth. Generally, we are ineligible for higher education, and thus are ineligible for the draft deferments which other college age youth take for granted, which is genocide.

I accuse the American welfare system of taking the self-respect from our Mexican families, forcing our youth to see the army as a better alternative to living in our community with their own families, which is genocide.

I accuse the law enforcement agencies of the United States of instilling greater fear and insecurity in the Mexican youth than the Viet Cong ever could, which is genocide.

I accuse the United States Congress and the Selective Service System which they have created of recognizing these weaknesses they have imposed on the Chicano community, and of drafting their law so that many more Chicanos are sent to Viet Nam in proportion to the total population than they send of any of their own white youth.

I accuse the entire American social and economic system of taking advantage of the machismo of the Mexican American male, widowing and orphaning the mothers, wives, and children of the Mexican American community, sending the Mexican men on to the front lines where their machismo has given them more congressional medals, purple hearts, and many times more deaths and casualties than any of the other racial or ethnic groups in the nation, which is genocide.

I accuse the legislature of the United States of gerrymandering the Mexican people out of their proper representation in the political system.

I have my induction papers, but I will not respect them until the government and the people of the United States begin to use the machismo of the Mexican male and the passion and suffering of the Mexican female to the benefit of themselves and of their own heritage, deferring all Chicano youth who serve our people, and providing the money and support that would make such work meaningful in social, political, and economic terms.

I will not respect the papers until the United States government and people can provide the funds and the willingness to improve the educational system so that all Mexican youth, the intelligent, the mediocre, and the tapados, just like the white youth, the intelligent, the mediocre, and the tapados, have the opportunity to go to college and get deferments.

I will not respect the papers until the welfare and other community agencies of the United States foster and allow for self-respect so that our youth can stay home and be men amongst our own families and friends.

I will not respect the papers until the systematic harassment of the law enforcement agencies has ended, and these agencies begin truly to protect and serve the Mexican-American community as well.

I will not respect the papers until the Armed forces, the largest domestic consumer of California table grapes, recognizes the United Farm Workers' Organizing Committee. Until that time, I cannot recognize the Armed forces, or any of its political uses of the American people. Until they begin to boycott the sellers and growers of California table grapes, I must boycott them!

CHALE CON EL DRAFT!

---

tapados— sell-outs
Chale con el draft! — Fuck the draft!

30 / Anonymous

Corrido de la Guerra

Por el suroeste ha llegado
la noticia muy alegre
que el Chicano es diferente.

Pues el Pueblo ya está en contra
los imperialistas ricos
que explotan a la gente.

Pero como hermanos somos
la lucha compartimos
con todos los del mundo.

Coro 1:
Viva la revolución
bajo con capitalismo
viva la lucha en general.

El veinte y nueve de agosto
para unirse en la batalla
salieron los Chicanos.

Y vamos a cumplir
con la marcha de la historia
para liberar al pueblo.

Coro 2:
Viva la lucha aquí
viva la causa en la historia.

La Raza llena de gloria
la victoria va a cumplir.

Nos dicen los generales
que la guerra siempre se hace
con bastantes mejicanos

y mandan 'los recruiters'
para enganchar a chicanitos
que se venden por frijoles.

Pero hombre de la Raza
oigan este canto
más muertos no queremos.

Ya saben los generales
que ni caro ni barato
comprarán nuestros hermanos.

Pero como es bien sabido
que pa' mantener la vida
la guerra no queremos.

ABAJO LOS IMPERIALISTAS
ARRIBA NUESTROS HERMANOS
QUE SE ACABE LA AGRESION.

(Throughout the Southwest, the news has spread that the Chicano has changed. Because now the people are against the rich imperialists who exploit the people. But since we are brothers, we share the struggle with everyone in the world.

Chorus 1: Long live the revolution, down with capitalism, long live the struggle.

The twenty-ninth of August, Chicanos came out to join the fray and we will fulfill the march of history in order to free our people.

Chorus 2: Long live the struggle here and in history. Covered in glory, the people will win the victory.

The generals tell us the war is always waged with lots of Mexicans, and they send recruiters to grab up chicanitos who sell themselves for nothing. But Chicanos hear this song: we want no more dead. Now the generals know that they cannot buy our brothers so cheaply. For it is well known that we reject war in order to sustain life. Down with imperialism. Up with our brothers. The aggression must stop.)   *Translation by George Mariscal*

31 / Elías Hruska y Cortez

Rocket Flight

I am flying on a rocket
      on a rocket
I am flying on a rocket over Viet Nam
    flying high
    flying high on a rocket over Viet Nam

there is rubble on the ground below
there are ants in the rubble on the ground below
there are ants dying on the ground below
DDT and Bombs on the ground below

but I don't care
'cause I'm flying on a rocket over Viet Nam
I'm flying to the moon over Viet Nam

there are children playing on the sand below
I see them on the beaches playing far below
I see a brother playing with his sister far below
I see my brother playing far below
my sister is calling from Viet Nam

I'm flying on a rocket over Viet Nam
flying high on a rocket over Viet Nam

I see toy soldiers far below
my brother playing war far below
my sister lies sleeping on the shore

my mother lies scattered on the dunes
the game was over long ago

I'm flying on a rocket over Viet Nam
flying high on a rocket over Viet Nam
flying high on a rocket to the Moon.

32 / Anonymous

Little Girls

Little girls
    and the sky-plane . . .
I see the sky . . .
    I see the flowers.
I see the little girls
    all on fire.
Little girls with eyes
    so brown.
Little girls
    strewn on the ground
The ground! The ground!
The napalm drenched
    ground.
As the sky-plane goes
    flying back to Saigon.
Who sent the sky-plane
    to kill little girls?
Who sent the sky-plane
    nobody knows.

We sent the sky-plane,
My neighbor and I.
Though we may shed
    many tears
And tell many lies,
We sent the sky-plane
My neighbor and I.

Hearts on Fire

1968,

that year you were born
in Saigon to Vietnamese dancer
and American soldier
you have never met, Nuoc,

some hearts broke
into chants, others
into flames.

I circled your birth
with thousands of students
chanting to Ho Chi Minh.

Thich Nhat Hanh intoned the heart sutra,
Brother Martin prayed with him, was silenced,
César and Dolores hummed the red earth mantra.

Cousin Rudy's prayers exploded
in a mine, next to a Vietnamese boy
whose father planted rice,
same as tío José,

green shoots turning to ashes
and grief.

Monks and nuns
opened their lotus hearts
and caught fire.

Heroes

All my tíos
marched off to war,
U.S. flag in their hearts,
straight
to the front lines.

Except one renegade
with fast feet, 20/20 vision
who went AWOL, who said
he didn't want to be
cannon fodder.

All my tías
waiting for heroes
welcomed him home.

34 / BÁRBARA RENAUD GONZÁLEZ

The Summer of Vietnam

So, what are you writing about? I ask Bill Broyles, the former *Newsweek Magazine* goldenboy. He's the Texas man who can write *anything* and get it published. Unlike me.

"Vietnam," he says. The worst answer. The only answer that can make me cry.

Instead, at night I remember.

Ernesto Sánchez is Vietnam to me. Born July 9, 1947. In a place called Kennedy, Texas. Died in the summer of 1967, somewhere in Vietnam. Somewhere in my 13th summer.

This is my Vietnam.

I sang love songs to them. Made up Ken dolls after them. Imagined kissing them. I still do. Marine-boys. Boys in dress green with stiff brass buttons that would catch your breaking heart when they gave you the biggest *abrazo* of your life. Then they died in Vietnam.

Always teasing me. "This last dance is for you, Barbara," they'd say. Taught me to dance those skip-steps of adolescence. Told me they'd wait for me. And they never came back from Vietnam to see how I'd grown up for them.

I knew they would not die. Heroes don't die in the movies, after all. The good guys always win. Who would dare extinguish the crooked smiles, football hands, and Aqua Velva faces I knew so well? My brothers-at-war.

---

abrazo – hug

Of the 3,427 Texas men who died in Vietnam, 22 percent were Latinos. And another 12 percent of the dead were African American. The minorities were *not* a minority in the platoons, but a majority of the frightened faces. And one-third of the body bags.

This at a time when Latinos constituted 12 percent of the population.

But the machismo goes a long way in war. We Latinos received more medals, thirteen of the prestigious Medal of Honor, than any other group.

We can count soldiers in the American Revolution (as Spaniards), the Roosevelt Rough Riders, both sides of the Civil War, and plenty of fathers and abuelitos in the world wars. Soldiering doesn't require U.S. citizenship, and no one cares how you crossed the border if you're willing to fight on our side.

We lost our best men in Vietnam. Isaac Camacho died first in 1963. Everett Alvarez was the first American pilot shot down, spending eight-and-a-half years as a POW. Juan Valdez was in the last helicopter leaving Vietnam. First in, and last out. They didn't go to Canada or Mexico. They went directly to Vietnam.

But from Oliver Stone, you would think that all our boys looked like Tom Cruise. Or agonized at China Beach. No. They were my brothers, uncles, cousins, my heroes.

Sometimes it looks as if they died for nothing. Impossible. It cannot be. Blood lost is blood redeemed, they say. What is the boy worth? If he died for all of us, then we must gain in proportion to the sacrifice. A Medal of Honor for the neighborhood school. Some Distinguished Service Crosses for family housing. Maybe the Bronze Stars for the judge or councilman. Flying Crosses for a good job. And a Purple Heart for a mother who still cries in Spanish.

---

abuelitos— grandfathers

35 / ARTURO SILVANO BOBIÁN

My Cousin Ralph

My brother Dan
warred an impersonal war
against the Asians.
He told me many stories
of how fear controlled him
not knowing who was friend or foe.

How does it feel to kill, I asked.
Like my dying, too, he said,
Every bullet in my gun
was aimed a little high
but one time I missed
and killed one of their guys.
At that moment, I feared god
more than all the armies of the world.

My cousin Ralph
fought along with other Marines
who had but one reason for fighting: their lives.
Given a choice, he would not have gone.
Ralph came back before the year was up,
but Ralph came back silent.

36 / Luis Valdez

From "Pensamiento serpentino"

César Chávez's NON-VIOLENCE
is one of the most
violent forces around
porque es positiva y porque
comienza con Dios.
Y a los que no les caiga
todo esto
pos hay 'ta
Vietnam
con todo su amor humano
precioso espíritu positivo
que no se ha dejado vencer
¿Y qué decía el Uncle Ho?
pues que a pesar de los
bombardeos
minas
biological warfare
sangre derramada en los
rice paddies de la nación
El pueblo Vietnamita todavía
abraza al pueblo norteamericano
que no culpa a los gabachos
porque solo el gobierno es culpable
El Nixon (que Dios lo perdone)
El LBJ (que Dios lo perdone)
El Kennedy (que Dios lo perdone)
no son los United States of America.
Y ésa es la verdadera victoria

de Vietnam: el no ser tragados por
EL ODIO cuando diariamente les cae
la muerte por encima.
Esa fuerza moral la tenemos todos
gracias a la resistencia
de esos heróicos campesinos.
En cara de esto,
how can we let the enemy robarnos of our humanity
with a little racism and police brutality
Compared to the Vietnamese,
our life in the hands of the gringo
has been
a tardeada con pura música de acordeón.

(César Chávez's NON-VIOLENCE is one of the most violent forces around because it is positive and because it origi-
nates with God. And for those who don't understand all
this, well, there's Vietnam with all its human love, its pris-
tine positive spirit which it will not allow to be conquered.
And what did Uncle Ho say? Well, that despite the bomb-
ings, mines, biological warfare, blood spilled in the nation's
rice paddies, the Vietnamese people continue to embrace
the people of North America, for they do not blame the
Americans because only their government is responsible.
Nixon (may God forgive him). LBJ (may God forgive him).
Kennedy (may God forgive him). They are not the United
States. And that is the true victory of Vietnam: to not be devoured by HATE when every day death rains down upon
them. We all have that moral strength thanks to the resistance of those heroic peasants. In the face of that, how can
we let the enemy rob us of our humanity with a little racism
and police brutality. Compared to the Vietnamese, our life
at the hands of the gringo has been an afternoon stroll set
to accordion music.)   *Translation by George Mariscal*

37 / María Herrera-Sobek

"Cinco poemas"

Vietnam

Vietnam
Was an obscene aberration
The young marched
To the rat-tat-tat
Of firing machine guns
Helicopter blades
Knifing the air
Others
Marched to the tune
Of peace
In their sandaled feet
Drugged and dazed
They chanted
"Hell no we won't go"
Meanwhile
Napalm clouds
Hovered
And danced
Their song
Of death.

Silver Medals

The silver medals
Purple hearts

medals of conquering heroes
Hung on Chicano homes
Another Mexican American hero
Brought home
Under the Stars and Stripes
Long gone the need
To prove his manhood
Long gone the need
To prove his red-blooded
American genealogy
And only the stars
Twinkle at our foolish pride.

Chicana Vietnam Blues

Kent was
the scream
heard around the world.
Flowers on rifle butts
Our emblem
We danced
Until we waved
good-bye to the moon
Drug dazed
We blinked at the sun
And lost our sanity
Wrists were at the ready
To make blood flow
In competition
With the killing fields
Of Vietnam
And no one left
The decade
Unscathed
Unscarred.

Untitled

We saw them coming
in funeral black bags
body bags they called them
eyes locked forever
they were our
brown men
shot
in a dishonest war
Vietnam taught us
not to trust
anyone over thirty
For *they* had the guns
and the power
to send our boyfriends
fathers, brothers
off to war
while they sauntered
in lily white
segregated
country clubs
a bomb was planted
in our minds
a bomb exploded
in 1969
Watts, East Los
Black Panthers
Brown Berets
Drank the night
and lighted up the sky
with homemade
fireworks
the war had come
to roost
in our own backyard
made in the USA guns
turned inward

and shot our young
Dead in the streets
Dead in the battlefields
Dead in the schools
and yet a plaintive song
Crashing against the crackling explosion
of a Molotov cocktail.
insisted
"We shall overcome."

Vietnam—A Four-letter Word

Vietnam
Was a four-letter word
The stench of napalm
In the air
seared our nightmares
California palm trees
Waving fronds of anti-patriotism
"Hell no, we won't go"
Was not a T.V. jingle
It was the chant
Of those who marched
To a different tune
Of those who wore peace
On their foreheads
Love on their sleeves
And American flags
On their behinds.

Blessed Amerika

When the campesinos embarked on
their struggle to unionize,
Blessed Amerika ate pinchi grapes.
Blessed Amerika is not a farmworker.

Fred Hampton and Mark Clark were
gunned down in cold blood;
Blessed Amerika sighed in relief.
Blessed Amerika is not a revolutionary.

When Los Siete de La Raza were jailed
supposedly for killing a cop,
Blessed Amerika agreed; maintain law & order.
Blessed Amerika does not live in a barrio.

Innocent individuals have met with death;
victims of justifiable homicide.
Blessed Amerika elected "responsible" crime fighters.
Blessed Amerika is not a "suspicious type."

Alcatraz was repossessed by a people to whom
much more than an island is indebted;
Blessed Amerika laughed.
Blessed Amerika has never suffered genocide.

---

pinchi— damned
Los Siete de La Raza—The People's Seven

Four blessed Kent State students are
murdered by trigger happy Guardsmen.
Blessed Amerika, that original wetback!
That as of late snoring giant!

Go ahead. Protest! Demonstrate!—
in the false Amerikan tradition.
Blessed Amerika, abhorring violence,
make peace your ultimatum!

There are many kinds of violence. . . .
. . . . . on many different fronts.

Juan Carlos González

Juan Carlos González
fue muy macho
le agradó mucho el ejército
EL TALLE DE SU UNIFORME
Y fue muy héroe
a los más chicos
de su vecindario.
al regresar con sus cintas
rojas, blancas y azules
les contaba
en gran detalle
el proceso por el cual
se hace un hombre
SOLDADO
Primeramente la correa
Cariñosamente ajusta
la hebilla al mismo
centro del estómago
Y luego la bayoneta
Es muy importante
amolarla científicamente
Un día
en tiempo de fiesta
recibimos la noticia
Juancho había muerto
Y nadie ni preguntó cómo
Pero sabemos
QUE FUE MUY MACHO.

(Juan Carlos González was very macho. He liked the army a lot THE CUT OF HIS UNIFORM and he was a big hero to the kids in the neighborhood when he came back with his red, white, and blue ribbons. He told them in great detail the process by which a man becomes a SOLDIER. First, you delicately adjust the buckle right in the middle of your stomach. And then the bayonet. It's important to sharpen it scientifically. One day, on a holiday, we got the news that Juancho had died and nobody asked how. But we know that HE WAS VERY MACHO.)

Translation by George Mariscal

Poema

El soldado crucificado ante su raza
Sale con su M-16, creyendo,
Creyendo que sus enemigos son los
amarillos.
Creyendo que es justicia matar.
Matar los oprimidos de este mundo.

El mismo oprimido por el sistema
no conoce las angustias,
no conoce las penas,
no conoce el espíritu
muriendo . . . muriendo.

Su M-16, la vida de su existencia,
su M-16, el opresor de su raza.
Matando, y él, matando su espíritu
aunque no lo sabe.
   Te
     Pido
       Señor
Dale conciencia, dale espíritu
porque ahora te doy mi alma
Crucificada ante toda mi raza.

(The soldier crucified in front of his people departs with his M-16, believing, believing that his enemy is the yellow man. Believing that it is just to kill. To kill the oppressed of this world. He himself oppressed by the system does not know the anguish, does not know the sorrow, does not know the spirit dying . . . dying. His M-16, the reason for his existence, his M-16, the oppressor of his people. Killing, and he, killing his spirit without knowing it. I ask you Lord. Make him realize, give him spirit because now I give you my soul crucified in front of my people.)

Translation by George Mariscal

41 / Anonymous

From "A Question Every Chicano Should Ask"

History calls me a Mexican (an excuse for wetback). It says that I am a lazy person who likes to take siestas, eat frijoles and tacos. It says we are uneducated and dumb.

The military calls me a Caucasian. The military says that, to the military, there is no such thing as white, black, or brown color; we are all the same. But it doesn't say how the military gives us and our black brothers the worst jobs. It doesn't say how the racist lifers try to separate us so we won't unite against them. It doesn't say how they try to brainwash us to keep us from finding out the truth about why we go to war. It doesn't say that they send us to Vietnam to fight people who are fighting the same enemy we are fighting in America: U.S. imperialism. It doesn't say that our purpose there is to protect the rich man's money and to make him richer.

Society calls me a Mexican American. They say I smoke marijuana, shoot heroin, and push drugs. They say I cause riots. They say I am lazy, uneducated, undependable to hold a job. They say I stay at home and live off welfare.

But they don't say that we smoke marijuana and shoot heroin because of despair, anger, being looked upon as less than human, being exploited and the only escape from this is by staying high in order to be happy. They don't say we push drugs to help support our families. They don't say that we cause riots in order to demand our rights, and to protest police brutality. They don't say how policemen arrest and beat our brothers for no reason at all. They don't say that the Declaration of Independence doesn't contain a single Chicano or black man's signature and that at that time a Chicano or black man was not considered human. They don't say we are uneducated because we don't have the opportunity to get an education like a white man has. They don't say that the rich pigs keep us on welfare to try and stop us from fighting against their so-called democratic government.

Yes, carnales, who am I? The answer is this.

My grandfather was a wetback because he didn't realize how the whites were using him and getting rich through his back-breaking work. My father was a Mexican American because he too was used and downgraded and exploited, and he didn't have the guts to stand up and fight for freedom. But me, carnales, I am a Chicano and I am proud of being a Chicano. I shall stand up to these rich pigs and fight for freedom and rights. I shall take arms if necessary. I will help the rest of the working people regardless of race and color. I am ready to give my life for this cause because my blood is the same as that of Che Guevara, Pancho Villa, Chicanos who died to give people their freedom.

Yes, carnales, this is what I am.

---

carnales – brothers

42 / ANONYMOUS (A Soldier de la Raza, overseas)

Carnal in Vietnam

Carnales:

Let me introduce myself. I am the voice of many soldiers overseas. I am the voice of Zapata screaming vengeance from his white horse. I am the voice of your camarada in Korea, or your brother in Vietnam, whose hatred is burning inside him like a passion. But most of all, I am the voice of the Chicano soldier.

We, the Chicano soldiers have something to say to the carnales of East Los Angeles.

We were proud when we heard of the East Los Angeles demonstrations. But why did you stop there? Why did you let the white bigots praise you to defeat you? Why has the death of Rubén Salazar gone forgotten?

You say that the accused is being held for trial. My carnales, in the old days to kill a Mexican was a sport. The only change now is that it's done by legal means. Carnales, open your eyes, and think about it. What is going to happen to the accused? Why did you stop at this point? What have you accomplished? Nothing.

The gabachos praised you in saying that you were well planned and organized. Now you sit back confident that you've accomplished something. Well, in our eyes you've accomplished nothing. You've only cleaned up your own mess, and lost a carnal. It took this long for the gabachos to make it a case against the law, only to satisfy your morale? Carnales, only to keep you quiet! A case of involuntary manslaughter, if it ever comes to trial, is not enough.

Carnales—Brothers
camarada—comrade
gabachos—white people

Carnales, we had faith in you! Don't let the gabachos stall around till this whole situation blows away in the wind. Remember the Sleepy Lagoon Case? Remember the Zoot Suit Riots? Ya basta! Carnales. Think about it? Who really won? We sit here impatiently waiting to get home. Forgive us if we cuss and cry out in anger, we are just lonely and are looking for a way home.

Ya basta! – Enough!

43 / ANONYMOUS

Vietnam: Gabacho's War

Dear Editor—

I am a Marine and I am fighting for a cause I was blind to see before I came over. I'm being treated like an animal over here. They don't give a damn if we live or die. All the gabacho is doing is protecting his money, money, money which he is too tight to give to the people of los barrios, I know this is not the Brown man's war and if I had a second chance I wouldn't have come over.

We have a war to fight against poverty, for equality, housing, and many other things. I just wish I could pass this message to all my brown hermanos and it is coming from my heart. I know what it is like to be here and many more have gone through the same thing. Viet Nam is not the Brown man's war. Let the gabachos fight for their own money.
QUE VIVA LA RAZA!

H & S Co. 2/5
Security PI#2

---

gabacho—white man
hermanos—brothers
Que viva la raza!—Long live the People!

La hora de todos

Nadie tiene derecho a seguir cantando,
Nadie tiene derecho a seguir riendo,
Y olvidarte y mirarte como algo lejano.
Vietnam, Vietnam, tu tragedia se extiende y escapa
Más allá de distancias y horas presentidas
Por los hombres que luchan y cantan
En todos los puntos de la tierra,
Más allá de la misma conciencia de esta hora.

Vietnam, Vietnam,
En tu justa y heróica lucha
Se decide también el destino de mi lucha
Que es la lucha del hombre por ser
Y salvar el derecho a vivir
Para todo lo humano y hermoso
que encierra la vida.

(No one has the right to continue singing, no one has the
right to continue laughing, and forget you and think of you
as something far away. Vietnam, Vietnam, your tragedy escapes and goes beyond, beyond all distances and future
days, for all men who struggle and sing everywhere in the
world, beyond the very consciousness of the present hour.
Vietnam, Vietnam, in your just and heroic struggle, the destiny of my struggle is decided as well, which is the struggle
for existence and the right to live for all that is human and
beautiful in life.) *Translation by George Mariscal*

45 / ALEJANDRO NEGRETE

Chicano Moratorium, December 20, 1969

As the march from First and Sunol Streets in East Los Angeles wound its path, within the "protective" ranks of a police escort, it was difficult to perceive that in the valleys and sand of Viet Nam other marches were in progress. Those unheralded marches of sweat and ammunition bands, steel helmets and loaded rifles, were even then trampling the soft hills and rice fields of the peasant countryside, searching for unsmiling faces of brown, burnt by the un-relenting sun, faces of beautiful almond-shaped eyes, faces crowned with lux-urious black hair and marked with the strange repose of centuries of toil. Search and destroy.

A young Chicana started a yell, was answered by a thousand "vivas" and joined in the "Chicano clap" as the procession approached Obregon Park.

And in that other place, as if in a different century, a young girl screamed as the reality of death left her an orphan. The volleys of gunfire and heat of burning grass huts were unable to penetrate her shock of total loss and lone-liness. She would not even recall how she was shunted to the side of the road and loaded into a US military dumptruck to be assigned to the nearest "New Life Hamlet," some 50 miles away, a distance she had never traveled in her 14 years with her family now "accidents of war."

When the speakers for the moratorium of frustration voiced their anger at the high death rate of minorities in Viet Nam, the crowd leaned forward, as if to see the full panorama of our brothers in the fields and the fallen in their graves, lives surrendered as martyrs in the "just course of an honorable conclusion."

La niña Lina en East Los Angeles

Lina chiquita y risueña
amidst the grass of green and the East L.A. sun
'Carnalismo' vibrating throughout the crowd.
Raza Sí! Guerra No! The time had come for us all.
Exalted spirits in bodies of brown,
passionate people proclaiming their humanity.
Viva La Raza! Que Viva la Causa! Viva la Liberación!
The 'Peoples Proposition' marches   RIGHT ON!!
                    Pinto Power   Peñalver Power   Pocho Power
Brown is Love! Brown is together!
A beautiful expression of unity.
And *then,* the POLICE were there!
And in the fleeing mass of confusion—Lina got lost!
Papá! Papá! ¿Dónde estás, Papá?
Run! Hide! "Get away from the teargas"
Burning eyes. Bewildered cries.
I found her and held her tenderly against my bosom,
while the riot squad ripped into the crowd.

Lina chiquita y risueña — Lina, small and laughing
Carnalismo — Brotherhood
Raza Sí! Guerra No! — The People, yes! War, no!
Viva la Raza! Que Viva la Causa! Viva la Liberación! — Long live the People! Long live the Cause!
    Long live freedom!
Pinto — prisoner
[Peñalver is a surname]
Pocho — assimilated Mexicans
¿Dónde estás, Papá? — Where are you, papa?

And in her innocence she clung to me for security.
She would not cry, and she would not let go.
I learned to love her in the long moments of chaos.
And I asked, "Why teargas?"
People are love! Lina is love!
"Why?" *Teargas.* Our men have been DYING!
Dying for *what?*—in Vietnam!
Dying for Lina, chiquita y risueña. Lina is LOVE.
Lina on the radio. Lina on television. KMEX. REPORTED LOST
    CHILD
Age three. Brown bundle of love. Answers to Lina.
3:00 o'clock—4:00 o'clock
Lina snuggles. Lina cuddles. Lina doesn't want you to leave her.
Lina sleeps while people riot in the streets.
Smashed windows, like smashed hopes, dignity reclaimed in
    rebellion
Pride bursts with flames of burning police cars, transporters of
    pigs.
Raza Sí! Guerra No! More tears for Rubén Salazar.
7:00 o'clock—8:00 o'clock
Lina eats a hotdog—drinks a coke—in amerika!
land of Kentucky Fried Chicken and disaster.
Can't call police—they're Parker's Pigs.
10:00 o'clock—11:00 o'clock
Doesn't anyone hear our call?
¡I won't take Lina to cold grey quarters!
Lina is love. Lina is brown. Lina chiquita y risueña.
RING   RING   RING
Brown man of concern calls.
Brown man burdened with worry comes to get Lina.
Take my love with you and leave me her memory to treasure.
Lina chiquita y risueña. Lina is love.
And the realization burns deep in my soul:
Lina was teargassed—because Lina   is   *brown!*

Chicano Is an Act of Defiance

In memory of Rubén Salazar

> *How simple death is: how simple,*
> *yet how unjustly violent!*
> *She refuses to go about slowly, and slashes*
> *when you least expect her wicked slash.*
>
> Miguel Hernández

On your tongue—the flowing of
accentuated ink: a challenge
for those who stereotype.

Chicano is an act of defiance—you'd say

Your last day,
laid out in protest.
In the rifles (hidden) waits
compact
death.

The accuracy of triggers/Senseless confrontation.
La Raza prays—breathing is a risk.
Blasts.
Random shots—
      La Raza prays.
Parafascist blasts
paramilitary blasts
blasts that kill pupils and

persistent throats.
The *Silver Dollar Cafe* is only for eating.
Someone didn't bother reading intents.
Three die.

In the wind.

You left your indelible, committed cry.
Perspectives went spreading through the streets.

One can decipher
a well-articulated cry.

Eulogy for Rubén Salazar [excerpt]

In journalism there is one axiom—be honest with the truth and relentless against false men and false reason. Many times a journalist must write about events which are unpopular and harsh. Many times he must weigh the delicate balance between the institution that gave him the opportunity and the people who gave him their faith and confidence. Today we are here to mourn a man who willed his career to the people he loved and understood. It is not ironic—rather, it is symbolic—that Rubén died in the streets of East Los Angeles covering the story that he vowed someday would come. Rubén Salazar is not the first journalist killed doing his duty, but he is the first Mexican American newsman to die articulating a courage we all claim to have but have been too timid to pursue.

Rubén Salazar was my colleague and friend. In journalism, Mexican Americans are few and far between and we get to know each other well. Rubén never wondered about the course he would take. He knew eventually he would return to California to write about a people whose story desperately needed to be told. It was our story, he said, and if we, who knew it, understood it and had the opportunity to tell it, didn't do so, then who would. I saw Rubén in Washington when he was already much involved in Chicano affairs for the *Los Angeles Times* and KMEX and he was doing it the way he said he would—with honesty, courage and foresight. We sat together at a Chicano Media meeting listening to polemics against the establishment media and I asked him if personal journalism compromised objectivity. Personal reporting, he said, was the neutralizer of establishment journalism and was a road toward the truth. Without truth, he said, there is no objectivity. I last saw Rubén in New York at a meeting with editors and publishers of the national news media. Rubén was pleading for more honesty, more public conscience and less indifference from the powers of the press. I recall him telling them that time was running out. The people were restless.

Rubén was the type of journalist who did not believe in covering a story by telephone from the city room. He went where the action was. He did not rely solely on official reports. He sought the sources that established the truth. He treated people as people rather than news items. He was there on Saturday not merely to cover a Vietnam Moratorium—which are plentiful these days—but to record in sound and words the fury and frustrations of the Mexican Americans. He was there to tell people that Chicanos were not there on a hot day because they like to shout and get beaten over the head. Rubén was there to tell the public that this is what it has come to and to ask if this is what Mexican Americans must do to be heard.

Last year, Rubén made a speech in San Antonio in which he predicted his fate. He admonished the press for stressing the sensational and ignoring the obvious. He said that the press was not saying the things that must be said in order to avoid violence. But if it comes, he said, "For God's sake, let us in the media be prepared to cover it adequately."

Rubén Salazar wrote his greatest story Saturday. The tragedy of it is that he had to write it with his blood.

Overkill at the Silver Dollar

It was nearly midnight, and the barrio strangely quiet, quiet with fear. I had just left the Carioca restaurant with a dozen tortillas de maíz in a paper bag. I was spending the night before the funeral at my mother's house, and she'd promised to cook my favorite breakfast of menudo con chile. The tortillas, naturally, were essential.

Suddenly a police car screeched to a stop at the curb. Two cops jumped out and pushed me against the wall, frisking me from top to bottom with rough, insolent hands. They said not a word, and neither did I. I was simply not macho enough to protest. A cop like these had blasted the skull of my friend Rubén Salazar, the Chicano columnist for the *Los Angeles Times,* in the Silver Dollar Café, and I was frankly afraid to cross them.

They have also arrested about three hundred Chicanos since the police riot that erupted during the East Los Angeles peace rally that Rubén was covering on the afternoon he was killed. I didn't want to be prisoner 301—and having flown all the way from New York, I certainly didn't want to miss Rubén's funeral. So I accepted the indignity of their frisk with a gut-souring meekness. This is all familiar stuff to anyone who has lived in a Chicano barrio. And when they yanked off my shoes and shook them upside-down, I clamped my mouth to hold back the sour saliva that I'd like to spit in their faces.

"What do you do?" one of them asked.

"I'm a lawyer and a writer."

"Oh—one of those guys."

Suddenly noticing the brown paper bag in my hand, one of these guardians of the peace grabbed it and quickly shuffled through the tortillas in an apparent search for marijuana or heroin. Finding none, he gave them back. Later on I threw the tortillas into a trash can—they must have a hundred cop fingerprints on them.

They let me go finally—a tribute to my meekness, to what I would rather call my old barrio wisdom. The pragmatism of fear. And in my confusion and resentment (or was it again a sense of prudent resignation?) I had not noticed their badge numbers. Nor would I be able to recognize their faces again. I'm afraid all cops' faces have begun to look alike to me. And that's tragic, in a way, because two years ago I wrote to Mayor Lindsay and the New York Police Commissioner, commending a police officer who had been extremely kind (fatherly-kind) to my ten-year-old daughter when she was injured near our apartment while we were away, the babysitter having gone astray. He had taken her to a hospital and stayed by her side for five hours. So it's not in me to be a cop hater.

Just below Soto and Brooklyn Avenue, while searching vainly for a cab on those deserted streets, I saw a police helicopter swishing over me like a giant insect, its bright, harsh searchlights probing the dark alleys and back yards of the barrio.

I wondered then if the police regard us Mexican Americans as a community of barricaded criminals. The phrase came easily at that moment because that very afternoon the *Times* had quoted an expert as saying that the kind of missile that killed Rubén "should be used only against a barricaded criminal." Gene Pember, a consultant for the Peace Officers Standards and Training Commission, had told newsmen that the high-velocity tear-gas projectile that pierced Rubén's skull should never be used for crowd control, that "the thing is like a young cannon, really." Such missiles, he said, could go through a thick stucco wall. "That's what they are for—to penetrate a house or an object behind which a dangerous suspect has barricaded himself. But even then they should never be fired at a person."

The ten-inch missile that killed Salazar was fired by a sheriff's deputy *through an open doorway* at a point-blank range of fifteen feet. The deputy who fired that missile may not have known it was Rubén Salazar he was shooting, but he certainly knew it was a Chicano.

Yet, not once during the entire week following this obvious example of heedless slaughter would Sheriff Pitchess admit that his men might have been even slightly negligent. Sam Houston Johnson once told me that his brother LBJ suffered from a profound inability to say "I'm sorry"—to admit any error, however inconsequential. Certainly a tragic flaw in a human being, and I wonder if the Los Angeles sheriff shares that affliction. Far from blaming any of his men, he keeps talking about "outside agitators."

Small wonder that my fellow Chicanos are willing to believe almost any accusation against the police. When the *Times* subsequently devoted its entire front page to blown-up photos from a community newspaper called *La Raza,* quoting at length from an article titled "The Murder of Rubén Salazar"— they may have begun to entertain even that suspicion.

Earlier that evening (several hours before the cops frisked me) I had attended a rally of Chicanos at the All Nations Auditorium, where I heard their collective rage and frustration—my own as well—burst from the throats of one speaker after another, the packed listeners periodically stamping their feet and raising clenched fists as a symbol of "Chicano power." The speeches were mostly in English but occasionally resorted to a schizolingual amalgam of English and Spanish to stress a vital point. Tough barrio language, most of it spoken with the bitterness of long years of resentment, some of it with a hushed, melancholy sense of bitter resignation.

When Corky Gonzales was introduced, a thunder of shoes stomped the floor and a chorus of "Viva Chicano power!" echoed from the walls, throbbing in my head, sending an expectant chill up my spine. But there was no flaming rhetoric from the much-loved leader of the Crusade for Justice—no call to arms, no threat of violence. There was instead an urgent plea for Chicano unity, for a grass-roots drive for political power, for a reclaiming of "the occupied territory of Aztlán"—that portion of the United States that once belonged to Mexico. It sounded more like a psychic take-back than a real one. The muted anger in his voice was spiced with humorous irony when he told the crowd, "I was busted at the peace rally and charged with suspicion of robbery because I had $325 in my billfold. To the gabacho cops, I guess it's suspicious for a Chicano to have that much bread."

Clearly moved by Corky's mesmeric hold on the audience, René Anselmo (an Anglo millionaire who owns three TV stations) instantly donated one hundred dollars to the bail-bond fund for the three hundred Chicanos who had been arrested since the riot. By coincidence, Captain Ernest Medina— defendant in the My Lai massacre case—was in Los Angeles during that same period, seeking donations for his defense from fellow Mexican Americans. I doubt that he could have raised two cents from the people who heard Corky, though I'm told that American Legionnaires in his hometown think him a hero.

---

gabacho—white

After the rally I went to the Carioca bar-restaurant to eat Mexican food. It was also a sentimental gesture. The last time I had seen Rubén Salazar we had come to this restaurant, mostly to hear the mariachi trio that entertains here. They had played our favorite "Adelita" and "Siete Leguas," songs of the Mexican Revolution that led us into a pleasant nostalgic mood. I had once written that my father was the only private in Pancho Villa's army, and he was now claiming that *his* father was the only private, smiling in that gentle way he had, his eyes shining with impish enjoyment. What better basis for a deep and abiding friendship than our mutual conviction that *each* of our fathers was the only private in that famous rebel Division del Norte?

Our conversation became serious after a while. Rubén was deeply concerned about the laggard pace of bilingual education programs for Chicano children in the early grades. Most educators know that everyone's greatest, most intense period of learning is from birth to the age of five. For a Chicano that fast-paced, crucial learning is acquired in Spanish or in a pocho combination of Spanish and English. But the day he enters kindergarten—a day of intense anxiety even for a child from the most secure Anglo environment— that learning tool is snatched away. He's not permitted to speak the only language he knows. So he sits in frustration, confusion, and fright as the teacher and the "more advantaged" kids talk in alien sounds, making him feel dumb and lost. The experience is repeated hour after hour, day after day, until he's ultimately defeated. There is no one more fragile than a five-year-old child on alien turf.

The Chicano brings failure to school with him; he has no chance of success, no possibility of the "reward and reinforcement" that child educators feel is indispensable. The high school dropout rate for Mexican Americans (58 percent in some Chicano ghettos—higher than the rate for black students) is a belated symptom of the dropping out that begins on the first day of kindergarten.

"Why can't they teach our Chicano kids in both Spanish and English?" asked Rubén, fingering an empty glass. "If they could have genuine bilingual classes—Spanish in the morning and English in the afternoon—there would be some trace of comforting familiarity between school and their home. They could feel successful in Spanish, capable of learning. They wouldn't feel dumb, they wouldn't quit trying as they do now. With a gradual transition in kindergarten and the first two grades, English would be easier."

His convictions were an echo of educational theories developed by

Dr. Jerome Bruner, director of Harvard's Center for Cognitive Studies, who has said that ghetto youngsters often face insuperable linguistic and environmental obstacles.

Ordering another round of margaritas that evening, we talked of other problems that bedevil Chicano kids. Thinking of the kid-glove treatment used on the Kennedy-Shriver cousins when they were arrested for possession of marijuana, we were both sure that a Chicano or black teenager would have been summarily convicted and sent to a reformatory for at least six months.

I told Rubén of my first encounter with the juvenile court system as a lawyer (I'd had several as a child). A Mexican American woman had called my office in a state verging on hysteria. Her thirteen-year-old son—let's call him Ramón Gómez—had been picked up by the police and whisked off in a squad car, but no one at the local precinct station would tell her where he was. Within half an hour we were at the Hollenbeck station in East Los Angeles and were informed that Ramón wasn't there. No record of his arrest. Then we hurried to the Juvenile Detention Home, where the desk captain said there was no booking on a Ramón Gómez. But as we were leaving, a young Chicano trusty told us that a boy answering Ramón's description had been taken from the detention home to the Los Angeles General Hospital. "He had a bloody bandage on his face." Checking the prison ward at the hospital, we learned two hours later that he'd received treatment for a fractured nose and then been returned to the detention home.

When we tried to see him at the so-called home, we were told he couldn't have visitors—nor could I see him in my capacity as his attorney. Angered by this refusal (any adult prisoner can see a lawyer), I went to a bail bondsman, who told me that kids weren't entitled to release on bail. Then I called several judges, who told me that they couldn't order his release on a writ of habeas corpus because children weren't entitled to that constitutional right.

When I finally saw the boy, he told me that he'd been accused of trying to break into a bubble-gum machine. "I put a penny in there and the gum didn't come out, so I was shaking it when the police came by. And when I tried to explain what happened, one of them slapped me. Then when I protested, they got me in the car, and one of them started punching my face with his closed fist, calling me a smart-aleck spic. That's how my nose got busted."

The Kafkaesque nightmare continued the next day at Ramón's hearing in juvenile court. The judge immediately informed me that I couldn't act as his lawyer "because this is not a criminal proceeding."

"Then why are you treating him like a criminal?" I asked. "Why has he been detained in that jail?"

"That's not a jail," he said rather testily. "It's only a detention home."

Paraphrasing Gertrude Stein, I said: "It has barred cells like a jail and barred gates to keep those kids inside, and a jail is a jail is a jail—no matter what name you give it."

But he still wouldn't let me appear as Ramón's lawyer, so his mother and I just sat there watching the nightmare proceedings of that quick-justice cafeteria called a "court." Not only were the juvenile defendants (almost all of them black or Chicano) denied lawyers; they couldn't face their accusers, they couldn't cross-examine witnesses against them, they couldn't object to rank hearsay testimony, they weren't protected by any of the normal rules of evidence. They were, in fact, unable to invoke any of the constitutional safeguards that are available to known gangsters.

And when I asked the judge for a transcript of the hearing after he had sentenced Ramón to six months in a reformatory, his mother pleaded with me not to appeal the case. "If we raise a big fuss," she said, "they'll only make it tougher on Ramón when he gets out. He'll be a marked man. We Chicanos don't have a chance."

Rubén had a film of tears in his eyes when I told him about Ramón. He said, "Think of all the other Ramóns who've been in the same bag."

Ramón Gómez must be twenty years old by now. He may have been one of the tight-mouthed militants in the angry crowd at the All Nations Auditorium on the night before Rubén's funeral, listening to one speaker comment on the tear-gassing of children at the peace rally, listening to the bitter irony in Corky Gonzales' voice. He's heard, as most Chicanos have, that Corky is a marked man, that the FBI probably shadows him from one state to another as he goes from campus to campus, from barrio to barrio, asking his brown brothers to join in common cause. Ramón knows from personal experience (as do too many Chicanos who have been brutalized by certain cops, by the juvenile court system, by those crime-breeding reformatories), knows with a sickening fear, that the police may some day crowd in on Corky, and that tragic violence may result.

But quite aside from his own not-likely-to-be-forgotten experience with the law, Ramón knows about inferior ghetto schools with indifferent teachers, about poor substandard housing, about high unemployment in the barrio, about radio and television shows that demean and insult his fellow paisanos. And he must be aware that local and federal government agencies largely ignore the plight of eight million invisible Mexican Americans. And he certainly knows that the television networks, national magazines, and news syndicates are generally deaf to the despairing voices of the barrio, although the more strident voices from black ghettos get ample notice.

Those same news media have been outraged by the alarming increase of cop killers—and it is well they should be, for any killing is abhorrent. But they should also know that the phrase is sometimes reversed in the ghetto— that Chicanos and blacks and poor whites often talk about killer cops with equal abhorrence.

Ramón and the rest of us Chicanos have been urged to turn a deaf ear to the dangerous cry of the militant, to listen instead to the voices of reason, to the voices of the people like Rubén Salazar. And though I myself felt slightly less than reasonable when those two cops shoved me against the wall on a dark lonely street, I would certainly agree that our only hope is reason and good will.

One must also hope that the police and other authorities will come to realize that reason flows both ways, that this fragile society can ill afford the frightening consequences of the kind of overkill that silenced the most reasonable voice of Rubén Salazar.

∫0 / Delfino Varela

A Walk in the Sun

We strolled down the street, my brother-in-law, a niece, my wife, our one-year-old baby in his stroller, and I. Behind us were but a few people, in front were thousands and thousands. All of us affirmed there were more thousands than we had ever seen. Brothers-in-law, nieces, wives, husbands, and one-year-old babies in their strollers, all strolling together in the noonday sun.

The voice of a friend who fled Germany kept coming back. "Marches here are so sloppy," she said. "Everybody just strolls along and there's no rhythm to it. You should have seen our marches in Germany," she said.

I was glad we were a motley crew, all out of step and with no rhythm. They'll never goose-step this crowd into fascism, I thought, these thousands of nieces, cousins, brothers-in-law, aunts and uncles, and the one-year-old babies in their strollers. They're too undisciplined, too massive, too uncontrollable for any Hitler.

Behind the few people in back of us was the end of the long, long line of countless thousands, some say twenty-five, some thirty, and behind all this rode two black busses massively built of steel and rubber with white roofs. These motorized vultures followed close, and their insides were filled with walking vultures. This long, long line of children, women, boys, and girls was followed closely by these two black busses, and the creatures inside them waited tensely for the battle and their noses quivered as they smelled the blood of our women, men, nieces, aunts and uncles and the one-year-old babies in their strollers.

In three and a half miles the long, long line was at the park. A quiet modest park, but well suited for the brothers-in-law, nieces, wives, and the one-year-old babies in their strollers, and for their sodas, candies, balloons, buttons, and picnic lunches. Today, this would be a people's park.

But the two black busses were close behind, and at the park they were joined by a third, full of armed men, full of dislike for the brothers-in-law, nieces, wives, and for the one-year-old babies in their strollers. Without a word they formed across the street from the park in long and silent lines, soon to move across the street toward the people in the park.

We were leaving but were ordered back into the park and the northern exit facing the police was closed to us. Soon, around us we heard them coming, the men from the black, black busses, from the west, and in back of all the brothers-in-law, wives, and one-year-old babies in their strollers.

Swinging clubs they came, without a word, just swinging clubs and throwing gas.

As we walked through the alleys, choking with the gas that was spread throughout the park and for several blocks away, I looked at my one-year-old baby in his stroller and his red and watery eyes. He seemed amazed, and looked in wonderment in all directions. He didn't know that men who come in big black busses threw things at little children to make them cry and run when they are in their strollers in the park.

51 / PATRICIA RODRÍGUEZ (age 7)

Chicano Moratorium

I saw a lot of people . . . about a hundred.
And then, I saw Henry R . . . so we
started marching
With him.
We marched from Atlantic Park to
Laguna Park.
on the way, somebody gave us
Cartons of water.

For one thing, I was bored and tired,
'Cause I just had to walk.
It was hot and . . .
I was uncomfortable.
My shoe laces kept getting untied, and
Every time we stopped . . .
I would look at my shoelaces and . . .
They were untied. So I bent down
And I tied them.

Some kids were throwing bottles and
things at the policemen . . .
So I got scared.
I was thinking that they,
The kids,
Were crazy.
I didn't want the kids to throw things
at the policemen . . .

Because I knew that the policemen
Were going to start . . .
Beating up people.

And . . .
My mother was staying there to watch . . .
So, I got even more scared.
So, I started telling my mother
To start walking.
She started ignoring me.
I just started marching
With Juan . . .
Because he drove us there
And he stayed there with us.
Then we got to Laguna Park.
Then we heard the sirens of the policemen.
So we started running out
To see what was happening.

And then . . .
We saw a whole mess of cop cars going by.
So, then, we
Crossed the street.
We met my sister there.
my sister wanted to see what was happening
So there was a green Volkswagen there
My sister got on top of the car.

Then we saw Carlos G.
We saw rocks and bottles being thrown
Up in the air
About a block away
From where we were
Standing.

We couldn't see good
From where we were.
I saw a police bus . . .

That was full of policemen . . .
Except for a couple of seats
That were empty.
And . . .
More cars of policemen
Went by.
Then,
I heard
Some shooting,
I couldn't see . . .
What the policemen were doing
Because it was loaded
With tear gas . . . and
It was too white to
See through it.

And then . . . I saw people running away
With their faces
All red, burned . . . and
Sweaty . . .
And their eyes red and tears
Running down their faces.

They were washing their faces
With the hose
In a lady's yard
Where we were standing.
Then Carlos and Juan helped us . . .
Get away.

And there is going to be . . .
Another march
On the 16th of September and
My brother and I
Are not going to be
There . . .
Because I think

It is going to be
Terrible again,
But my Mother
Is going to go . . .
ALONE.

52 / Katarina Davis del Valle

Song to a Thousand Faces / My People in the Streets

Remembrance   August 29, 1970   hot afternoon

Marching across an ancient land now Whittier Boulevard
hot street beneath tired feet
and voices lifted to the sky
speaking just whispered comfort

We are here and we are One for now

marching across an ancient land now Whittier Boulevard
(knowing we speak to ourselves much more than to anyone else
the shouts higher every step)

tunnel over our heads
archway of the ancient gods now freeway overramp
vibrations stirring bodies for miles

A thousand faces
A thousand brown faces
brown from birth
from that same birth that gave birth to the corn husk in Yucatan
(We didn't need to wait for the sun)
marching across an ancient land now Whittier Boulevard
just under that
archway of the ancient gods now freeway overramp
I turn and see a face
in an instant I know

It is We who make the streets sacred.

53 / ABELARDO DELGADO

Due Process of Law

when justice itself is on trial
outmoded law must change in style,
i swear by aztec and christian gods
it will not have another chance,
another while,
you take a simple misdemeanor
charge
of carrying a concealed weapon,
c.c.w., for short, apply that law
to a chicano taller and stronger
than the California sequoias
and watch the whole southwest
tremble stronger than the recent
quake,
i do not envy judges or jurors
or prosecutors for their yardstick
called law crumbles in their very
hands
at the weight of past misjudgments
and a justice dispensed not out
of fair blindness but out
of 20-20 blue eyes with dollars for
lashes
and so it was that symbolically
el jefe would get like christ

---

el jefe— the boss (Corky Gonzales)

forty days and forty nights
and zeta acosta to the almost
last court in heaven or in hell
or until the whole story tell
who is really guilty of what
and leave those truly guilty in
their consciences to rot.

---

zeta acosta— Oscar Zeta Acosta, Chicano attorney and novelist

$\mathcal{54}$ / Roberto Rodríguez

From *Assault with a Deadly Weapon*

By then, Chicanismo—pride in being Chicano, in being Mexicano, was sweeping through all the barrios of L.A. Montebello seemed to be untouched by this movement. The majority of Mexicans from Montebello it seemed were surfers who thought they belonged to another race. I don't think I had ever really come into contact with a totally brainwashed Mexican until I went to school at Montebello High. The thing too was that not that many of us from Eastmont Jr. High seemed to be going there. There was a revolution going on in the streets a few blocks away—and it seemed like there was a gigantic barrier on Garfield Blvd. or something because it didn't seem to have any effect on many students there.

As a thirteen, fourteen and fifteen year old—I knew there were walkouts going on around and I knew that people were protesting police brutality and things like that but nothing that had happened till then, besides crossing the border, had really made any impact on me. On August 29th, 1970 it was as though reality set in on East L.A. There was a big riot that day. It was to protest the high rate of Chicanos being killed in Vietnam. I think that the organizers had one thing in mind and the plebe had another. The event set the stage for a cataclysmic volcano. East L.A. erupted and till this day, it will never be the same again. If Rubén Salazar, noted journalist for the *L.A. Times* and News Director for Channel 34, hadn't been killed, who knows how we would've looked back on that day. To the youth, like myself, we had other things to think about. It might have gone down as just another riot during a turbulent era. That was the time of the Vietnam War, but youngsters didn't really care about it until they got to be of drafting age. The reason this day became different is because inadvertently, Rubén Salazar became an instant martyr. Everyone still remembers the Silver Dollar and Laguna Park. Now, it is the New Silver Dollar, and Laguna was renamed "Rubén Salazar Park."

Consciously or subconsciously, I know that that event influenced me probably more than anything that had ever happened to me.

♪♪ / Luis J. Rodríguez

From *Always Running: La vida loca, Gang Days in L.A.*

When the hanging's done and the embers at the burning
stake are grayed and cold, the conquered bodies of martyrs
become the unconquerable ideas.   Nelson Peery

August 29, 1970: Tens of thousands gathered in East L.A.'s Belvedere Park to protest the Viet Nam War. The organizers placed flyers on lampposts and bus stops with the following statistics: 22 percent of the war's casualties came from Spanish-speaking communities—although this population made up less than six percent of the U.S. total!

The ensuing march and demonstration—called the Chicano Moratorium Against The War—became the largest anti-war rally ever held in a minority community.

I jumped on a bumpy bus from South San Gabriel and exited on Beverly Boulevard and Third Street, toward Belvedere Park. When I arrived, people carried signs denouncing the war, including a few which said "Chicano Power." The Brown Berets, both men and women, in military-style tan, fatigue clothing, marched in cadence on Third Street. A man with a bull horn shouted slogans: "No More War," "¡Chale! We Won't Go" and "¡Qué Viva La Raza!"

The slogans incited the crowd to chants. Signs and fists pierced the sky. Conga drum beats swirled around a grouping of people at one end of the park. I melded among the protesters, dressed in street attire and my favorite blue Pendleton shirt. When the marching started, I threw a fist into the air.

We advanced down Atlantic Boulevard, past stretches of furniture stores, used car lots and cemeteries. Store owners closed early, pulling across rusty

---

¡Chale! – No way!
¡Qué Viva La Raza! – Long live the People!

iron enclosures. Young mothers with infants in strollers, factory hands, gang-bangers, a newly-wed couple in wedding dress and tuxedo—young and old alike—strolled beside me.

We snaked around to Whittier Boulevard where people from the neighborhood joined in the march; some offered us water and food. Battles between police and young dudes flared up in alleys and side streets. Thrown bottles smashed the windshields of squad cars.

The protesters pulled into Laguna Park in the heart of the largest community of Mexicans outside of Mexico. A stage thundered with speeches, theater and song. Music permeated the air. I spotted Cuervo and Eight Ball from Lomas. They had reds and we dropped a few. There was a liquor store on the corner of Indiana and Whittier where we scored on some brew. But Cuervo and Eight Ball stole a case, forcing the store owner to close up shop. Soon a crowd gathered outside the store demanding to get in. Somebody banged on the glass door. Suddenly a shotgun pressed against my skull.

"Move or I'll blow your fuckin' head off," a sheriff's deputy ordered. I returned to the park, wandering through feet and bodies, coolers and blankets.

A line of deputies at the park's edge—armed with high-powered rifles, billy clubs and tear gas launchers—swaggered toward the crowd. They mowed down anybody in their path. A group of people held arms to stop the rioting police from getting to the families. I turned toward the throng of officers. One guy told me to go back: "We'll fight tomorrow."

But there were no more tomorrows for me. I had had enough at the hands of alien authority.

Come on, then, you helmeted, wall of state power. Come and try to blacken this grass, this shirt of colors, this festive park filled with infants and mothers and old men, surging forth in pride. Come and try to blacken it with your blazing batons, shotguns and tear gas canisters. I'm ready.

A deputy in a feverish tone shouted for me to move.

"*Chale,* this is my park."

Before I knew it, officers drove my face into the dirt; there was a throbbing in my head where a black jack had been swung. On the ground, drops of red slid over blades of green. The battle of Laguna Park had started.

Bodies scurried in all directions. Through the tear gas mist, I saw shadows of children crying, women yelling, and people lying on the grass, kicking and gouging as officers thrust black jacks into ribs and spines. Deputies pursued several people into the yards and living rooms of nearby homes. In a murderous frenzy, they pulled people out of back yards and porches, beating and arresting them.

A deputy pushed me into the back of a squad car. Somebody lay next to me, his hair oiled in blood. I didn't want to look in case his brains were coming out. I gave him a piece of my favorite shirt, soon to be soaked.

The first round of arrestees were crowded into a holding tank for hours in the East L.A. jail—the same jail where in a year's time, seven prisoners reportedly "committed suicide."

Later that night, we were piled into black, caged buses and taken to the Los Angeles County Jail, the largest in the country, then to juvenile hall and again to the county jail. At one point, officers sprayed mace into the windows of the bus while we sat chained to one another. Our eyes and skin burned as we yelled, but no one could hear us.

There were three other young dudes with me: another 16 year old, a 15 year old and his 13-year-old brother. In the county jail, deputies placed us in with adults—with murder, drug and rape suspects. We weren't old enough to be incarcerated there, but they didn't care about this. There was an uprising in East L.A. and we were part of it. One black guy recalled the Watts rebellion and shook our hands. I watched deputies come into the cells and beat up prisoners—breaking the arm of one guy.

At one point, the four of us juveniles were hauled to the Hall of Justice jail, known as the Glasshouse. The deputies threw us into "murderers' row," where hardcore offenders were awaiting trial or serving time. I had a cell next to Charles Manson.

They threw me in with a dude who had killed a teacher and another who had shot somebody in the Aliso Village housing projects. One of the dudes pressed a stashed blade to my neck. But I knew, no matter what, never show fear. I stood up to him, staring without blinking. Then he backed off. Soon we played cards, told jokes and stories.

That night, we heard the "East L.A. riot"—this is what the media was calling it!—had escalated throughout much of Whittier Boulevard. Stores were burned down and looted. Police had killed people. Fires flared in other Chicano communities such as Wilmington and Venice.

Then a radio reporter announced that sheriff's deputies had killed Chicano journalist Rubén Salazar. Salazar had been a lone voice in the existing media for the Mexican people in the United States (he was a former *Los An-*

geles Times reporter and KMEX-TV news director). At word of his death, the tier exploded into an uproar. Inmates gave out gritos and cell bars rattled; mattresses were set on fire.

The next day, Manson, who stayed in an enclosed cell with only a small glass-and-bar opening to see him through, had to attend a hearing. Early that morning, guards woke up everybody and made us face the walls of our cells. Some protested. The dude next to me said it was at Manson's request.

"Fuck this," I said, but we were forced to comply.

At midday, they allowed us to roam the tier. I talked to inmates from the other cells, most of whom were black or Chicano. For the most part, the four of us young dudes from the unrest were treated with respect. When it was time for Manson to walk the tier, however, the guards made everyone else go back into their cells. Manson emerged from his enclosed box. He ranted and raved about "niggers and spics," about how whites should kill us all. The other inmates yelled back, threatened his life, but Manson knew the guards wouldn't let anyone get to him.

I disappeared in the criminal justice system. I was being held without a hearing. Whenever one was scheduled, my parents would show up and then the courts canceled it. Dad and Mom searched for me everywhere. They checked for my name in court records and arrest sheets. They fell into a maze of paperwork and bureaucrats. At least once, I was being pulled away in chains while my mom and dad sat confused in a hearing room. Days built up on days while they waited word about my release.

Finally in the middle of the night, a guard awakened me, pulled me out of the cell and led me down brightly-lit corridors. Through a thick-glassed window, I saw my mother's weary face.

They brought me out in my old clothes, caked with dirt and blood. Mama forced a smile.

"I ain't no criminal, ma," I reassured her.

"I know, m'ijo," she replied. "I know."

---

gritos – shouts
m'ijo – my son

56 / Lucha Corpi

From *Delia's Song*

"Don't you think that everyone has a right to a safe environment and to an equal share in the benefits of his labor?" Mattie insisted.

There was ineluctable logic in Mattie's words—platitudes, Delia thought. She had heard them all her life, but was it really so? Did all people in the U.S. share alike? She and her family had had few choices. She was at Berkeley because an Anglo nun in high school had managed to open some doors for her.

Her brother, Sebastián, had not been so lucky and had died of a drug overdose in a damp, putrid-smelling shooting gallery. Her second brother, Ricardo, had gone into the Army because he was afraid he would suffer the same fate as Sebastián.

"What a choice," she had told Ricardo when they kissed for the last time. "You either die like Sebastián or you die on a battlefield."

Ricardo smiled and tried to be hopeful. "There won't be a war, *hermanita,* and I might just come back with a career." A year later, he was lying dead in a swamp in Southeast Asia.

Delia felt a pang of anger. *What does she know about me and my people Does she really care* "For Mexican-Americans there are no choices," she uttered in anger and her tone surprised and scared her; yet she felt exhilarated. . . .

March 21 1969   I didn't write anything after that Silence   Fog   When the wind becomes a whisper   Fog rolls in   The first day of spring Silence   The blank pages   The walls empty   TWLF   Washed away Samuel   Julio   The Marines Yeah Your brother and I musta' been there at the same time He was in the Army You say Ricardo Treviño   How was it over there Julio I   Suena callous But maybe your brother was one of the lucky ones You know

---

hermanita— little sister
Suena— it sounds

To have died right away Look at Güero that vato is in bad shape Vivo pero muerto It
was hell It was hell all right Those of us who came back alive We'll never be the same
again You loved him very much He was my brother He was my best friend too Know
what you mean Mi carnala y yo We're good friends too If my mom had asked him not
to go But she didn't   Nothing she could do He wanted to go Somos cabrones Men
Warlords Creemos que somos lo más chingón This time the gun backfired on us. . . .

   What does Mamá want   Why don't you ask her   She won't tell me She says
I ask too many questions Is that bad   No darling it's not bad She probably feels it's
too late for her   Too late Why We all have dreams that sometimes never come true
Dreams   The lethal dose swallowed   What did she dream of doing She lies in the
cradle of unfulfilled dreams She lulls herself to sleep And I thought all her dreams had to
do with us Ricardo Where does the dream end and the nightmare begin   She once
had two sons The man came and took one away Sister listen to my story Sister holding
back my tears I demand from him   Go on Lay your platitudes on my table   And
she gave him   Tell me that to die for God and country is right She could have said
no but she didn't Tell me that the killing must go on to ensure the welfare of the world
There won't be a war hermanita and I might just come back with a career Tell me that I
was wrong to bring up men of peace   Why do mothers allow their sons to go to war
But before you come for my sons man Build a concrete wall around you For my heart
knows inch by word your dark designs And you You're in danger Beg   Fight
Go to jail Organize   Mattie is right   Brown brother against brown brother
Young Chicanos will buy again the politics of self-destruction   Central America
If we could Organize Chicano mothers   How   Aunt Marta   Camille They
don't have children   My mother   Maybe she could do it   No she probably
wouldn't   Just another dream   Another dream   Or another nightmare
nightmare   Why not   Even if it is   What if it doesn't do any good   It
didn't do any good ten years ago   It seemed all so useless No   Jeff is right It's useless not to try to do something   It wasn't fair But then life has nothing to do with
fairness   No He hasn't done anything for Chicanos   I haven't either Okay We
got beaten over the head I will get beaten and I'll get up again and again and again
I'm here to stay

---

vato— dude
Vivo pero muerto— Alive but dead
Mi carnala y yo— My sister and I
Somos cabrones— We're bad asses
Creemos que somos lo más chingón— We think we're the baddest

♪7 / Rick Browne

Young Chicano's Death Described
(on Moratorium of January 30, 1971)

I was a close-up witness Sunday to the last violent moments in the life of a young Chicano. [The deceased was in fact Austrian exchange student Gustav Montag, from East L.A. College—Ed.]

I arrived on Whittier Blvd. shortly before 4 P.M., just minutes after rioters had moved down that East Los Angeles business artery, smashing the store windows that weren't boarded up, ripping down protective iron gratings, looting a music store here, a dress shop there. About a dozen sheriff's deputies, in full riot gear and most of them carrying shotguns, were walking west on Whittier toward Arizona Ave. in an inverted wedge formation. The deputies moved hesitantly under a heavy barrage of rocks, bottles, lengths of pipe, concrete chunks, and other objects that were being thrown by about 40 young Chicanos stationed on both sides of the Whittier-Arizona intersection.

It was the first confrontation between deputies and Chicanos all day. Uniformed officers were conspicuous by their absence at the 'police brutality' protest in Belvedere Park and at the subsequent attack on cars in the parking lot of the East Los Angeles sheriff's station. The deputies and Chicano assailants were about 40 feet from each other on Whittier Blvd. when I heard about 10 shotgun rounds fired into the air, apparently as a warning. I was more or less in line with the advancing deputies but was hugging storefront walls on the north side of Whittier. As I got to within 30 feet of the intersection, I saw one Chicano in a white t-shirt throw a chunk of concrete and another Chicano—heavy-set and wearing a sweater—throw a big metal plate.

At the same instant, I heard four or five explosions and saw dust and concrete fly off the corner of the building at Whittier and Arizona. I turned and saw a sergeant bring his revolver down and holster it—and saw two deputies in a crouch, pumping the spent cartridges out of their shotguns. The sergeant's right hand and helmet were bloody. I turned back quickly and saw the heavy-set Chicano sprawled face down over the curb and the Chicano in the t-shirt lying motionless in the middle of the street, blood spurting from his neck.

The mortally wounded man was cared for by several friends, who waved the missile-throwers away and tried to stanch the flow of blood by applying pressure to the wound in his neck. A priest rushed up and several Chicanos gingerly lifted the dying man and, inexplicably, started to carry him to the other side of Whittier and down a block to set him down. In the minutes before the ambulance arrived, several Chicanos who were gathered around the dying man yelled at the deputies, "Murderers!" and "Killer Pigs!" The sergeant who had fired his revolver—I didn't get his name—commented later, "I don't think I hit him. My shot hit the corner of the building."

58 / ALBERTO RÍOS

The Vietnam Wall

I
Have seen it
And I like it: The magic,
The way like cutting onions
It brings water out of nowhere.
Invisible from one side, a scar
Into the skin of the ground
From the other, a black winding
Appendix line.
                    A dig,
                    The way archeologists explain.
The walk is slow at first
Easy, a little black marble wall
Of the dollhouse,
A smoothness, a shine
The boys in the street want to give.
One name. And then more
Names, long lines, lines of names until
They are the shape of the U.N. building
Taller than I am: I have walked
Into a grave.
And everything I expect has been taken away, like that, quick:
                    The names are not alphabetized.
                    They are in the order of dying,
                    An alphabet of—somewhere—screaming.
I start to walk out. I almost leave
But stop to look up names of friends,
My own name. There is somebody

Severiano Rios.
Little kids do not make the same noise
Here, junior high school boys don't run
Or hold each other in headlocks.
No rules, something just persists
Like pinching on St. Patrick's Day
Every year for no green.
                    No one knows why.
Flowers are forced
Into the cracks
Between sections.
Men have cried
At this wall.
I have
Seen them.

59 / Naomi Helena Quiñonez

America's Wailing Wall

There was a sixties hitch
and we were it.
The world around us
launched an all-out defensive
and you were sent to
screaming eagles.
I defied tradition.
There was movement
and we pushed hard
against new skin.
Out here the world
was a carnival
of blind purpose
and anger.
The striated hues
of social change
became vivid
and finally
bold with reason.
In your twilight zone
of death
you drained
into pale submission.
The moss green
of your jacket
a fibrous tumor

on your good spirit.
A blood belt of outrage
bonded us
before the barrios
became a pond
fat with fish
for military consumption.
"Carnal"
I named you affectionately
"Carnalita" you responded.
Each day
one more young man
disappeared off the streets,
hooked on the bait
dropped before carnales like you.
Jail or war
Poverty or war
Victim or war
Later your letters appeared.
Words lined the pages
like tired weeds.
I answered
giving all the details
to my life of infamy
describing my own war
of wombs and justice.
You gave me few clues
but your letters
smelled of death
and between the stiff
upper lip
of your lines
I read your daily horrors.

Carnal—Brother
Carnalita—Sister

Today I walk to the wall
we have constructed for you
the thousands of names
solidified
into a polished monolith.
Your name stands there
someplace
on America's wailing wall.
On America's wailing wall
your name stands there
someplace
between millions of names
of those
sentenced to death.
Your name scratched into
stone
like the placa you etched
on a church wall
in the vain illusion
of the por vida
we shared.
There is no bringing you
back
carnal.
But your spirit reminds
those who dare to remember
that the wars
worthy of the deaths
of men and women like you
are best fought
on our own turf
against a common enemy.
Ignorance
will be attacked

---

placa— graffiti
por vida— forever

until there are no more
dogs of war
until there are no more
wailing walls
until there are
no more wars.

60 / Enrique R. Lamadrid

Enemy Way

Ricardo knew it would take months to get used to the silence. Back in Albuquerque the pace of his life had become so frantic that coming to the pine and sage mesa country of *Tloh' Chin To* was like stepping off into a void. Not that he had really gotten away from anything. The war and his struggle with the draft hung just as oppressively over his thoughts. Drawing a ten on the draft lottery had thrust him into the middle of a dangerous whirlwind on an unknown course. "It's the only damned drawing I've ever come that close to winning," he thought, the usual wisp of humor creeping back into his thoughts. "With luck like that something was telling me that I'd got some Asians in my future." He was glad that they would be Navajo instead of Vietnamese. He was feeling more in control of his destiny now than the night when Selective Service played TV sweepstakes with his life.

The red glow was fading from the sandstone cliffs behind his cabin as Ricardo stumbled back inside to light the lamps and start a fire. As he was fumbling with the matches he heard the bellowing and popping of Benny Chato's new GTO as it lurched up the dirt road. "God, not again," Ricardo cringed. The length of the horn blasts were the measure of Benny's drunkenness.

"*Haa t'ish ba naa ni nah,* Benny, how've you been?" Ricardo shouted tentatively.

"Hey, *Naakai,* how about we cruise some a little bit?" came the standard reply. Benny always used the Navajo word for Mexican with him, a sign of guarded trust.

"Take it easy, you want to get me killed?" Ricardo joked to ease the tension.

"Watch it, maybe I do, so just get in *Naakai,* I'm telling you."

Ricardo sank reluctantly into the front seat and Benny shoved a can of beer into his lap. Ricardo drank it slowly as Jimi Hendrix blasted out of the tape deck.

"Well, aren't you going to ask me anymore about Nam?" Benny scowled. He still didn't know what to think of the outsider who had set up in his uncle's summer cabin.

"I just can't believe you signed up again, Benny, what's in it for you?" Ricardo complained, his uneasy frankness beginning to show.

"That's where the action is, you know, it's too damn quiet up here. I get too nervous hanging around."

Actually, Benny had only spoken once about Viet Nam, briefly muttering something about "those fucking Gooks and their shit smeared booby traps." It was chilling to hear the slurs coming from such a high cheeked, bronze face. Usually outspoken in condemning the war, Ricardo held back his feelings with the Navajos. They all seemed so much in favor of it, even to the point of having "Love it or Leave" bumper stickers and double eagle decals on their pick ups. It was hard enough around Chicanos, so many of his own cousins and friends had enlisted. Speaking your mind was risky business, especially when people thought you were condemning your own family.

Strangely, Benny spoke freely about his uncle in World War II, how he had been one of the famous Navajo code talkers. The silence about his own experience made Ricardo think that he must consider it in less than heroic terms. The times he asked about Ricardo's military background, Ricardo always managed to change the subject. He feared what would happen when Benny found out.

"Those bullshit hippy traitors. I wish you could've seen the one I pounded last month in Gallup," he said, slugging the dashboard. "But all you *Naakai,* you're different, more like us." He started the engine and Ricardo jumped out, relieved to see the dusty lights disappearing.

On the way to school the next morning, Ricardo felt a gnawing frustration. "How am I going to survive here if I can't tell anybody where I stand. I wish I could get it across to the Navajos what bloody mercenaries they are by joining up and going along with everything the government dishes out." Around the bend near the Chapter House, he started, braking reflexively upon seeing Benny's GTO halfway down the embankment resting square on a smashed juniper. "To think I almost went with him last night!" he sighed after making sure that nobody was in the vehicle.

At school he hurried down to the math classroom where Gloria Chato,

Benny's sister-in-law, was an aide. Without even pausing to greet her, Ricardo whispered, "Is he OK? I saw his car by the Chapter House."

She made a confusing gesture, nodding and shaking her head at once, "He walked away from this one too. Didn't make it to his mother's till after midnight. Did you see him last night?"

"He came by around sundown. Gloria, I think he's really trying to kill himself." Ricardo paused, amazed they had exchanged so many feelings with so few formalities. He hardly knew her.

In his classroom, he stared out the window at the pale autumn light, waiting for the students. Ricardo had an innate sense of how to belong in a new place with new people. He felt close to what he knew of Navajo ways, but his growing awareness had its price. True differences separate peoples; there are cultural gaps that might never be bridged. Yet, his students sensed that as a *Naakai,* he was somehow more approachable, more familiar than the uptight *"Bilagaana"* teachers from back east.

It was ironic that not that long ago the Spanish had also made their attempt to dominate the Navajo. Instead, the Navajo assimilated the Spanish, taking only what they needed from them: horses, sheep, coffee and a few cultural odds and ends. Ricardo was delighted that he could communicate so well with the older people who knew more Spanish than English. Since World War II, the children had been learning English so his bond with the younger Indians was a little harder earned. Even though he taught biology, his kids were always asking him what all their Spanish surnames meant. It was embarrassing to have to tell them that Chato was "flat face" and Cojo was "lame one," but he added that these were names used by great chiefs. Fortunately most of them had more traditional names like Martínez, Pino or García.

"Morning, Mr. Cha-Cha" the kids taunted as they piled gleefully into the room. It was only a month into classes and they had a nickname for every teacher in the school. After the class the boys cornered him with the usual questions.

"Come on Mr. Chávez, you said you would tell us about when you were in the service. Was it the Army?" He shook his head, "The Navy?" They never asked about the Marines or Air Force because of his glasses.

"All right, all right, I'll tell you but you've got to sit down first. I wasn't in the service and I won't ever be."

"Eh yah," they squealed. "Was it because you were chicken or something?" one of them laughed. A hush fell over them again as Ricardo managed an appropriate frown.

"No, I just told them I wasn't going to go when they tried to get me to. You want to know why?" They fixed their eyes on him. "Because if it was a hundred years ago and I let them take me, you know who I would be fighting with?" He paused again for dramatic effect. "You guys . . . and I'm not about to do that either, then or now!"

They rushed up and surrounded him, their raven heads bobbing up and down shouting, "Why us, why us?"

"Because back then you guys were the enemy, you guys were the Gooks, and Kit Carson had us killing your sheep, burning your hogans, and cutting down your peach trees." Ricardo drove his point home hard. It was they who had told him the human details of the Long Walk of the Navajos, how their parents still knew the songs that were sung by the people as they were driven with their sheep across the desert.

"So that's why I didn't go to the service. How could I shoot you guys?" he said laughing, poking them in the stomach with his finger to break the mood.

As they stampeded out the door, Ricardo stood there shaking his head, unable to believe that he had just spilled his guts to them. It was so easy and they seemed to understand the way he had made his point. "Did you say too much? Did you blow it?"

The rest of the week went by more quickly than usual. Now that the word was about him, what more could happen? His sense of confidence was gradually returning. Knowing the Navajo community as he did, he figured his words would come back to him. "But from where?" The doubts kept rolling back through his mind. "If you could only explain it to the adults as easily as you did to the kids . . ."

Ricardo spent a quiet weekend grading papers and splitting wood. On Sunday afternoon he almost acted on his urge to go to town, especially since that was Benny's favorite time to drop by. This time when he heard the rumble of the souped up engine, he was ready for anything.

"*Yaa'a t'eh,*" Benny said, barely honking as he drove up. Not only was he early, but Ricardo was surprised to see he hadn't been drinking. "Let's go, *Naakai,* I want to talk to you." With a shrug, Ricardo jumped in.

They turned down the road towards Zuni. Benny handed him a thermos of coffee and Ricardo poured out a cup.

"We're going to an Enemy Way over by Broken Rock. I wanted you to be there. A friend of mine is just back from Nam and they're doing it for him."

"What are they going to do, Benny?"

"It's a Squaw Dance, there'll be food."

"Yeah, but why your friend? Will we see him?"

"No, they'll have him stashed away inside his hogan with the medicine man. He got fucked up in Nam, and they're going to straighten out his head. The action for us will be outside."

They drove part way toward Gallup and cut far west on a red dirt road. The shadows were lengthening into rusty velvet as Ricardo's thoughts bounded ahead of the car. Something had changed in Benny.

It was dark by the time they turned into a clearing with a hogan behind a square log house. Already a huge bonfire was licking up into the night, making it seem even darker. An assortment of dusty pickups was parked around the fire. People were seated in them, eating, hardly speaking, laughing quietly. They loaded up on roast lamb ribs, mutton stew and fry bread. There were two brand new garbage cans on small fires, simmering to the brim with coffee. Ricardo had never seen so much coffee.

"How are these people going to drink up all that *gohweh?*" he said, emphasizing the last word, a Navajo version of the Spanish *café*.

"They will," laughed Benny, "they will." After seven or eight cups, Ricardo knew what he meant. The crystal-headed clarity of the caffeine intoxication was something he had never experienced to that degree.

By then a group of singers had gathered and another bonfire was lit. Although the songs sounded serious, Ricardo noticed there were a few words tossed in to accompany the usual seed syllables of the chant. Now and then quiet laughter would ripple through the spectators.

"Are those words, Benny?" He nodded with his lips. "If this is about your wiped-out friend, why are the people giggling and enjoying themselves?"

"Listen to this one, Ricardo: 'I'm so horny, won't you let me take you home, take you home, in my one-eyed Ford, hey yanna ho, hey yanna eh!'"

"You've got to be kidding, I thought this was supposed to be serious."

"It is. They're fixing up my friend, Danny Peshlakai. Meanwhile, we're supposed to be putting in our good feelings. Hey look, there goes the sage girl. Watch what she does. You better find something to give her."

Dressed in velvet and silver, a young woman was doing a measured side step around the circle. She was clutching sprigs of sage in each hand, gently swaying them as she danced. She would pause every few steps, picking men out of the crowd with her eyes. They would come forward and do a few stately turns around her with their eyes lowered. As she dismissed them with a flick of her chin they dropped coins and dollar bills into her sash.

Ricardo was so entranced with her beauty and the pulsing songs of the chorus that before he knew it she was looking directly at him. He started slinking back into the shadows, embarrassed to be the only outsider there. Benny whispered, nudging him forward into the full glow of the bonfire, "Go on, go on, she wants you. Be sure to give her these." He dropped a handful of quarters into Ricardo's fist.

Shouts from the crowd applauded him as he circled around her. The dark folds of her dress blended with the night sky and firelight glinted from the constellations of silver buttons on her breast. Ricardo stared into her eyes for a moment too long and she brushed his face with the sage, smiling. He almost forgot to drop the coins in her sash as he stepped back into the crowd.

"Hey, *Naakai,* remember I said you would like this?" Benny said, jabbing him in the ribs.

After a few more cups of coffee, Ricardo turned towards his companion, "Benny, did they ever do an Enemy Way for you?"

"Hell no, everyone knows I'm too crazy. Besides, I didn't bring you here to have you ask me that." A frown formed then vanished from his face.

"Why did you bring me then?" Ricardo thought, not daring to speak. They both stared at the ground.

"It's time we should go. Look how late it is," Benny said. "Besides, in an hour or so they'll start shooting off their rifles to mark the end of the ceremony. You don't want to be here for that part."

They walked back to the car and started back down the dirt road to the highway. At the turn off they both noticed a shooting star coming right out of the constellation of the seven sisters. Ricardo thought of the sage girl and everything he had experienced that night.

"I think I know why you brought me, Benny," he said, struggling with his apology. "It was beautiful. So much good energy for a returning soldier. I've never seen anything like it." He held his breath while Benny kept looking straight out the windshield. "I think I've been much too critical of your people and the war. I should shut up and learn something from you. You've been great warriors for centuries and who am I to say anything?"

"It's what you said the other day, Cha-Cha, that's why I brought you." Benny gunned the engine and spun onto the highway.

"What do you mean?" Ricardo said, alarmed at the burst of speed and the swerving of the car.

"It's my brother. Gloria told me. Gloria my sister-in-law, you know." Ricardo didn't move. "Some kids told her what you said to them." Ricardo's heart sank.

"Benny, I didn't mean any harm. I was just explaining to them why I wouldn't fight." Surprisingly the car slowed down.

"It's all right, *Naakai,* I understand. I don't want to fight you either." Ricardo couldn't believe his ears. Benny continued. "It's my brother. See if you can help him out. He and Gloria have two kids and he just got his draft notice. He doesn't want to go."

"He got his draft notice? Do they know he has a family?" Benny nodded. "That's crazy, no way those bastards can get away with that. He's got rights. I'll talk to him tomorrow."

"Thanks, *Naakai,* I hoped you could understand," Benny said with awkward relief. "Come on, we've got to get home and work on getting some sleep tonight after all that coffee." He reached under the seat and handed Ricardo a warm beer. They opened it and passed it back and forth silently as they sped off into the velvet and silver night.

61 / Gregg Barrios

Chale Guerra

Chale Guerra de Corpus Christi came home
with his body broken and crippled and hanging from his neck
he had an AirCom medal, a bronze star, a foreign service
medal, and a broken purple heart. What else?
Oh, a broken back, a silver plated brace,
a nervous tic, and a stainless wheel chair to race.
When he came home there was no xmas, no news,
no new year, no gas, no men in little white hats,
no love, no welcome home, no nothing.

Now Carlos Guerra sits in his tiny room and plots
now that his nerves are a bundle of rotten knots
and no job offers come his way, and no one gets
in his way, and he can't even get his rocks off
cause no young girl wants a cripple mess
to slob over her luscious *teen-age* bod.

But Charlie was young once and in his barrio
on Leopard Street he was bien pinche—"Chale
el jale" as he was known because he loved to party
back then he wanted to be a marine and prove himself
as a real macho and fight for the country that never gave
him a damn thing except a warped sense of who he was
and what he could do with himself.

---

bien pinche—very flaky

Now he can't do anything for himself. Now he can't do
anything. Anything. You wanna drink of water, Chale?
You have to piss, Chale? You have to scratch your ass,
Chale! No Jane Fonda in the middle of the night to
offer him some afternoon delight. No one to make him
feel like a man of might.

So they put Carlos on the Domingo Peña Show
right between the Butter Krust Bread and Joe Bravo
commercials. And he looked like a real war hero
some kind of secret agent orange colored spy
as he told his tale live as thousands gasped
and they gave him a dozen loaves of bread and
the VA promised to find him a special hospital bed
and he went home that night got drunk and tried to fight
and in the morning they came and took him away.

And now all the vatos in the barrio talk about poor
Chale and listen to the jukebox in the PASTIME pool
hall as "Ya Volví de Vietnam" churns out loud
and hell, Chale might as well be dead but god would
have it that he spend the rest of his days a freak.
My aunt went to see him and when she returned
she could hardly speak about it. Chale Guerra.
That poor sonovabitch from el barrio de Leopard St.

---

vatos – dudes
Ya Volví de Vietnam – I just got back from Vietnam

A time to raise questions

Alex Ortega's story made the news
as one of the 'Hispanics'
killed in Lebanon
his death—a tribute
to all Hispanic-Americans.

He was not alone:
Johnnie, Juan, Danny, Randall, Ronald,
Louis, Richard, Rafael, Camera,
Gómez, García, Hernández,
Ortiz, Quirante, Rodríguez,
Santos, Silva, and Valle.

Never quite understanding
the war in Lebanon,
our foreign policy. . . .
reading lists like this
my mind/soul reflects
on sobrinos-nephews
that have joined the service.

Why do we not honor
those that believe
in justice and peace,
those that have refused
to go into foreign lands
to kill innocent people

because presidents and generals
pass the order?

Why do we not honor those
that have given their life
to better educating themselves
in order that they might return
to their barrios
to make it a better world
for the unfortunate, the poor?

Why do we not honor those
that have refused to take up arms
but instead creatively
use their talents for the kingdom?

Why do we not honor those
that did not go to Lebanon
because they believed
that this is not the way
to bring about peace!

The death of Raza—of our brothers
and sisters
is a time to give tribute to Hispanic
Americans.
It is also a time—for all of us
to raise questions
about our participation in unjust wars—
the annihilation of peoples
for the interest
of a few,
the rich!

EPILOGUE: Treinta años después
(Thirty years later)

Politicians now court the Hispanic middle class, and corporate managers have discovered the "Hispanic market," but social and economic conditions for the majority of Chicanos and Mexicanos have not substantially improved in the past thirty years. The redistribution of wealth upwards, the long recession in the 1980s, job flight, deindustrialization, and the worsening crisis in the urban cores have all contributed to xenophobia in the Southwest. From Texas to California, we have seen immigrant bashing, the militarization of the U.S.-Mexico border, the inaction of government officials to the 1992 L.A. riots, and attacks on affirmative action. Proposals from the progressive side are vague and ineffectual. In the think tanks and universities, intellectuals "theorize" poverty, "minority discourse," and "race" but cannot act. Coalitions among disempowered groups are tenuously constructed, as various groups spin off into separatist identity politics.

The Chicano Movement finds itself fragmented as well. Among Chicano/a youth, the rampant careerism bred in the Reagan years clashes with a renewed ethnic nationalism that sits uncomfortably next to broader multiethnic projects such as the "Four Winds" movement in Los Angeles, a group of high school and college students who led walkouts to protest Proposition 187 and attacks on affirmative action. The massive influx of new immigrants since 1970 from Mexico and Central America has forced a rethinking of *chicanismo* and the consideration of pan-Latino alliances. A small elite class of Chicano/a professionals continues to increase its ranks, but it is not clear what their allegiance will be, if any, to the less-privileged communities in which many of them were raised.

At the observation of the twenty-fifth anniversary of the Chicano Moratorium in 1995, organizers were disappointed to learn that public interest was scant. A month later two Chicano intellectuals published an article in the *Los Angeles Times* that declared the *movimiento* dead: "The death throes of the Chicano Movement signal a new consciousness among Latinos. As politically and economically marginal as many of us are today, we are more defined by hope than anger. And as more than one-third of California's population, we are now more concerned with renewing a society in decline than in preserving a minority movement."[1] The tone of this article suggests the rather comfortable and self-congratulatory attitudes of the Hispanic middle class, which, like other bourgeoisies, equates passionate commitment with mere anger and then attributes it to their less-civilized compatriots. Given the dismantling of the public sphere, explicit acts of racism, continuing evidence of police brutality in major urban centers, and anti-immigrant legislation—in short, given a rollback of most of the gains made in the late 1960s and early '70s—it is difficult to understand how the authors of the article could be hopeful.

Because the Chicano Movement was a product of the turbulent Viet Nam era, the new Mexican Americans feel they must disavow it in order to ingratiate themselves with the corporate elite. According to this self-congratulatory mythology, the sixties were simply chaotic; people were irresponsible and acted badly for no reason. So goes the neo-conservative revision of history.

To take one example: In "The Last Angry Brown Hat," L.A. playwright Alfredo Ramos creates a Chicano "Big Chill" in which cynical former Brown Berets wallow in nostalgic memories of their youth. The character "Rude Boy" is a Viet Nam veteran, a former drug addict and current alcoholic who is content to live on unemployment checks and handouts. Halfway through the play, Rude Boy rewrites his own personal trajectory and that of his community:

> Damn it! Who in the hell do we think we are? Did we think we were
> gonna make a difference by putting on those brown hats and yelling,
> "Chicano power!" (*Fist in air*) Hell no! Where was the movement when I
> got shipped over to Viet Nam, huh?
>
> *Rude Boy takes a drink from the tequila bottle.*
>
> Here I am, just barely eighteen years old, fighting in some strange
> country. Shit, until then, I'd never even been outside of East L.A.[2]

With the exception of one reference to the Moratorium demonstration on August 29, 1970, "The Last Angry Brown Hat" erases the Chicano anti-war movement by leaving unanswered Rude Boy's question, "Where was the movement when I got shipped over to Viet Nam, huh?" JoJo, a Hollywood screenwriter, promises he will write a screenplay about the Brown Berets and the Movement, but Ramos's play makes it clear that, even if JoJo keeps his promise, there is no place in the mass media market for treatments of Chicano history, especially those that convey an excess of "anger."

According to the same *L.A. Times* article mentioned earlier: "Ramos claims he and his peers have gone beyond reckless bravado and are a part of a 'new breed' of young Latinos. They're too confident to be defensive. They care about social issues, yet are not driven by anger. They will fight their battles in their own ways. 'We're new and improved,' says Ramos with a laugh."[3] In a typical neo-conservative move, Ramos dismisses the acts of Viet Nam–era activists as "reckless bravado"—as though Chicanos and Chicanas took to the streets in a frenzy of foolishness. What is missing in Ramos's revisionism, of course, is any mention of a war that sent thousands of young men of color into the killing fields of Southeast Asia. The "new and improved" middle-class Hispanic of the 1990s can afford not to be angry since he has never faced conscription, battlefield combat, police or border patrol violence, or the killing of his friends.

In the revisionism of the late 1990s, then, the "Viet Nam experience" is forgotten or else rewritten and repackaged. But the question asked at the end of Oswaldo Rivera's novel *Fire and Rain* has yet to be answered. Comparing the solidarity experienced in combat to the racial divisions experienced in the rear, Rivera's narrator explains:

The tent was not like any hooch in the war zone. . . . This was the world, the one he had left behind. The old components were here. They could never be brought out in the field. The element of self-preservation negated that instinct. Here in the Brig the real danger subsided, and old grievances flared. . . . They stood on their side and we stood on ours. A time-worn equation: them and us. . . . In the rear areas there was a nonexistent durable barrier that no one ever trespassed unless he was an outcast from his peer group; the whites, the blacks, the spics, and within the spics an agglomerate of Mexicans, 'Ricans, Cubans, etc. . . . He thought of the clique back in his old platoon where everyone was lumped together for mutual protection. How long would that little circle last in the outside world? He need not ask. . . . Everybody sticks with his own because he feels more comfortable. Combat distorted this basic relationship in some way. Or was it that the basic relationship was always there and a lack of combat distorted it? We cooperate with outlanders out of the necessity to survive. But what *was* the basic relationship?[4]

The suggestion made in Rivera's novel—that combat precludes narrow separatisms (what today we call identity politics)—should not be written off as mere nostalgia. In difficult times the project to establish the kind of "mutual protection" sought by Rivera's characters will have to be a pan-ethnic, cross-gender enterprise. Narrow nationalisms may be comforting and familiar, but only strong coalitions will see us through.

With the passage of time, representations of what happened during the war will supplant history and be received as factual. The consumption of television programs and movies about the war has in many ways determined what those born after the war know about it. Whenever I speak at local high schools or teach an undergraduate course on the war and the students learn I am a veteran, they invariably ask if I had problems readjusting, if I was addicted to drugs, if I suffered psychologically upon my return. I attribute such questions to the effects of the dominant stereotype of the disturbed Viet Nam vet, a stereotype so pervasive that for these students it overwhelms the apparent fact that I am a university professor with a doctorate who at least is not visibly psychotic.

The power of the stereotype is such that even a writer as sensitive as Ana Castillo can reproduce it with ease, much as earlier stereotypes about Mexicans were reproduced:

> Now, it happened that for some time just hearing that a vato had been in Vietnam, twenty years ago or not, set off a little warning signal in Sara's head. Back in those days when they first came back, Sara was already married, so she didn't have to experience them personally. But still, she heard stories through friends, for instance, how at a family get-together, all of a sudden the Vietnam vato would go off and start throwing things around and beating up on his mother. Things like that.
>
> Anyone can only imagine what those vatos went through in Vietnam. At seventeen or nineteen years old they went off, leaving their little villages and barrios, kissing la Mary Sue or la Debbie goodbye and coming back to give Mary Sue and Debbie a life of hell because they could not shake those six months in the Vietcong jungle.[5]

The beserk Chicano veteran, so violent that he beats his mother, adds one more brick on the edifice of Rambo culture and stereotypical machismo. To reduce all veterans to one type is, of course, dangerously misleading.

The structures of experience that I have discussed in the earlier sections of this book—the sense of solidarity between exploited people of color, for example—are now endlessly crosscut by a vast array of movies and TV programs and, to a lesser extent, novels and poems produced after the war. At the level of mass culture, Oliver Stone, Sylvester Stallone, and their brethren are rewriting the history of the Viet Nam period.

But we also have the Viet Nam Memorial, where the many Spanish surnames remind us of the Latino sacrifices. If a pilgrimage to the Wall is a first step in understanding who has been left out of the historical accounts of the period, follow-up trips to less well-known memorials in the Southwest might fill in the picture. I am thinking in particular of the Viet Nam Veterans National Memorial near Angel Fire, New Mexico. Built in 1971 in the northern section of the state, in the virtual heart of Aztlán, the chapel rests among the foothills of the Sangre de Cristo Mountains overlooking the Moreno Valley. There, far from Washington, D.C., and the myopia of government officials and East Coast historians, one can contemplate Mexican American participation in and against the Viet Nam War. It is to be hoped that this memorial will inspire the telling of Chicano and Chicana experiences of the war in intellectual circles and popular cultural outlets. But even if those experiences are finally represented, they will still not be safe. For until Americans of Mexican descent achieve some resemblance of economic justice and social equality, there is always the possibility that our history will be appropriated and manipulated.

I want to end this volume with a lesson taught by Walter Benjamin, who, as a Jew living in Nazi Germany, understood the plight of marginalized groups and their relationship to official history. In "Theses on the Philosophy of History," he wrote: "Historical materialism wishes to retain that image of the past which unexpectedly appears to man singled out by history at a moment of danger. The danger affects both the content of the tradition and its receivers. The same threat hangs over both: that of becoming a tool of the ruling classes."[6] As receivers, makers, and interpreters of images of the American war in Viet Nam, in particular the effects of that war on the Mexican American community, we are confronted with the threat identified by Benjamin. To what extent will we allow the content of that image to be misappropriated in order to feed a renascent xenophobia and a nostalgic imperial patriotism? To what extent should we allow it to serve as fodder for an overly abstract and mystifying cultural criticism? These and other urgent questions merit our attention because for the vast majority of Chicano and Mexicano people, the moment of danger is now.

Coda

On August 30, 1997, I attended a reunion of some of the original members of the National Chicano Moratorium Committee. The gathering was hosted by Rosalío and Roz Muñoz in their home overlooking the lights of East Los and to the west those of downtown L.A. Old friends recalled the details of the Viet Nam era, shared stories, and debated political theory. Twenty-seven years after that momentous day in 1970, I saw no sign of a "Big Chill" among these former "militants." Keenly aware of the issues facing Spanish-speaking and working-class people, they continue to organize in the trade union, educational equality, and indigenous rights movements. As a Viet Nam veteran, I thank all those present that evening for the risks they took a generation ago in order to end the destruction. They wrote an important chapter of our collective memory and stand as reminders to young Latinos and Latinas that they too must be prepared to take an active role in the making of history.

NOTES

In the introductory essays, I use "Viet Nam," which is the spelling preferred by the Vietnamese, rather than the colonial French usage, "Vietnam."

Aztlán and Viet Nam

1. José Monleón, "Mesa redonda con Alurista, Rudy Anaya, María Herrera-Sobek, Alejandro Morales y Helena Viramontes," *Maize* 4 (1981): 8.

2. Two histories of the anti-war movement and the 1960s that do discuss Chicano/Latino participation are George Katsiaficas, *The Imagination of the New Left: A Global Analysis of 1968* (Boston: South End Press, 1987) and Terry H. Anderson, *The Movement and the Sixties* (Oxford: Oxford University Press, 1996).

3. H. Bruce Franklin includes one of Pedro Pietri's poems in his anthology, *The Vietnam War in American Stories, Songs, and Poems* (Boston: St. Martin's Press, 1996), 298–300.

4. Felix Rodríguez, *Shadow Warrior* (New York: Simon & Schuster, 1989). Two memoirs by Mexican citizens who fought with the U.S. military are Francisco Javier Munguía's *Un mexicano en Vietnam* (see Reading 10) and Guillermo Quintero's *Semper Fidelis* (Mexico City: Coordinación de difusión cultural, UNAM, 1993).

5. Ruben Treviso's oft-quoted assertion that one of every five "Hispanics" was killed in action and one of every two served in a combat unit may be accurate but is impossible to verify. See "Hispanics and the Vietnam War," in Harrison Salisbury, ed., *Vietnam Reconsidered* (New York: Harper & Row, 1984).

6. What is lacking is a companion to Raul Morín's *Among the Valiant: Mexican-Americans in WW II and Korea* (Alhambra, Calif.: Borden, 1996). Morín fought in World War II and his son Eddie, like so many other sons of World War II veterans, served in Viet Nam. Morín offers a poignant affirmation of the discourse of assimilation: "We feel just as proud of the Colin Kelleys, the Dobbie Millers, and the Sadio Munemoris as we are of the Martinez', Garcias and Rodriguez'" (p. 9).

7. See Trujillo's introduction to his *Soldados: Chicanos in Viet Nam* (San Jose, Calif.: Chusma House, 1990). There has, however, been a market for oral histories of GIs from various regions of the United States; see, for example, James W. Wilson, *Landing Zones: Southern Veterans Remember Vietnam* (Durham: Duke University Press, 1990) and Owen W. Gilman, *Vietnam and the Southern Imagination* (Jackson: University Press of

Mississippi, 1992). Lea Ybarra's *Too Many Heroes: Oral Histories of Chicano Vietnam Veterans* (University of Texas Press, forthcoming), a collection of personal accounts by Chicano veterans, will be a major contribution.

8. One example of this powerful desire for recognition is the Eugene A. Obregón Congressional Medal of Honor Foundation, an ongoing project to construct in Los Angeles a monument to all thirty-eight Latino winners of the Medal of Honor.

9. Sol Marroquin, *Part of the Team: Story of an American Hero* (Mission, Tex.: Rio Grande Printers, 1979). In 1995 the U.S. Navy commissioned the U.S.S. Gonzalez, a guided missile destroyer, in tribute to Gonzalez.

10. John Flores, "The Ballad of Freddy Gonzalez," *Hispanic Magazine* (November 1996).

11. *El Grito del Norte* 2 (October 10, 1969). "Valentina" was in fact Valentina Valdez, a nineteen-year-old Chicana from San Luis, Colorado, who had been active in the Tijerina land grant movement in New Mexico. Telephone interview with Valentina Valdez, May 27, 1997. Another local periodical that regularly addressed the issue of the war was the *Chicano Times,* published in San Antonio by José Luis Rodríguez. In summer 1970 Mario T. García edited a special number on the war of *La palabra,* a journal published at San Jose State College in California.

12. *El Grito del Norte* 2 (August 29, 1970).

13. Telephone interview with Elizabeth Martinez, July 2, 1996.

14. *El Grito: A Journal of Contemporary Mexican-American Thought* 3 (Fall 1969). The issue opened with a poem by Pedro B. Anchondo (see Reading 6). On the role of *El Grito* in the deconstruction of the social sciences from a Chicano perspective (long before French poststructuralism arrived in the United States), see Raoul Contreras, "The Ideology of the Political Movement for Chicano Studies," Ph.D. dissertation, UCLA, 1993.

15. For an introduction to the anti-war writings of African American intellectuals, see Clyde Taylor, *Vietnam and Black America: Anthology of Protest and Resistance* (New York: Anchor Press, 1973). Taylor's description of his book has guided my own work: *"Vietnam and Black America* is not meant to be a collection of souvenirs and mementos. The intention is to offer an assemblage representative of the intellectual as well as physical resistance Blacks mounted against the war" (p. xx).

16. Juan Manuel Bernal, in *Cenzontle: Chicano Short Stories and Poetry,* Seventh Chicano Literary Prize, Irvine, 1980–81 (Santa Ana, Calif.: Quality, 1981), 107. My translation.

17. Jack López, "Easy Time," in Gary Soto, ed., *Pieces of the Heart: New Chicano Fiction* (San Francisco: Chronicle Books, 1993). Dagoberto Gilb, "Nancy Flores," in *The Magic of Blood* (New York: Grove Press, 1993). Rosaura Sánchez, "The Ditch," in *Requisa Treinta y Dos* (La Jolla: UCSD Chicano Studies Program, 1979).

18. Despite the Spanish first name of the protagonist and the suggestion of a

Southwest location in Larry Heineman's award-winning *Paco's Story* (1987), little in the text suggests that Paco Sullivan is of Mexican descent. Critics have noted that it is precisely the combination of names that makes Paco an everyman figure. In any case, character and race relations in the novel remain neatly situated within the traditional black/white opposition. Philip D. Beidler astutely points out, however, the racial and ethnic meanings of Paco's Spanish nickname: "The first name, on the other hand, Paco, is distinctly a given one of those who have this time borne the burden in a new war of needless slaughter and uniform pain in waste"; *Re-Writing America: Vietnam Authors in Their Generation* (Athens: University of Georgia Press, 1991), 103.

19. John M. Del Vecchio, *The Thirteenth Valley* (New York: Bantam, 1982), 53. In an uncanny coincidence, *The Thirteenth Valley* is based on a real military operation— Operation Texas Star near Khe Ta Laou, South Viet Nam—that ended on August 30, 1970, the day after the Moratorium demonstration in Los Angeles.

20. Isabel Allende, *The Infinite Plan,* trans. Margaret Sayers Peden (New York: Harper Perennial, 1994), 192. To my knowledge, Haskell Wexler's *Latino* (1985) is the only film to date whose protagonists are Chicano Viet Nam veterans. Several years after returning from Southeast Asia, Special Forces advisors Eddie Guerrero and Ruben Treviño are shipped to Central America, where they train the right-wing Contras in their attempt to overthrow the Sandinista government of Nicaragua. Structures of recognition between the "sensitive" Chicano GI, Eddie, and the Latino "enemy" appear throughout.

21. Joe Klein, *Payback* (New York: Knopf, 1984), 140. In an interesting short story by C. W. Truesdale, a teacher whose brother serves in Viet Nam is troubled by the fact that his Chicano students are "like" the Vietnamese: "I think Miguel fully understood the pain I felt over my brother's serving in Vietnam as a Green Beret and my knowing, all too well, that given the right circumstances my brother would have been duty-bound to search out Miguel (or people very much like him in Vietnam) and kill him. . . . It seemed to me then (as it still does) that Vietnam was the Indian Wars all over again and that Miguel was a Latino version of the great Chief Red Cloud or Chief Joseph of the Nez Percé and that my brother was somebody like Custer or Major Reno"; "El Angel de la Guerra" in Vivian Vie Balfour, ed., *The Perimeter of Light: Short Fiction and Other Writing about the Vietnam War* (Minneapolis: New Rivers Press, 1992).

22. Captain Brandon Swenson, "Latino Officers in the Marine Corps," *El Sol* (San Diego, Calif.), April 3, 1998: 10.

23. Angie Chabram, "Conceptualizing Chicano Critical Discourse," in Hector Calderón and José David Saldívar, eds., *Criticism in the Borderlands: Studies in Chicano Literature, Culture, and Ideology* (Durham: Duke University Press, 1991), 127–48.

24. Fredric Jameson, paper delivered at the conference "Viet Nam Now: The War, Its Fictions and Realities," held at the University of California, Irvine, May 1980.

Standing at the Wall

1. For the complete poem, see Reading 34. Although Stone's *Platoon* (1987) contained Latino characters, they were depicted as stereotypes; see Gregg Barrios's review, "A 'Platoon' Without Latinos," *L.A. Times,* Calendar (April 19, 1987): p. 2.

2. From the *Congressional Record;* reprinted in *La Luz* 1 (1972): 48–49. Despite such sentiments, McGovern alienated many Chicano voters a month before the election when his campaign accused La Raza Unida Party, a Chicano political organization that had not endorsed McGovern, of taking money from the Republicans. As a result, Nixon fared much better than expected in traditionally Mexican American Democrat strongholds.

3. Olivia Chumacero, "Untitled," *Caracol: La Revista de la Raza* 4 (November 1977): 5. My translation.

4. Rolando Hinojosa, *The Useless Servants* (Houston: Arte Público, 1993), 41.

5. Daniel Cano, *Shifting Loyalties,* 87. Another *tejano* character in the novel remarks: "Man, you guys from Califas can't speak Spanish for shit, huh?" (187).

6. Martin Luther King, Jr., "A Time to Break Silence" (speech delivered on April 4, 1967) in *The Eyes on the Prize Civil Rights Reader,* eds. Clayborne Carson and others (New York: Penguin, 1991), 387–93.

7. Daniel Patrick Moynihan, quoted in Lawrence M. Baskir and William A. Strauss, *Chance and Circumstance: The Draft, the War, and the Vietnam Generation* (New York: Knopf, 1978), 125.

8. John F. Kennedy, "Statement Establishing the Task Force on Manpower Conservation" (September 30, 1963) in *One-Third of a Nation: A Report on Young Men Found Unqualified for Military Service* (January 1, 1964), Appendix A: A-1.

9. Lewis B. Hershey, "Letter to Selective Service Personnel" (October 31, 1963) in *One-Third of a Nation,* A-49.

10. Robert McNamara, quoted in "Readjustment of Project 100,000 Veterans," Hearing before the Subcommittee on Oversight and Investigations of the Committee on Veterans Affairs, House of Representatives, One Hundred First Congress, first session (February 28, 1990): 1. In his 1995 "reevaluation" of the Viet Nam debacle and his role in it—*In Retrospect: The Tragedy and Lessons of Vietnam*—McNamara does not make any mention of Project 100,000. On May 15, 1995, four Chicano Viet Nam veterans, the Bolaños brothers of El Paso, Texas, all recipients of the Purple Heart, filed suit against McNamara to prevent him from earning profits from his book. Daniel Patrick Moynihan, the project's other architect, does not list Project 100,000 in his review of social programs since the 1960s in *Miles to Go: A Personal History of Social Policy* (Cambridge: Harvard University Press, 1996). Major studies of the war, including those by progressive historians, have devoted little attention to Project 100,000.

11. See Lisa Hsiao, "Project 100,000: The Great Society's Answer to Military Manpower Needs in Vietnam" in William M. King, ed., *Viet Nam Generation, Special edition: A White Man's War: Race Issues and Vietnam* 1 (Spring 1989): 14–37. Both the task force and the Selective Service used only two racial/ethnic categories: Caucasian and non-Caucasian.

12. "In Pursuit of Equity: Who Serves When Not All Serve," Report of the National Advisory Commission on Selective Service (Washington, D.C.: U.S. Government Printing Office, 1967), 26.

13. *Marginal Man and Military Service,* Department of the Army (December 1965).

14. Charles Durden, *No Bugles, No Drums* (New York: Viking Press, 1976), 43.

15. Memo from George Ball to President Johnson, July 1, 1965, quoted in Marvin E. Gettleman and others, eds., *Vietnam and America: A Documented History* (New York: Grove Press, 1995), 282. It is not clear whether the phrase "white army" was common bureaucratic usage. Ball, who refers to the memo in his memoir—*The Past Has Another Pattern: Memoirs* (New York: Norton, 1982), 398—was also concerned about unspecified "problems" related to the Chicano/Latino community: "Apart from the question of illegal immigrants, I can foresee formidable social and economic problems resulting from the increasing political influence of Hispanic-Americans" (489).

16. Nancy Zaroulis and Gerald Sullivan, *Who Spoke Up?: American Protest Against the War in Vietnam, 1963–1975* (New York: Doubleday, 1984), 374.

17. Renny Christopher, *The Viet Nam War/The American War: Images and Representations in Euro-American and Vietnamese Exile Narratives* (Amherst: University of Massachusetts Press, 1995), 6.

18. Fredric Jameson, paper delivered at the conference "Vietnam Now: The War, Its Fictions and Realities," held at UC Irvine, May 1980.

19. Haitian scholar Michael-Rolph Trouillot puts it this way: "What happened leaves traces, some of which are quite concrete—buildings, dead bodies, censuses, monuments, diaries, political boundaries—that limit the range and significance of any historical narrative. This is one of many reasons why not any fiction can pass for history: the materiality of the socio-historical process (historicity 1) sets the stage for future historical narratives (historicity 2)." *Silencing the Past: Power and the Production of History* (Boston: Beacon Press, 1995), 29.

20. Raymond Williams, *Marxism and Literature* (Oxford: Oxford University Press, 1977), 129.

21. *Hispanics in America's Defense* (Washington, D.C.: Office of Deputy Assistant Secretary of Defense for Equal Opportunity and Safety Policy, 1984). See also Patricia A. Robles, "Hispanics' Contributions to the U.S. Military: An Annotated Bibliography," *Latino Studies Journal* 5 (May 1994): 96–103.

22. Luis Valdez, *Early Works* (Houston: Arte Público Press, 1990), 132. Principal

photography on a film adaptation of *Soldado Razo* (by Kinan Valdez) was begun in 1995. On the Teatro Campesino's Viet Nam plays, see "The Chicano in War at Home and Abroad" in Jorge A. Huerta, *Chicano Theater: Themes and Forms* (Tempe, Ariz.: Bilingual Press/Editorial Bilingüe, 1982); Edward G. Brown, "The Teatro Campesino's Vietnam Trilogy," *Minorities Voices* 4 (Spring 1980): 29–38; and Guillermo E. Hernández, *Chicano Satire: A Study in Literary Culture* (Austin: University of Texas Press, 1991).

23. Little Joe y la familia, "Soldado Razo," *16 de septiembre,* Sony Records. We can also trace these themes back in time. In a poem written to a nephew who was preparing to ship out during World War II, Florencio Trujillo, a World War I veteran, said: "Trujillo le contestó / ya vamos para las frentes / ahora lo que hemos de hacer / pues es mostrarnos valientes" (Trujillo answered him, we're off to the front, so what we must do is show that we are brave); "Soldaditos del '45" in *De colores* 2 (1975): 12.

24. Rolando Hinojosa, "Feliz Cumpleaños, E.U.A.," *La palabra* 1 (1979): 56.

25. Luis Valdez, *The Dark Root of a Scream,* in Luis Omar Salinas and Lillian Faderman, eds., *From the Barrio: A Chicano Anthology* (San Francisco: Canfield Press, 1973), 90.

26. The classic account is Raul Morín's *Among the Valiant: Mexican-Americans in WW II and Korea,* 3d ed. (Alhambra, Calif.: Borden, 1966). José Montoya, a poet and Korean War veteran, reminds us: "Los Chicanos en Korea / Se portaron con honor / Ganaron muchas medallas / Hasta liberty en Japón / Pero al volver al cantón / Derechito a la prisión" ("Chicanos acted with honor in Korea. They won many medals and took leaves in Japan. But when they returned home, they went straight to prison"); "Chicanos en Korea" in *Information: 20 Years of Joda* (San Jose, Calif.: Chusma House, 1992), 251. Louie Mendoza, the protagonist of Arturo Islas's last novel, is a Korean War veteran who loves to hear World War II veterans tell stories because "they made out like they knew how come they killed other guys"; *La Mollie and the King of Tears* (Albuquerque: University of New Mexico Press, 1996), 124. See also Beatriz de la Garza, *Pillars of Gold and Silver* (Houston: Arte Público, 1997) in which the principal character's journey is precipitated by the death of her father in Korea. Literary accounts of Chicano experiences during World War II and Korea include Américo Paredes, *The Hammon and the Beans;* Tomás Rivera, . . . *y no se lo tragó la tierra;* and Rolando Hinojosa, *Klail City, Korean Love Songs,* and *The Useless Servants.*

27. Charley Trujillo, *Soldados: Chicanos in Viet Nam* (San Jose, Calif.: Chusma House, 1990), 27. In their anti-draft literature, Nina Genera and Lea Ybarra made the following point to Mexican American parents: "Parents must begin to place the love of their sons before their fear of the government." *La batalla está aquí: Chicanos and the War* (El Cerrito, Calif.: Chicano Draft Help, 1972), 7.

28. Ramón Ruiz, "Another Defector from the Gringo World," *The New Republic* (July 27, 1968): 11.

29. *La Raza* 1 (1970): 7. This premier issue of *La Raza* was offered "in memory of

Chicanos who have died in the horror of the Vietnam War—a war created by their very own oppressors in the U.S. to further oppress and exploit those people it deems inferior."

30. Letter to Douglas MacArthur Herrera, dated October 25, 1967. Original correspondence in the John Herrera Collection, Houston Metropolitan Research Center, Houston Public Library. For the difficult decisions faced by Chicano conscientious objectors, see the accounts in Lea Ybarra, *Too Many Heroes: Oral Histories of Chicano Vietnam Veterans* (University of Texas Press, forthcoming).

31. Octavio I. Romano V., *Geriatric Fu: My First Sixty-Five Years in the United States* (Berkeley: TQS, 1990), 62 and 70.

32. Everett Alvarez, Jr., and Anthony S. Pitch, *Chained Eagle* (New York: Dell, 1989). The sequel to *Chained Eagle* is Everett Alvarez, Jr., and Samuel A. Schreiner, Jr., *Code of Conduct* (New York: Donald I. Fine, 1991). Craig Howes describes how Alvarez's story becomes the literary and ideological model upon which subsequent POW autobiographies were based; *Voices of the Vietnam POWs: Witnesses to Their Fight* (Oxford: Oxford University Press, 1993).

33. Delia Alvarez, quoted in Dorinda Moreno, *La Mujer—en pie de lucha ¡y la hora es ya!* (Mexico City: Espina del Norte, 1973), 86. Delia Alvarez became a highly visible anti-war protestor; she attended a world peace conference in Paris and appeared on national television in the United States.

34. Alvarez rejects the term "Chicano": "To me words like Chicano and La Rasa [*sic*] meant people who had come from Mexico. Period. I didn't like the sounds of a 'Chicano movement' or a 'Chicano manifesto'" (*Code of Conduct*, 25).

35. Roy P. Benavidez and Oscar Griffin, *The Three Wars of Roy Benavidez* (San Antonio: Corona, 1986), 75–76. Benavidez has also published an extended version of his autobiography: *Medal of Honor: A Vietnam Warrior's Story* (Washington, D.C.: Brassey's, 1995).

36. Martin Luther King, Jr., on the program *Issues and Answers,* ABC News, June 18, 1967.

37. J. Glenn Gray, *The Warriors* (New York: Harper, 1967), 27.

38. Lou Lacariere, quoted in Paul Gabel, *The Vietnam War: HyperCard History Book,* Regeneration Software (Santa Barbara, Calif.: Intellimation, 1989), 534–35.

39. Quoted in William King, "Our Men in Vietnam: Black Media as a Source of the Afro-American Experience in Southeast Asia" in *Viet Nam Generation, Special Edition: A White Man's War: Race Issues and Vietnam* 1 (Spring 1989): 109. See also Anthony Griggs, "Minorities in the Armed Forces," *Race Relations Reporter* 4 (July–September 1973): 9–14, 26–29; James E. Westheider, *Fighting on Two Fronts: African Americans and the Vietnam War* (New York: New York University Press, 1997); Peter Levy, "Blacks and the Vietnam War," in D. Michael Shafer, ed., *The Legacy* (Boston: Beacon Press, 1990).

40. Quoted in Malcolm Boyd, *My Fellow Americans* (New York: Holt, Rinehart

and Winston, 1970), 183. Boyd, an Episcopalian priest and writer of some celebrity in the late '60s, devoted a chapter of this book to Corky Gonzales and the Chicano Movement.

41. Quoted in Ybarra, *Too Many Heroes*, 77. It is worthwhile here to recall something Angela Davis wrote in 1974: "When white people are indiscriminately viewed as the enemy, it is virtually impossible to develop a political solution"; from "On Becoming a Fugitive," cited in Deirdre Mullane, ed., *Words to Make My Dream Children Live: A Book of African American Quotations* (New York: Anchor, 1995), 105.

42. Stanley Goff and Robert Sanders, with Clark Smith, *Brothers: Black Soldiers in the Nam* (New York: Berkley Books, 1985), 67.

43. Joe Rodríguez, *The Oddsplayer* (Houston: Arte Público, 1989), 62. Other examples focused narrowly on race (with gestures toward poor whites) appear in numerous texts: "This ain't our war. Our war's at home. When we get back on the block, we still ain't going to be nothing but nappy-headed niggers, along with the rest of the shithead greasers and spics, raggedy-ass honkies, and blanket-ass Indians"; Charley Trujillo, *Dogs from Illusion* (San Jose, Calif.: Chusma House, 1994), 106.

44. Marilyn Young, *The Vietnam Wars: 1945–1990* (New York: Harper Collins, 1991), 175.

45. See Michael Bilton and Kevin Sim, *Four Hours in My Lai* (New York: Penguin, 1992). Attempting to explain the Chicano Movement to the East Coast intelligentsia, historian John Womack wrote: "So many young men have borne so well the uses made of them in the armed services, for 'action' in Indochina or 'intelligence' in Latin America, that by now the roster of junior commissioned officers is studded with names like Ernest L. Medina (now retired)"; *New York Review of Books*, "A Special Supplement: The Chicanos," (August 31, 1972): 14.

46. Valdez, *Early Works*, 116. This scene was reproduced decades later in novels such as Trujillo's *Dogs from Illusion*, in which a Chicano combat soldier says of the Vietnamese: "I kind of even look like them. They're mostly farm-workers just like my family" (177). It is not clear to what extent these scenes are quotations from earlier writings or drawn from actual experience. On the homefront, David Sánchez, prime minister of the Brown Berets, improvised a stunning piece of anthropology in a 1968 interview: "We figure that since Chicanos came down through the Bering Straits, we're part Oriental, and then that honkie, what's his name?, Cortez, came across over and raped our women, so we're half mongoloid and half caucasoid, that makes the Viet Cong our brothers"; quoted in F. Chris Garcia, ed., *Chicano Politics: Readings* (New York: MSS Information Corporation, 1973), 211.

47. Hruska y Cortez is of Bohemian and Cuban heritage, but I have included his poem in this anthology because of his long-time involvement with the Chicano community in San Francisco.

48. Valdez, *Early Works*, 133. Most of the *actos* were not written by Valdez, but

were collaborative efforts on the part of the entire company. *Soldado Razo,* for example, was based on a true story told to the company by one of its female players; see Yolanda Broyles-González, *El Teatro Campesino: Theater in the Chicano Movement* (Austin: University of Texas Press, 1994), 132. Because the directorship of El Teatro has not granted scholars access to their archives, we do not know how many incidental pieces dealing with the war were performed by the company.

49. Joe Olvera, Leo Rojas, and Raul Estrada, *A Barrio Tragedy* in *Caracol* 4 (March 1978): 18. At the play's opening, the character Johnny has killed a Vietnamese woman. Upon his return to the states, he accidentally kills his own mother. The other Johnny's nightmare from *Soldado Razo* in this play becomes reality, and the recognition between the Chicano soldier and the Vietnamese is reaffirmed.

50. Valdez, *Early Works,* 115; Nephtalí de León, *The Death of Ernesto Nerios* in *Five Plays* (Denver: Totinem, 1972), 25. In Ed Vega's "Casualty Report," Puerto Rican veteran Sonny Maldonado has the experience of "looking at himself in the mirror and not recognizing the image because it was dark and as foreign as the enemy's had been"; *Casualty Report* (Houston: Arte Público, 1991), 38. The situation of the Latino GI from rural Puerto Rico was especially charged since not only did he "recognize" the skin color and *campesino* culture of the Vietnamese, but the physical surroundings of the war zone were uncannily like those of home. In Jaime Carrero's play *Flag Inside* (1966), the absent son Alberto writes home: "El aire tropical de Vietnam y su vegetación es parecido al de la isla" ("The tropical air of Vietnam and its vegetation is like that of the island"); *Flag Inside* (Río Piedras, P.R.: Ediciones Puerto, 1973, 19).

51. Valdez, *Early Works,* 117.

52. Erwin R. Parson, "The Gook-Identification and Post-Traumatic Stress Disorders in Black Vietnam Veterans," *Black Psychiatrists of American Quarterly* 13 (1984). Charley Trujillo has suggested to me that the Chicano GI's recognition of his own situation in that of the Vietnamese, rather than leading to a heightened critical awareness, in fact produced exaggerated forms of violence. The possible dynamics of self-hatred inherent in this interpretation are too complex (and unpleasant) for me to investigate here.

53. Joel Osler Brende and Erwin Randolph Parson, *Vietnam Veterans: The Road to Recovery* (New York: Plenum Press, 1985), 156. Unfortunately, Brende and Parson rely too heavily on ethnic stereotypes ("Hispanic machismo," "Asian fatalism") in their analysis of minority GIs.

54. The experience in Viet Nam of Asian Americans has yet to be discussed extensively in any scholarly forum. See *Amerasia Journal* 17 (1991) for the recollections of Darrell Y. Hamamoto and Lewis Kawahara and also Peter Nien-Chu Kiang's essay "About Face: Recognizing Asian and Pacific American Vietnam Veterans in Asian American Studies." See also the novel by Korean American Ernest Spencer, *Welcome*

to *Vietnam, Macho Man* (New York: Bantam Books, 1989); the account of Mike Wong, a Chinese American resister, in William Short, *A Matter of Conscience: GI Resistance During the Vietnam War* (Andover, Mass.: Addison Gallery of American Art, Phillips Academy, 1992); and Maxine Hong Kingston's "Brother in Vietnam" in *China Men* (New York: Knopf, 1980), in which a Chinese American in the U.S. Navy dreams he is a participant in a massacre: "When he stops, he finds that he has cut up the victims too, who are his own relatives. The faces of the strung-up people are also those of his own family, Chinese faces, Chinese eyes, noses, and cheekbones" (291). In Frederick Su's unpublished novel "An American Sin," the character David Wong says: "I killed because I was Asian fighting in an Asian War. How else could I prove I was American?" Excerpts from this novel are available at http://www.vena.com/authors/1027bi.html.

55. Shojiro Yamashita's story is among those reproduced on the Berkeley Viet Nam Veteran's Memorial website: http://www.ci.berkeley.ca.us/vvm.

56. "Wounds of Vietnam Heal Slowly for Asian American Veterans," *Asian Week* (December 9, 1983): 20. See also Victor Merina, "The Glory and Pain of Fighting for Your Country," *Rice* (April 1988): 35–38. Thanks to Lily Lee Adams and Cher Nicholas for bringing these articles to my attention.

57. Anne Keegan, "Oriental GIs in Vietnam: Living with Face of the Enemy," *Chicago Tribune* (November 11, 1988): 1, 18. A Japanese American Viet Nam War Memorial was unveiled in Los Angeles on November 11, 1995. Names on the memorial may be accessed at http://koma.org/apa/jaccc.

58. "Interview with Sam Choy," *Getting Together* 1 (April 1970): 12.

59. One of the most celebrated cases was that of David Fagen, an African American soldier who deserted to the Filipino rebels in 1899; see Michael C. Robinson and Frank N. Schubert, "David Fagen: An Afro-American Rebel in the Philippines, 1899–1901," *Pacific Historical Review* 64 (February 1975). Consider also Malcolm X's ironic (?) remark in his autobiography that in 1943 he was "frantic to join . . . the Japanese army." Thanks to George Lipsitz for bringing these two cases to my attention.

60. Trujillo, *Soldados,* 177.

61. Daniel Cano, *Shifting Loyalties* (Houston: Arte Público, 1995), 78. Later in the novel, Peña's former platoon-mates speculate on his whereabouts: "There were a few nutty stories that he was traveling with the VC. Some guys said they saw him selling fish tacos in the Mekong Delta. Others said he was running drugs near the DMZ. You know, just a big joke, stupid stuff, like he probably started a *mariachi* in Hanoi or owned a burrito stand near Haiphong" (100–101).

62. Durden, *No Bugles,* 123. On the home front, Huey Newton of the Black Panther Party had written a letter to the leadership of the NLF (dated August 29, 1970, coincidentally the date of the largest Chicano Moratorium demonstration) in which he offered to send Panther "troops" to Viet Nam to assist "in your fight against Ameri-

can imperialism." Roth's *Sand in the Wind* (Boston: Atlantic Monthly Press, 1973) features a trio of Chicano characters, one of whom refuses to carry out orders by the end of the novel.

63. See the chilling account by an anonymous Chicano informant in Ybarra, *Too Many Heroes.*

64. Walter Dean Myers, *Fallen Angels* (New York: Scholastic, 1988), 52 and 124. Lea Ybarra's research suggests that real-life cases of recognition between Chicanos and the Vietnamese were few. Of the twenty-five veterans interviewed, only three alluded to such recognition; "Perceptions of Race and Class Among Chicano Vietnam Veterans" in William M. King, ed., *Vietnam Generation 2*, Special issue: A White Man's War: Race Issues and Vietnam: 68–93. I would argue that for most veterans an admission of "recognition" with the Vietnamese continues to be difficult, if not taboo.

65. Quoted in Ybarra, "Perceptions of Race," 83. In Chicano-authored fiction about earlier wars, a similar recognition produces hybrid identities and acts of crossing over. Américo Paredes's short story "Idhiro Kikuchi," for example, tells the story of a Mexican-Japanese soldier fighting for Japan in World War II who is captured by U.S. forces and saved from execution by a Chicano GI. In Rolando Hinojosa's *Korean Love Songs,* a Mexican American GI, David "Sonny" Ruiz, deserts to Japan and becomes Mr. Kazuo Fusaro.

66. See Westheider, *Fighting on Two Fronts,* 156–57.

67. Quoted in Peter Goldman and Tony Fuller, *Charlie Company: What Vietnam Did to Us* (New York: William Morrow, 1983), 117. Goldman and Fuller present portraits of three Latino GIs: Richard Garcia, a California Chicano who died in Viet Nam; Antonio Rivera from Puerto Rico; and Alberto Martinez, a Cuban citizen who volunteered "to fight communism," returned a broken man, and committed suicide in 1982.

68. Michael Herr, *Dispatches* (1977; reprint, New York: Random House, 1991), 250.

69. Parallel stories appear throughout Asian American accounts of the war. U.S. Marine Mike Nakayama writes: "The last night I spent in the field, we were overrun by a large NLF force. Out of the twelve wounded, I was one of three emergency cases who are supposed to have priority for medical treatment. I was the last to be treated. When I asked what was taking them so long, the corpsman explained that he thought I was a 'gook'"; "Nam & U.S.M.C.," *Gidra* 3 (May 1971): 17. Donald Lau recalls: "Every now and then I would hear of an Asian American who was killed because of mistaken identity. Upon coming home I was told of an Asian American who was wounded and taken to an evac hospital. . . . He was dying and a racist surgeon who made the decisions on who got priority treatment looked at him and said, 'Let's treat the Americans first.' The Asian American soldier was conscious enough to know what was going on, so he flicked the safety switch off of his pistol and fired the entire mag-

azine into the ceiling. He then got immediate attention"; Mark J. Jue, "Asian Viet Vets Want Memorial to Honor Own War Dead," *East/West* (February 20, 1985).

¡Raza sí, guerra no!

1. On the August 29 Moratorium demonstration, see the classic account in Armando Morales, *Ando sangrando [I Am Bleeding]: A Study of Mexican American–Police Conflict* (La Puente, Calif.: Perspectiva, 1972). See also Rodolfo Acuña, *A Community Under Siege: A Chronicle of Chicanos East of the Los Angeles River, 1945–1975,* monograph no. 11 (Los Angeles: Chicano Studies Research Center of UCLA, 1984) and *Occupied America: A History of Chicanos,* 3d ed. (New York: Harper & Row, 1988), 346ff.; Marguerite V. Marin, *Social Protest in an Urban Barrio: A Study of the Chicano Movement, 1969–1974,* 201–18; Juan Gómez Quiñones, *Chicano Politics: Reality and Promise, 1940–1990* (Albuquerque: University of New Mexico Press, 1990). David García's prize-winning documentary *Requiem 29* (1970) is archived at the Chicano Studies Library of UCLA. Other films include Francisco Martinez's *August 29, 1970,* Thomas Myrdahl's *Chicano Moratorium: A Question of Freedom,* and *March in the Rain,* a record of the February 1970 demonstration produced by Claudio Fenner-López and Los Angeles Public Television station KCET.

2. *La Raza Yearbook* (May 11, 1968): 3.

3. *La Raza* 2 (December 1969): 3.

4. Abelardo Delgado, *The Chicano Movement: Some Not Too Objective Observations* (Denver: Totinem, 1971), 31–32.

5. Nephtalí de León, *Five Plays* (Denver: Totinem, 1972), 49. After spending five months in the U.S. Army, de León deserted to Mexico. Upon his return he was sentenced to hard labor and solitary confinement before being discharged. Telephone interview with Nephtalí de León, March 15, 1996.

6. Thanks to Christine Marín of Arizona State University for bringing to my attention this group, which for a short time in the early 1970s published "El Amanecer Rojo" ("The Red Dawn").

7. Telephone interview with Lea Ybarra, June 2, 1997. The real Richard Campos, a Californian, was killed by small-arms fire in South Viet Nam on December 6, 1966.

8. The printing of photos depicting atrocities perpetrated by U.S. soldiers had been a tactic of the earliest anti-war literature in the Chicano community. In 1968, for example, a group called the Chicano Liberation and Peace Movement had published such a photo in the L.A. newspaper *Chicano Student* (June 12, 1968) with the caveat: "The reason for printing this picture is not to put down GIs but just to point out the fact that the Army can mess up your mind if you let it" (2).

9. See Lawrence J. Mosqueda, *Chicanos, Catholicism, and Political Ideology* (New York and London: University Press of America, 1986), 98ff. The official slogan of Católicos por la Raza was "Señalar y combatir los defectos de la Iglesia es servirla" ("To point out and fight against the Church's defects is to serve her").

10. Oscar Zeta Acosta, *Revolt of the Cockroach People* (New York: Vintage, 1973), 13. San Francisco poet Roberto Vargas wrote: "It seems . . . just the other day / FireBrimstone MacIntyre assucked / Saigon's Cowed Cao Ky to come / make war here   Rally round / The Flag boys—from the halls / Of Montezooma   (Column Right Ho)"; "Elegy Pa Gringolandia" in *Primeros Cantos* (San Francisco: Ediciones Pocho-Che, 1971), 33.

11. Telephone interview with Father John Luce, December 11, 1996. An unsung hero of the Movimiento, Father Luce remained in Los Angeles until 1974. Today he continues to support Latino causes in the New York area.

12. Telephone interview with Eliezer Risco, December 12, 1996. Risco was the model for the character of the same name in Acosta's *The Revolt of the Cockroach People*. He was ordained an Episcopalian priest in 1994.

13. Telephone interview with John Dauer, March 16, 1997. Mario Salas, an organizer of African American and Latino heritage, was one of the few activists who participated simultaneously in Chicano organizations, SNCC, and the Black Panther Party. In 1997 he won a seat on the San Antonio city council. Charlene Ortiz, the sole Chicana in Women for Peace, went on to become executive director of a community-based health organization in San Antonio.

14. Paul Houston and Ted Thackrey, Jr., "Man Slain as Violence Erupts in East L.A. after Chicano Rally," *Los Angeles Times* (February 1, 1971): A16.

15. Cesar Chavez, quoted in Jacques E. Levy, *Cesar Chavez: Autobiography of La Causa* (New York: Norton, 1975), 197.

16. Chavez, in an interview with Bob Fitch, *The Christian Century* (February 10, 1970), reprinted in F. Chris García, ed., *Chicano Politics: Readings* (New York: MSS Information Corporation, 1973), 174–82.

17. Chavez, quoted in Richard Griswold del Castillo and Richard A. García, *Cesar Chavez: A Triumph of Spirit* (Norman: University of Oklahoma Press, 1995), 118.

18. *Congressional Record* (April 22, 1969), vol. 115, pt. 8: 9951–54.

19. The MAPA membership did adopt an anti-war resolution in 1968. On the divisions within MAPA, see Mario T. García, *Memories of Chicano History: The Life and Narrative of Bert Corona* (Berkeley: University of California Press, 1994), 273–75.

20. On the changing attitudes of the GI Forum, see Acuña, *Community Under Siege*, 361, n. 83, and Carl Allsup, *The American G.I. Forum: Origins and Evolution* (Austin: University of Texas Press, 1982), 151–52.

21. On the incidents at Fort Dix and in Houston, see the report by participant

Carlos Rodríguez in *El Grito del Norte* 2 (n.d.) and David Cortright, *Soldiers in Revolt: The American Military Today* (New York: Anchor, 1975).

22. Videotaped discussion with Noriega and Muñoz at the University of California, San Diego, April 13, 1994.

23. The complete speech is reproduced in this volume as Reading 29. A short film of the day's events, *Chale con el draft*, was made by Neil Reichline. Muñoz's father, Rosalío Muñoz, Sr., was a veteran of World War II and one of the first Mexican Americans to receive a doctoral degree in the United States. He supported his son's anti-war activities throughout the period. On the origins of the Moratorium Committee, see Ernesto Chávez, "Creating Aztlán: The Chicano Movement in Los Angeles, 1966–1978" (University of California, Los Angeles, Ph.D. dissertation, 1994); F. Arturo Rosales, *Chicano!: The History of the Mexican American Civil Rights Movement* (Houston: Arte Público Press, 1996); Lorena Oropeza, "¡La batalla está aquí!" (Cornell University, Ph.D. dissertation, 1996); Jaime Pelayo, "The Chicano Movement and the Vietnam War" (Yale University, Department of History, Senior Essay, 1997).

24. After meeting with several anti-war groups in early 1968, Robert F. Kennedy referred to the Chicano activists as "gentle revolutionaries"; quoted in Ralph Guzmán, "Brown Power," *Los Angeles Times Magazine* (January 26, 1969): 12. A march and memorial service for Kennedy were held at East Los Angeles City College on June 8, 1968. Speakers included Cesar Chavez, Father John Luce, and Bert Corona.

25. Ed Davis, "Viva la Raza," CBS documentary (1971). After the events of August 29, Davis offered a classic Cold War "analysis": "Ten months ago, the Communist Party in California said it was giving up on the blacks to concentrate on the Mexican Americans"; *Los Angeles Times* (August 31, 1970).

26. On Chicano informers, see Josie Carillo, "Infiltration into the Chicano Movement," *Regeneración* 4 (1972): 20; Edward J. Escobar, "The Dialectics of Repression: The Los Angeles Police Department and the Chicano Movement, 1968–1971," *The Journal of American History* (March 1993): 1483–1514; and Pelayo, "The Chicano Movement," on the LAPD mole Sergio Robledo. In discussing the assassinations of Malcolm X and Dr. King, James Baldwin commented, "The fates of both men were radically altered (I would say frankly, sealed) the moment they attempted to release the black American struggle from the domestic context and relate it to the struggles of the poor and the nonwhite all over the world"; "Malcolm and Martin" (1972) reprinted in David Gallen, ed., *Malcolm X: As They Knew Him* (New York: Ballantine, 1992), 308.

27. On August 26, 1970, Salazar met with two members of the U.S. Civil Rights Commission to report the LAPD's continual harassment of him and his family and to express his fear of possible assassination attempts. For more on Rubén Salazar, see Mario T. García, ed., *Border Correspondent: Selected Writings, 1955–1970* (Berkeley: University of California Press, 1995), which includes Jesús Sánchez's "Corrido de Rubén Salazar" (1970).

28. Abelardo Delgado, "Rojo" in *Los Cuatro* (Denver: Barrio Publications, n.d.), 6. Nephtalí de León, *¡Chicanos! The Living and the Dead!* in *Five Plays* (Denver: Totinem, 1972), 47. Roberto Vargas, *Primeros Cantos* (San Francisco: Pocho-Che, 1971), 35.

29. A rather mysterious analysis of the events surrounding Salazar's death was circulated at the University of California, San Diego in November 1970. At the time, the philosopher Herbert Marcuse was in residence, and a pamphlet, "Riot and Representation," appeared under his name proposing to analyze the events of August 29. The pamphlet defended violent demonstrations and, glossing Voltaire, concluded: "Humanity won't be happy until the last bureaucrat is hung with the guts of the last capitalist." Marcuse, already under attack by Governor Ronald Reagan and university officials, quickly denied having written the broadside: "A pamphlet entitled 'Riot and Representation, by Herbert Marcuse (the significance of the Chicano riots)' is being distributed on campus. This pamphlet is an outright forgery. I neither wrote it nor contributed to its writing, nor do I know who is responsible. Herbert Marcuse" (UC San Diego *Triton Times,* November 13, 1970). The true author remains unknown; it may have been written by a Marxist Chicana/o anti-war activist or by a saboteur determined to undermine the growing strength of the Movimiento. In any event, the attempt to involve a leading Marxist philosopher in the events of August 29 suggests that Chicano-led activities were attracting national attention.

30. Members of the Socialist Workers Party erroneously claimed that the Moratorium Committee had organized the September 16 event. See Mirta Vidal, *Chicano Liberation and Revolutionary Youth* (New York: Pathfinder Press, 1971) and Olga Rodríguez, ed., *The Politics of Chicano Liberation* (New York: Pathfinder Press, 1977). The concern that coalition-building might weaken Chicano agendas was expressed in *El plan de Santa Barbara* (1969) and was reproduced in the earliest histories of the Chicano Movement written by key participants. Juan Gómez Quiñones, for example, wrote in 1978: "A 'Third World' tendency attempted to deny the Mexican national thrust and full development of the student movement by subordinating it to Black and Anglo movements"; *Mexican Students Por La Raza: The Chicano Student Movement in Southern California* (Santa Barbara, Calif.: La Causa, 1978), 30.

31. In 1969 Martínez had agreed to serve the ATF as a provocateur in order to beat an illegal firearms conviction for which he had been serving time in Houston. For an eyewitness account of the activities of the Brown Berets, see David Sánchez, *Expedition through Aztlán* (La Puente, Calif.: Perspectiva, 1978). In one incident, an LAPD agent who had attempted to convince Moratorium organizers to carry firearms was subsequently beaten up by police during a raid on Moratorium headquarters and "charged" with carrying a concealed weapon. Interview with Rosalío Muñoz, April 14, 1995.

32. Joey García, "Juan's Epitaph" (1970) in Jorge Huerta, ed., *El Teatro de la Esperanza: An Anthology of Chicano Drama* (Goleta, Calif.: El Teatro de la Esperanza, 1973),

9. García read these lines at a rally in Oxnard on September 19, 1970; some eight hundred demonstrators attended.

33. "Setiembre del año 1970" in *Los Cuatro,* 32.

34. Gerald Horne, "Blowback: Playing the Nationalist Card Backfires," in Christopher Newfield and Ronald Strickland, eds., *After Political Correctness: The Humanities and Society in the 1990s* (Boulder, Colo.: Westview Press, 1995), 85. On the Mexican American left, see the forthcoming work of Jeff Garcilazo of the University of California, Irvine.

35. Lyndon Johnson, speaking in 1970, quoted in Doris Kearns, *Lyndon Johnson and the American Dream* (New York: Harper & Row, 1976), 251–53.

36. Roger Alvarado and others, *La Raza! Why a Chicano Party? Why Chicano Studies?* (New York: Pathfinder Press, 1970), 11.

37. *El grito del norte* 4 (June 5, 1971): 9. On the cultural origins of Mexican/ Chicano "machismo" in its modern form, see Carlos Monsivais, "Mexicanerías: ¿Pero hubo alguna vez once mil machos?" *Escenas de pudor y liviandad,* 6th ed. (Mexico City: Grijalbo, 1988). See also Alfredo Mirandé, *Hombres y Machos: Masculinity and Latino Culture* (Boulder, Colo.: Westview Press, 1997). The most succinct theoretical statement on Movement gender relations is Angie Chabram-Dernersesian, "I Throw Punches for My Race, but I Don't Want to Be a Man; Writing Us—Chica-nos (Girl, Us)/Chicanas—into the Movement Script," in Lawrence Grossberg, Cary Nelson, Paula Treichler, eds., *Cultural Studies* (New York: Routledge, 1992), 81–95. For an interesting reading of the sexual politics of Oscar Zeta Acosta's writing, see Carl Gutiérrez-Jones, *Rethinking the Borderlands: Between Chicano Culture and Legal Discourse* (Berkeley: University of California Press, 1995), 123–39. Despite his disclaimer— "The movement was obviously far more complex, in intentions and effects, than Acosta's treatment allows"—Gutiérrez-Jones leaves the impression that Acosta's deplorable attitudes were typical of all Movement activists.

38. Chavez, quoted in Levy, *Cesar Chavez,* 286.

39. By the mid-1970s, Marta Cortera had developed a complex feminist analysis of Chicano/a culture in essays and papers delivered at meetings such as the "Chicana Identity Conference" held in Houston in 1975. At that conference Cortera argued that the feminism of many Chicanas predated their participation in the Movimiento: "I feel that most women were feminists when they came to the Chicano Movement"; *The Chicana Feminist* (Austin: Information Systems Development, 1977), 31.

40. Telephone interviews with Irene Tovar, November 15, 1995, and Katarina Davis del Valle, June 2, 1997. For an important reading of the women Brown Berets and early Chicana feminism, see the forthcoming work of Dionne Espinoza of the University of Wisconsin, Madison.

41. Jorge Ruffinelli, "Alurista: Una larga marcha hacia Aztlán," *La palabra y el hombre* 17 (1976): 33.

42. Susan Jeffords, *The Remasculinization of America: Gender and the Vietnam War* (Bloomington: Indiana University Press, 1989), 183. Or consider Lisa Lowe's contention that "the American soldier, who has in every way submitted to the nation, is the quintessential citizen and therefore the ideal representative of the nation," which ignores the long history of resistance within the U.S. military; *Immigrant Acts: On Asian American Cultural Politics* (Durham, N.C.: Duke University Press, 1996), 6. Elsewhere in her book, Lowe's opposition of Viet Nam veterans and Asian Americans relegates to a footnote the important figure of the Asian American Viet Nam veteran.

43. Leroy Quintana, *Interrogations* (Chevy Chase, Md.: Viet Nam Generation & Burning Cities Press, 1990): 100–101. In the first cinematic rendering of the Persian Gulf War, Edward Zwick's *Courage Under Fire* (1996), it is the character of a Viet Nam veteran turned journalist who seeks the truth of what "really happened" in a friendly fire incident. The appropriation and exploitation of Viet Nam veterans in the aftermath of the Gulf War, in which once again many Latinos served, has yet to be analyzed.

44. Cynthia Enloe, *Ethnic Soldiers: State Security in Divided Societies* (Athens: University of Georgia Press, 1980), 54.

45. Frank Delgado, in Trujillo, *Soldados,* 27.

46. Quoted in Rubén Darío Sálaz, *Cosmic: The La Raza Sketchbook* (Santa Fe, N.M.: Blue Feather Press, 1978), 131. One of the GI Resistance's more "humorous" demands was made in 1971 in the underground Marine Corps journal, *All Ready on the Left,* published at Camp Pendleton, California: "The right of Black Brown, Yellow, and Red GIs to form their own armies"; quoted by Barbara L. Tischler, "Breaking Ranks: GI Antiwar Newspapers and the Culture of Protest" in Harry W. Haines, ed., *Vietnam Generation* 2, Special issue: "GI Resistance: Soldiers and Veterans Against the War: 32. At their August 1972 convention, the Raza Unida Party called for draft deferments for all Chicanos and Native Americans based on the disproportionate casualty rates suffered by both groups.

47. J. Glenn Gray, *The Warriors: Reflections on Men in Battle* (New York: Harper & Row, 1959), 242.

Epilogue

1. David E. Hayes-Bautista and Gregory Rodriguez, "The Chicano Movement: More Nostalgia Than Reality," *Los Angeles Times* (September 17, 1995).

2. Alfredo Ramos, "The Last Angry Brown Hat," unpublished manuscript.

3. Hayes-Bautista and Rodriguez, C12.

4. Oswaldo Rivera, *Fire and Rain* (New York: Four Walls Eight Windows Press, 1990), 47.

5. Ana Castillo, "Vatolandia," in *Loverboys* (New York: Plume/Penguin, 1997), 67. The passage continues: "The thing about a Vietnam vato that Sara Santistevan learned right away was that he does not trust no one. When a Vietnam vato looks you dead in the eye and says he doesn't even trust his abuela [grandmother], believe him. She respected what a Vietnam vato went through, but she kept away from him."

6. Walter Benjamin, *Illuminations,* ed. Hannah Arendt, trans. Harry Zohn, 5th ed. (New York: Schocken, 1978), 255.

Sources

Although every effort has been made to contact the copyright holders for the works published in this anthology, because of the age and the nature of the sources, it has not always been possible to locate them. The editor apologizes for any omissions and welcomes information that would allow him to give proper credit in future printings of this book.

Alvarez, Jr., Everett, and Anthony S. Pitch, *Chained Eagle* (New York: D. I. Fine, 1989). Copyright © 1989 by Everett Alvarez, Jr., and Anthony S. Pitch. Excerpt used by permission of Donald I. Fine, an imprint of Penguin Books USA Inc.

Amézquita, Ricardo Mario, "I Just Got Back from Vietnam, Baby." First published in *Revista Chicano-Riqueña* 8:4 (Fall 1980). Reprinted by permission of Arte Público Press–University of Houston, publishers of the *Americas Review* (which continues the *Revista Chicano-Riqueña*).

Anchondo, Pedro B., "Lonely Vietnam." First published in *El Grito* 3 (Fall 1969).

Anonymous, "Carnal in Vietnam." First published in *La Raza* 1:6 (1970). Reprinted courtesy of Raúl Ruiz.

Anonymous, "Corrido de la guerra." First published in Lea Ybarra and Nina Genera, *La batalla está aquí* (El Cerrito, Calif.: Chicano Draft Help, 1972). Reprinted courtesy of Lea Ybarra and Nina Genera.

Anonymous, "Little girls." First published in *La Raza Yearbook* (Los Angeles: La Raza, 1968). Reprinted courtesy of Raúl Ruiz.

Anonymous, "A Question Every Chicano Should Ask." First published in *El Grito del Norte* 4 (June 5, 1971). Reprinted courtesy of Elizabeth Martinez.

Anonymous, "Vietnam: Gabacho's War." First published in *La Raza* 1:4 (1970). Reprinted courtesy of Raúl Ruiz.

Avila, Magdaleno (Juan Valdez), "Sea of Freedom" and "My Uncle Sam." First published in Magdaleno Avila, Abelardo Delgado, Reymundo "Tigre" Pérez, and Ricardo Sánchez, *Los Cuatro* (Denver: Barrio Publications, n.d.).

Barrios, Gregg, "Chale Guerra." First published in *Puro Rollo (A colores)* (Los Angeles: Posada, 1982). Reprinted by permission of the author.

Barrón, Robert, "Viet Nam Veteran." First published in *El Grito* 1 (Spring 1968). Reprinted by permission of the author.

Benavidez, Roy, *Medal of Honor: A Vietnam Warrior's Story* (Washington, D.C.: Brassey's, 1995). Excerpt used by permission of Brassey, Inc., copyright © 1995.

Bobián, Arturo Silvano, "My Cousin Ralph." First published in *And this is what we said...* (Lubbock, Tex.: Trucha Press, 1975). Reprinted by permission of the author.

Browne, Rick, "Chicano Moratorium, January 30, 1971." First appeared in the *Los Angeles Times* (February 1, 1971). Copyright © 1997 Los Angeles Times. Reprinted by permission.

Calderón, Tomás M., "Untitled." First published in *Caracol* 2 (July 1976).

Cano, Daniel, *Shifting Loyalties* (Houston: Arte Público Press–University of Houston, 1995). Excerpt and epigraph used by permission of the publisher.

Cano, Daniel, "Somewhere Outside Duc Pho." First published in Gary Soto, ed., *Pieces of the Heart* (San Francisco: Chronicle Books, 1993). Reprinted by permission of the author.

Cantú, Norma Elia, *Canícula: Snapshots of a Girlhood en la Frontera* (Albuquerque: University of New Mexico Press, 1995). Excerpts used by permission of the publisher.

Conde, Carlos, "Eulogy for Rubén Salazar." First published in *Journal of Mexican American Studies* 1 (Fall 1970). Reprinted by permission of the author.

Corpi, Lucha, *Delia's Song* (Houston: Arte Público Press–University of Houston, 1989). Excerpt used by permission of the publisher.

Davis del Valle, Katarina, "Song to a Thousand Faces / My People in the Streets." This first publication by permission of the author.

Delgado, Abelardo, "Due Process of Law." First published in *El Gallo* (May 1971). Reprinted by permission of the author.

Durden, Charles, *No Bugles, No Drums* (New York: Viking Press, 1976). Epigraph used by permission of Penguin Books USA Inc.

García, Ignacio M., "Unfinished letter to Terry." First published in *Saguaro* 3 (1986). Reprinted by permission of the author.

Gutiérrez, José Angel, "22 miles." Epigraph used by permission of the author.

Herrera-Sobek, María, "Cinco poemas." This first publication by permission of the author.

Hruska y Cortez, Elías, "Rocket Flight." First published in *This Side and Other Things* (San Francisco: Pocho-Che, 1971). Reprinted by permission of the author.

Lamadrid, Enrique R., "Enemy Way." First published in Rudolfo A. Anaya, ed., *Voces: An Anthology of Nuevo Mexicano Writers* (Albuquerque: University of New Mexico Press, 1988). Reprinted by permission of the author.

Lenoir, J. B., "Vietnam Blues." Epigraph used by permission of Evidence Music, Conshohocken, Pennsylvania, © 1995.

López, Enrique Hank, "Overkill at the Silver Dollar." First published in *The Nation* (October 29, 1970). Copyright © The Nation Company, L.P. Reprinted with permission from *The Nation* magazine.

Molina, Ralph, "Dos Recuerdos." This first publication by permission of the author.

Montoya, Mushroom, AIA. "Too many targets, too high a body count." This first publication by permission of the author.

Montoya, Jr., Proceso R., "Poema." First published in *El Grito del Norte* (May 19, 1970). Reprinted courtesy of Elizabeth Martinez.

Morante, José. "Corrido del padre de un soldado." From the Arhoolie CD 396 by Flaco Jimenez, *Un mojado sin licencia* (1977). Lyrics reprinted courtesy of San Antonio Music Publishers, Inc.

Moreno, Dorinda Guadalupe, "La niña Lina en East Los Angeles." First published in Dorinda Moreno, ed., *La Mujer—en pie de lucha ¡y la hora es ya!* (Mexico City: Espina del Norte, 1973); and *Tejidos* 3:1 (Spring 1976). Reprinted by permission of the author.

Munguía M., Francisco Javier, *Un mexicano en Vietnam* (Mexico City: Harper & Row Latinoamericana, 1986). Excerpt.

Muñoz, Rosalío, "Speech refusing induction." Printed by permission of the author.

Negrete, Alejandro, "Chicano Moratorium, December 20, 1969." First published in *Machete* 2 (January 8, 1970).

Ortiz Vásquez, Pedro, "Las cartas de Martín Flores." First published in *Saguaro* 3 (1986).

Paiz, Patricio, "En memoria de Arturo Tijerina" and "Get It On." First published in *De colores* 2 (1975).

Perea, Robert, "Dragon Mountain." First published in *De colores* 4 (1978).

Portilla de la Luz, "La hora de todos." First published in *El Grito del Norte* 5 (May 19, 1972). Reprinted courtesy of Elizabeth Martinez.

Quiñonez, Naomi Helena, "America's Wailing Wall." First published in Michelle T. Clinton, Sesshu Foster, and Naomi Quiñonez, eds., *Invocation L.A.: Urban Multicultural Poetry* (Los Angeles: West End Press, 1989). Reprinted by permission of the author.

Quintana, Leroy V., *Interrogations* (Chevy Chase, Md.: Viet Nam Generation and Burning Cities Press, 1992). Poems reprinted by permission of the author.

Ramirez, Juan, "History of a Chicano Vietnam Veteran." Excerpt; this first publication by permission of the author.

Renaud González, Bárbara, "The Summer of Vietnam." First published in Charles Tatum, ed., *New Chicana/Chicano Writing* (Tucson: University of Arizona Press, 1992). Reprinted by permission of the author.

Reyes, Ben, "Juan Carlos González." First published in *El Grito del norte* (October 8, 1968). Reprinted courtesy of Elizabeth Martinez.

Reyes, Jacinto, "The Tortilla Mission." Excerpt; this first publication by permission of the author.

Ríos, Alberto, "The Vietnam Wall." First published in *Journal of Ethnic Studies* 16 (Summer 1988). Reprinted by permission of the author.

Rodríguez, Joe, *The Oddsplayer* (Houston: Arte Público Press–University of Houston, 1989). Excerpt used by permission of the publisher.

Rodríguez, Luis J., *Always Running: La vida loca, Gang Days in L.A.* (Willimantic, Conn.: Curbstone Press, 1993). Excerpt used by permission of the publisher.

Rodríguez, Michael W., "Party on the Mountain." This first publication by permission of the author.

Rodríguez, Patricia, "Chicano Moratorium." First published in *Regeneración* 1 (1970).

Rodríguez, Roberto, *Assault with a Deadly Weapon* (Los Angeles: Rainbow Press, 1984); reissued as *Justice: A Question of Race* (Tempe, Ariz.: Bilingual Press, 1997). Excerpt used by permission of the author.

Salinas, Luis Omar, "Death in Vietnam." Previously published in Joseph Sommers et al., eds., *Chicano Literature: Text and Context* (Englewood Cliffs, N.J.: Prentice-Hall, 1972), and H. Bruce Franklin, ed., *The Vietnam War in American Stories, Songs, and Poems* (Boston: St. Martin's Press, 1996). Reprinted by permission of the author.

Sánchez, Saúl, "El Entierro." First published in *hay plesha lichans tu di flac* (Berkeley: Editorial Justa Publications, 1977). Reprinted by permission of the author.

Sánchez, Jr., Trinidad, "A time to raise questions." Previously published in *Poems* (Lansing: El Renacimiento/Renaissance Publications, 1985), and *Why Am I So Brown?* (Chicago: March Abrazo Press, 1991). Reprinted by permission of March Abrazo Press, copyright © 1991.

Tafolla, Carmen, "Los Corts." First published in Rosa Raquel Elizondo, ed., *Encuentro artístico femenil* (Austin: Casa/Tejidos, 1978). Excerpt used by permission of the author. This first publication of "La siembra" is also by permission of the author.

Trujillo, Charley, *Dogs from Illusion* (San Jose, Calif.: Chusma House, 1994). Excerpt used by permission of the author.

Trujillo, Charley, *Soldados: Chicanos in Viet Nam* (San Jose, Calif.: Chusma House, 1990). Excerpt used by permission of the author.

Valdés, Gina, "Hearts on Fire." First published in *Alternative Visions* 13 (1997), special issue, "Giving Tongue." Reprinted by permission of the author. This first publication of "Heroes" is also by permission of the author.

Valdez, Luis, "Pensamiento serpentino," from *Luis Valdez—Early Works: Actos, Bernabé, and Pensamiento Serpentino* (Houston: Arte Público Press–University of Houston, 1971). Excerpt used by permission of the publisher.

Varela, Delfino, "A Walk in the Sun." First published in *Regeneración* 1 (1970). Reprinted courtesy of the author's son, Delfino Varela, Jr.

Vargas, Adrian, "Blessed Amerika." First published in *La palabra* 6 (1970). Reprinted by permission of the author.

Villanueva, Tino, "Chicano Is an Act of Defiance." First published in Philip D. Ortego, ed., *We Are Chicanos: An Anthology of Mexican American Literature* (New York: Washington Square Press, 1973). Reprinted by permission of the author.

Designer: Sandy Drooker
Compositor: G&S Typesetters
Text: 11/14 Columbus
Display: Pepita
Printer/Binder: Haddon Craftsmen